DOING DEMOCRACY
IN "THIRD PLACES"

DOING DEMOCRACY IN "THIRD PLACES"
Youth Citizenship Education

Edited by Stéphanie Gaudet
and Caroline Caron

In collaboration
with Sophie Théwissen-LeBlanc

University of Ottawa Press
2025

Les **Presses** de l'Université d'Ottawa
University of Ottawa **Press**

Les Presses de l'Université d'Ottawa / University of Ottawa Press (PUO-UOP) is North America's flagship bilingual university press, affiliated to one of Canada's top research universities. PUO-UOP enriches the intellectual and cultural discourse of our increasingly knowledge-based and globalized world with peer-reviewed, award-winning books.

www.Press.uOttawa.ca

Library and Archives Canada Cataloguing in Publication

Title: Doing democracy in "third places" : youth citizenship education / edited by Stéphanie Gaudet and Caroline Caron ; in collaboration with Sophie Théwissen-LeBlanc.
Other titles: Faire l'expérience de la démocratie. English.
Names: Gaudet, Stéphanie, editor | Caron, Caroline, 1973- editor | Théwissen-LeBlanc, Sophie, editor.
Description: Translation of: Faire l'expérience de la démocratie : les tiers-lieux de l'éducation à la citoyenneté des jeunes au Québec. | Includes bibliographical references and index.
Identifiers: Canadiana (print) 20240540298 | Canadiana (ebook) 20240540336 | ISBN 9780776641751 (softcover) | ISBN 9780776641744 (hardcover) | ISBN 9780776641768 (PDF) | ISBN 9780776641775 (EPUB)
Subjects: LCSH: Civics—Study and teaching—Québec (Province) | LCSH: Democracy—Study and teaching—Québec (Province) | LCSH: Social justice and education—Québec (Province)
Classification: LCC LC1091 .F3513 2025 | DDC 370.11/5—dc23

Legal Deposit: Second Quarter 2025
Library and Archives Canada

CIRCEM

CRSH ≡ SSHRC

Production Team

Translation	Mihaila Petricic and Carmen Ruschiensky
Copyediting	Scott Irving
Proofreading	Tanina Drvar
Typesetting	Nord Compo

Cover Image
Stéphanie Gaudet, *Baskatong*, mixed media (collage, acrylic paint, and ink) on canvas. An abstract expression of the cartography of Quebec's lakes and reservoirs; 40 x 48 inches.

This volume was published with the financial support of the Centre for Interdisciplinary Research on Citizenship and Minorities (CIRCEM).

uOttawa

The University of Ottawa Press gratefully acknowledges the support extended to its publishing list by the Government of Canada, the Canada Council for the Arts, the Ontario Arts Council, the Social Sciences and Humanities Research Council and the Canadian Federation for the Humanities and Social Sciences through the Scholarly Book Awards (ASPP), and by the University of Ottawa.

Canada

Canada Council   Conseil des arts
for the Arts   du Canada

ONTARIO ARTS COUNCIL
CONSEIL DES ARTS DE L'ONTARIO
an Ontario government agency
un organisme du gouvernement de l'Ontario

Ontario

Democracy is the faith that the process of experience is more important than any special result attained. [...] Since the process of experience is capable of being educative, faith in democracy is all one with faith in experience and education.

Democracy is a way of life controlled by a working faith in the possibilities of human nature. [...] This faith may be enacted in statutes, but it is only on paper unless it is put in force in the attitudes which human beings display to one another in all the incidents and relations of daily life.

John Dewey

Preface

In Quebec, a range of civil society initiatives are introducing thousands of young people to the concept of democratic togetherness. These initiatives represent "third places" of citizenship education. The organizations behind them advocate for children's rights, feminist social action, community movements, alternative globalization, and public action in schools and local governments. As part of a collaborative research project, we worked with seven of these organizations to better understand their practices, their contributions to the democratic ethos, and how they embody citizenship. This book examines their invaluable contribution to Quebec's democratic vitality.

The adults working in these organizations are dedicated to action and strive to identify the best practices to adopt day to day. They expressed a particular need to better define the multilayered concepts of democratic citizenship and youth engagement. This book responds to that need by contributing to the ongoing theoretical debates on youth democratic citizenship. Diverse discourses on democratic citizenship run through the initiatives covered in this book: liberal, participatory, deliberative, multicultural, agonistic, critical, eco-citizen, and the feminist discourse on care. We defend the idea that, to reach young people, this diversity is necessary and desirable.

We learned several lessons from the practices we observed, including that it is important to welcome young people into warm, inclusive spaces; to encourage them to dream together and expand their political horizons; for adults to engage them in concrete, authentic, and meaningful action; and for organizations and funding bodies to recognize the work of initiative facilitators and help ensure their success.

This book is written in an accessible style to reach a broad audience, including staff at youth organizations, youth policy workers, graduate students, and anyone interested in the issues surrounding youth citizenship in the twenty-first century.

Table of Contents

List of Figures

List of Tables

Acknowledgements

This research project spans several years, which is why our list of acknowledgements is long. We are grateful to the many organizations and individuals we met in a series of encounters. We begin at the beginning. Caroline Caron and Stéphanie Gaudet—the editors of this book—met at a conference on citizenship that Stéphanie co-organized with the Institut du Nouveau Monde[1] (INM) as part of the 2012 Acfas congress.[2] Since then, we have worked together on several projects. Collaborating with the INM is also part of a long-standing relationship dating back to the early 2000s. We would like to thank the former and current INM staff members who helped shape this book. We are particularly grateful to Miriam Fahmy, who worked on the Education and Democracy Symposium, where this project took root, as well as to Michel Venne, Stéphane Dubé, François P. Robert, Marie-France Duranceau, Malorie Flon, Julie Caron-Malenfant, Marie-Dina Salvione, Louis-Philippe Lizotte, Emmanuelle Biroteau, and Dominic Vézina. We are also grateful to Judith Gaudet for her invaluable assistance with the Delphi method.

We thank all the young people we met during our case studies and the team of young students who participated in various stages of the project. Special thanks go to Stéphanie Boyer, who coordinated the symposium and the beginning of the project; Emilie Drapeau, who coordinated the project for four years; and Sophie Théwissen-LeBlanc, who took over next and assisted us from start to finish in the various stages of knowledge production and mobilization. We would like to thank the many assistants who worked with us on the case studies, including Hérold Constant, Alexandre Cournoyer, Jessica Anne Déry, Evelyn Forero, Esther Frigon, Jose Fuca, François Marchand, and Hilda Joyce Portilla. Additionally,

Rosemarie Côté-Pitre, Gabrielle Jodoin, Yannick Masse, and Ziad Nsarellah made contributions at various stages of the research.

Special thanks go to our colleagues, who participated in this project, helped shape it, and contributed to the research and data analysis. Many thanks go to Mariève Forest, the senior researcher on the Commission jeunesse de Gatineau[3] case study; Brieg Capitaine, the senior researcher on the Oxfam-Québec case study; and Chantale Mailhot, who supervised the Exeko case study and was present during the INM case study. Thanks to our colleagues Nathalie Bélanger, Laurence Bherer, Paul Carr, Nicole Gallant, Gilles Labelle, Mona Paré, Michel Sasseville, Gina Thésée, and Joel Westheimer, who participated in the symposium and influenced our interpretations and analyses.

We would like to express our gratitude to our partners, particularly Maxime Goulet-Langlois, researcher and Exeko representative, and Nadia Duguay. We thank Jean-Pierre Denis, Geneviève-Gaël Vanasse, and François Gervais from Oxfam-Québec as well as Josiane Cossette and Isabelle Miron from the Commission jeunesse de Gatineau. Thank you to Soraya Elbekkali, Julie Roussin, Noémie Brière-Marquez, and Martine Boies-Fournier from the Forum jeunesse de l'île de Montréal[4] and Concertation Montréal; to Danielle Mongeon and Anne-Marie Bureau from the Centre de pédiatrie sociale de Gatineau; and to Aula Sabra, Laurence Arbogast, and Andréann Lahaie from YWCA Montréal.[5]

During this project, the research team also met with other organizations and individuals to develop partnerships and gain insights. For their time, we extend our gratitude to Monica Rosales and Catherine Lebossé from Élections Québec; Francis Sabourin from Concertation Montréal; Esther Lapointe from Groupe Femmes, Politique et Démocratie;[6] Ducakis Désinat from Exeko; and Dominic Vézina from Lab22.

This project would not have been possible without the support of several institutions. We would like to acknowledge the Centre for Interdisciplinary Research on Citizenship and Minorities at the University of Ottawa, which supported our grant applications to the Social Sciences and Humanities Research Council of Canada (SSHRC). SSHRC awarded us a Connection Grant to organize the Democracy and Education Symposium as well as a Partnership Development Grant for our research. The Faculty of Social Sciences at the University of Ottawa and the Department of Social Sciences at the University of Quebec in Outaouais also supported us with research time stipends. Finally, the Vice-Dean of Research of the Faculty of Social Sciences at the University of Ottawa awarded us a grant to publish and translate this book.

Notes

1. New World Institute.
2. *5ᵉ Colloque science-société sur la participation des citoyens : Logiques, trajectoires et processus d'engagement dans la vie quotidienne* (Fifth Science-Society Conference on Citizen Participation: Logic, Trajectories and Means of Engagement in Daily Life).
3. Gatineau Youth Commission.
4. Montreal Youth Forum.
5. Gatineau Social Pediatric Centre.
6. Women, Politics, and Democracy Group.

Introduction

Stéphanie Gaudet and Caroline Caron

During the 2019 Global Climate March, Greta Thunberg chose to campaign in Montreal for two reasons: first, because young Quebecers were actively responding to the political crisis that had gripped the world; and second, because they were participating in Fridays for Future, the school strike for climate movement that she had started (Shields, 2019). The march was a resounding success. Around 500,000 people, mostly youth, attended the event, making it the largest citizen gathering in Canadian history (Baillargeon & Shields, 2019). The commitment of young Quebecers to the cause can be explained by Quebec's tradition of youth activism, which reached its peak during the 2012 Quebec student protests, also known as the Maple Spring. Quebec is also home to civil society organizations and semipublic environments that support democratic projects and experiments. These organizations provide young people with opportunities to _do_ democracy (see Dupuis-Déri, 2020a, 2020b; Gaudet, 2021; Simard, 2013).

The term "doing democracy" was inspired by American philosopher John Dewey's vision of citizen participation in education (1916/2018). Dewey's work had a strong influence on the research presented in this book, which encompasses seven case studies in Quebec. Our research team consisted of the seven partner organizations in our case studies, ten researchers, and a dozen student research assistants. We believe that individuals working together as a collective to solve a problem is one of the most important forms of democratic education. Based on this premise, we set out to observe how young people in French-speaking Quebec—comprising children, adolescents, and young adults—experience democratic education in various places, settings, and initiatives. What do young people experience in such programs and how do these experiences teach them to live in democracy? What do they learn from the organizations and teams they are welcomed into? What democratic skills can they develop? How do they feel about the quality of their experience? How do their experiences differ in different settings? What are the best ways to recruit and retain young people in voluntary initiatives?

This book presents findings from our collaboration with various stakeholders in Quebec's ecosystem of youth initiatives in democratic citizenship education. We wrote with youth workers and our partner organizations in mind; besides documenting and raising awareness of their impact on youth development and democratic community life, we hope this book will provide them with valuable insights on how to strengthen their programs, recruitment strategies, and practices—areas they are typically concerned with improving. We also hope that this book is easy to understand, and that the practical knowledge we have gathered can inspire and encourage non-profit organizations and their dedicated staff in this regard.

In our research, we have taken an ethnographic rather than an evaluative approach. The goal of building partnerships with various organizations was to generate new knowledge about people's experiences in the initiatives we studied (see Gaudet, 2020). Currently, the bureaucratic tendency is to fixate on weighing the costs and benefits of government-funded youth programs. Instead, our team advocates observing for the sake of understanding. In other words, we set out to understand what young people experience in these programs and how these experiences help them learn what it means to live in a democracy. We believe that both researchers and society at large have much to learn about the role that civil society organizations play in young people's lives and the promotion of democratic values in local communities. This book is unique for its comprehensive approach. It seeks to raise awareness about youth experiences, make them visible, and to highlight the local and intergenerational community practices that welcome young people, support them, and initiate them into social, civic, and political action. To our knowledge, no published work of this kind exists in Quebec, and few works offer such an extensive and diversified range of case studies (see Gaudet et al., 2020). We hope that the methodology and conceptual vocabulary, which combine research from both the French and English geolinguistic spaces, will offer readers a fresh perspective on youth participation.

Overview

The book is divided into two parts: a theoretical introduction (chapters 1 and 2) and an empirical section (chapters 3 to 9).

Part 1, the "Theoretical Background," summarizes the scholarship on two major interdisciplinary subjects and introduces the plurality of young people's democratic experiences in the places and settings we observed. Chapter 1 identifies these places and settings as socialization spaces using Ramon Oldenburg and Dennis Brissett's (1982) concept of third places of education. These spaces help young people integrate into democratic society by complementing their primary and secondary socialization at home and school. The different spaces we studied are sites of concrete citizen experiments that are helping shape civic and local democratic cultures in Quebec society. Chapter 2 focuses on citizenship, in particular examining youth participation in the programs and initiatives covered in Part 2. We challenge common preconceptions by using a citizenship studies approach embedded in a critical interdisciplinary perspective to reject the idea of young people as citizens in the making (see Boyer & Gaudet, 2021; Caron, 2011, 2018). Although many organizations claim to adopt a "by youth, for youth" approach, scholarly publications have repeatedly shown that many young people feel excluded from decision-making processes and believe they are being instrumentalized by adults in programs designed to promote their engagement and participation (see Hart, 2007; Liebel, 2010). In this chapter, the concept of citizenship brings together the concepts of participation, involvement, and experience. Rather than promoting an idealized notion of citizenship based on adult norms, we adopt a nuanced notion of youth citizenship rooted in children's rights as viewed through the lens of the *Convention on the Rights of the Child*. We argue that empowering young people requires providing them with authentic and meaningful participatory opportunities that are dedicated to their growth and development.

Part 2, "Case Studies," is divided into three sections on democratic citizenship education experiences.

Section A comprises two chapters on education in participatory democracy—often linked to participatory citizenship—emphasizing the role of individuals and groups in decision-making and joint action. It highlights the importance of discussion, deliberation, and practices that ensure accessibility, inclusion, and equal participation rights (Sant, 2019). We present case studies on the Summer School program hosted by the Institut du Nouveau Monde (Chapter 3) and Oxfam-Québec's World Walk (Chapter 4) initiative.[1] We examine the experiences of young people in Montreal and other parts of Quebec who were invited to participate in collective practices related to participatory democracy, including discussing social and political issues, deliberating, and making decisions with a view to taking action.

Section B is a collection of three chapters that present experiments in citizenship education for social change. Despite their differences, the experiments share several characteristics: They all involve educating young people, sensitizing them, and making them aware of their rights, of social problems resulting from social inequality, of social struggles to counteract inequality, and of ways they can assert rights. YWCA Montréal (Chapter 5), the Centre de pédiatrie sociale de Gatineau[2] (Chapter 6), and the Montreal-based organization Exeko (Chapter 7) offer young people the opportunity to experience a culture of social solidarity, one that is deeply rooted in Quebec's community tradition and has played an important role in shaping modern Quebec (Ampleman et al., 2012). Through advocacy, activism, and community projects, young people learn that civil society is the foundation of a democratic, dynamic, and empathetic society committed to equality and social inclusion.

Finally, section C includes two chapters that present case studies in citizenship education based on representative democracy and public action. At the Commission jeunesse de Gatineau[3] (Chapter 8) and the Forum jeunesse de l'île de Montréal[4] (Chapter 9), young people gain experience in elected representation by participating in local government committees and school board student assemblies. They have a unique opportunity to learn about mechanisms and procedures that resemble those in the formal processes and institutions that govern liberal democracies. They can experience an election, exercise leadership, deliberate, and take concrete action based on consensus.

The number of case studies we present reflects the vitality, diversity, and richness of experiences in democratic citizenship education that civil society organizations are offering young people in Quebec. It is our hope that this body of knowledge will contribute to existing research and raise awareness and recognition of this too-often-kept secret. Some organizations go to great lengths to ensure participants have a meaningful, impactful experience. The partner organizations in our study run programs that enrich individuals and communities alike, helping to strengthen social bonds and democratic culture. It is essential to understand and raise awareness of the real impact that such organizations are having on young people, especially at a time when the legitimacy of contemporary democracies is being increasingly challenged (Bachelet, 2022). We hope that this book will be useful to youth organizations and help policymakers understand the contribution they make to a strong democratic culture and how to make informed decisions about how best to meet their significant and ongoing financial needs.

References

Ampleman, G., Denis, L., & Desgagnés, J.-Y. (Eds.). (2012). *Théorie et pratique de conscientisation au Québec*. Presses de l'Université du Québec.

Bachelet, M. (2022, August 3). *La crise et la fragilité de la démocratie dans le monde* [Speech transcript]. Opening workshop for the International Association of Jesuit Universities, Boston College. https://www.ohchr.org/fr/statements-and-speeches/2022/08/crisis-and-fragility-democracy-world

Baillargeon, S., & Shields, A. (2019, September 28). 500 000 citoyens emboîtent le pas à Greta Thunberg. *Le Devoir*. https://www.ledevoir.com/environnement/563659/marche-historique

Boyer, S., & Gaudet, S. (2021). La citoyenneté démocratique des enfants à l'école primaire. *Revue des sciences de l'éducation, 47*(2), 174–196. https://doi.org/10.7202/1083983ar

Caron, C. (2011). Getting girls and teens into the vocabularies of citizenship. *Girlhood Studies, 4*(2), 70–91. https://doi.org/10.3167/ghs.2011.040206

Caron, C. (2018). La citoyenneté des adolescents du 21e siècle dans une perspective de justice sociale : pourquoi et comment ? *Lien social et Politiques, 80*, 52–68. https://doi.org/10.7202/1044109ar

Dewey, J. (2018). *Démocratie et éducation* suivi d'*Expérience et éducation* (A. Colin, Trans). Armand Colin. (Original works published 1916 and 1938)

Dupuis-Déri, F. (2020a). Histoire des grèves d'élèves du secondaire au Québec : démocratie et conflictualité. *Revue des sciences de l'éducation, 46*(3), 67–94. https://doi.org/10.7202/1075988ar

Dupuis-Déri, F. (2020b). Mobilisations de la jeunesse pour le climat au Québec : analyse des dynamiques conflictuelles à l'école. *Sociologie et sociétés, 52*(2), 303–325. https://doi.org/10.7202/1088759ar

Gaudet, S. (2020). Sur le terrain de la sociologie publique : enjeux éthiques d'une recherche collaborative sur les expériences d'éducation citoyenne des jeunes. *SociologieS*. https://doi.org/10.4000/sociologies.15416

Gaudet, S. (2021). Les initiatives jeunesse au Canada : des tiers-lieux de l'éducation démocratique. *Revue internationale d'éducation de Sèvres, 88*, 93–104. https://doi.org/10.4000/ries.11586

Gaudet, S., Drapeau, É., Marchand, F., & Forest, M. (2020). Repenser le rapport social d'âge sur le terrain : ethnographies de la Commission Jeunesse Gatineau et du Comité des droits de l'enfant du Centre de pédiatrie sociale de Gatineau. In Côté, I., Lavoie, K. & Trottier-Cyr, R.-P. (Eds.), *La recherche centrée sur l'enfant : enjeux éthiques et innovations méthodologiques* (pp. 219–246). Presses de l'Université Laval.

Hart, J. (2007). Empowerment or frustration? Participatory programming with young Palestinians. *Children, Youth and Environments, 17*(3), 1–23. https://www.jstor.org/stable/10.7721/chilyoutenvi.17.3.0001

Liebel, M. (2010). *Enfants, droits et citoyenneté : faire émerger la perspective des enfants sur leurs droits* (in collaboration with P. Robin & I. Saadi). L'Harmattan.

Oldenburg, R., & Brissett, D. (1982). The third place. *Qualitative Sociology, 5,* 265–284. https://doi.org/10.1007/BF00986754

Sant, E. (2019). Democratic education: A theoretical review (2006–2017). *Review of Educational Research, 89*(5), 655–696. https://doi.org/10.3102/0034654319862493

Shields, A. (2019, August 28). Montréal figure dans les plans de Greta Thunberg. *Le Devoir*. https://www.ledevoir.com/environnement/561444/climat-montreal-figure-dans-les-plans-de-greta-thunberg

Simard, M. (2013). *Histoire du mouvement étudiant québécois 1956-2013 : des Trois Braves aux carrés rouges*. Presses de l'Université Laval.

Notes

1. New World Institute.
2. Gatineau Social Pediatric Centre.
3. Gatineau Youth Commission.
4. Montreal Youth Forum.

PART 1

THEORETICAL BACKGROUND

CHAPTER 1

Democratic Citizenship Education in Quebec's Third Places

Stéphanie Gaudet and Caroline Caron

Abstract

This chapter describes seven youth citizenship initiatives as third places—physical, relational, and dialogical spaces in which young people experiment with collective discussion and decision-making. The initiatives are inspired by multiple discourses on democratic citizenship education—the liberal, deliberative, participatory, critical, multicultural, agonistic, eco-citizen, and care-based discourses. We explain the methodology behind our research and how the seven initiatives foster experiences in participatory democracy, representative democracy, public action, and social change.

B eyond the political institution it represents, democracy embodies a way of being and participating in society. It is a dynamic practice termed the "democratic ethos." It is both a way of life, expressed through routine actions, and a state of mind that reflects our values. We learn and experience this ethos in different areas of daily life. It connects individuals to society and involves younger generations in intergenerational transmission. The success of a democratic political project relies on a community's ability to define its goals and develop ways of living and acting that make this way of *doing society* achievable over time.

Citizens of all ages are experimenting with the art of living democratically as a way of doing society. In their daily lives, they are called upon to emancipate themselves individually and collectively, to seek

common solutions, to question norms, and to propose ways of responding to shared challenges. A democratic society, then, relies on social
change, which involves a constant tension between the instability
of redefining collective values and the stability of the democratic
institution.

Democratic education involves more than just being taught
national history, civics, and other institutionalized knowledge; it also
involves learning ways to think and act that make it possible to reflect
on the social good, social change, and collective decision-making. The
goal of democratic citizenship education is therefore to introduce citizens to a democratic ethos as a way of preserving it (Honneth, 2015).
Involving and welcoming young people into the culture is a crucial
part of the project. The initiatives young people are joining provide
them with spaces to experience a democratic ethos with their peers,
and with adults who create environments that encourage discussion,
deliberation, and collective decision-making. We set out to visit Quebec
organizations to evaluate young people's experiences in these spaces.

1.1. Democratic Citizenship Education

In North America, discussions on democratic education typically
centre around liberal democratic political systems and institutional
and representative democracy. The goal is to prepare future voters
to participate in elections. Democracy, here, assumes an individual-
istic view of human nature in which freedoms are protected by a
state that minimizes its intervention. This discourse is widespread
in our society because it forms the basis of the system of electoral
political representation in Western democracies, which promotes
equality among individuals, sovereignty of the people, and the rule
of law.[1] It is important to clarify that this discourse is not to be con-
fused with liberal and neoliberal economic discourses, which apply
market values such as competition, surplus value, and performance
to society and to the state (Dardot & Laval, 2010).

North American schools promote liberal democratic education.
According to research by Joel Westheimer and Joseph Kahne (2004), most
of the curriculum taught in US schools follows two models. The first
model is that of the responsible citizen who works, pays taxes, and obeys
laws. The second is the model of the participatory citizen, which stresses
the importance of community engagement, learning about democratic

institutions, and participating in them politically. Westheimer and Kahne note that these models are not exclusive to democratic culture: Totalitarian regimes also pass these models on to young people through institutional history and civic engagement. Democratic citizenship education focuses more on normative political action. This involves making decisions based on ethical and moral goals while navigating the tension between institutional stability and the instability of social change that is inherent to the democratic model. According to Westheimer and Kahne, the goal of normative political action should be social justice.

In democratic contexts, normative social change is common and often challenges the dominant liberal political philosophy. In fact, the democratic ethos encourages discussion and multiple discourses on normative democratic ideals; this is what makes it so rich. In our observations, we found many different discourses and practices contributing to the vitality of youth initiatives and experiences.

In a systematic literature review, Edda Sant (2019) identifies six pro-democratic discourses that dominate education: (1) liberal, (2) deliberative, (3) participatory, (4) critical, (5) multicultural, and (6) agonistic (see Figure 1.1). Discourses are social constructs that have been developed in scientific literature and professional circles, which is why Sant studies them. They all have their strengths and weaknesses and vary according to their epistemological and ontological assumptions. To the six democratic discourses Sant identifies, we add eco-citizen (7) and care-based (8). In Quebec, these two discourses are increasingly influencing education, politics, and action. Figure 1.1 groups these discourses based on how they influence the individuals in our case studies. Their practices appear to be inspired by a variety of complementary notions of democracy. As in our research, we highlight this diversity, not to identify the best discourse but to consider the different theoretical concepts that counterbalance liberal pro-democratic discourse.

Liberal pro-democratic discourse (1) emphasizes political representation and individual rights, while deliberative pro-democratic discourse (2) emphasizes the importance of teaching discussion, critical thinking, and considering different points of view (Lefrançois & Éthier, 2010; Sasseville, 2009). As in Jürgen Habermas's discourse ethics, deliberative pro-democratic discourse assumes that participants are rational. The approach prioritizes rational discussion over emotions and power dynamics, emphasizing a form of collective intelligence. Recent research in mindfulness and philosophy for children, however, has begun to consider participants' emotions (Malboeuf-Hurtubise et al., 2021).

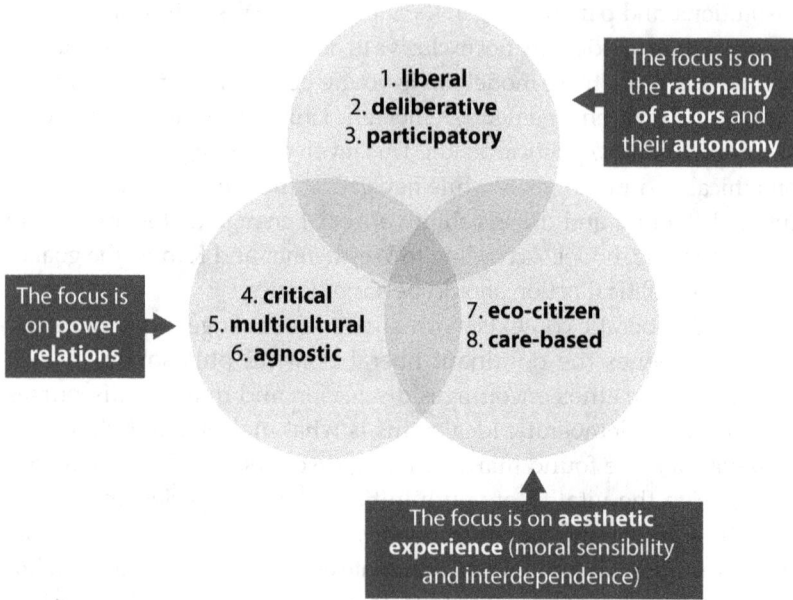

FIGURE 1.1. Eight discourses on citizenship education.
Source: Inspired by Sant (2019).

Participatory citizenship education (3) is another dominant discourse. It is based on the assumptions of deliberative discourse (2), except that it is focused on making and implementing decisions that result from discussion. This approach is in keeping with the legacy of John Dewey, who believed that education should be pragmatically rooted in everyday life and prepare individuals to participate democratically (Biesta et al., 2014). All the initiatives we studied partake in this educational discourse. They offer young people practical spaces where they can deliberate and make decisions, whereby participatory citizenship education begins to resemble participatory democracy (Blondiaux, 2008). The above discourses present individuals as co-creators of decisions and actions. Liberal discourse, in contrast, emphasizes representative democracy and is often supported by the elite. These three discourses—liberal (1), deliberative (2), and participatory (3)—are based on a rationalist anthropological framework in which human beings are primarily seen as rational beings who, through reason, become free and independent.

The other three discourses Sant (2019) identifies are rooted in a critical sociological framework, according to which citizenship cannot be understood simply in its ideal, universalistic form—that of independent rational beings. This view also plays into social relationships, which involve cultural factors and power dynamics. Critical discourse (4) calls into question liberal democracy's ability to guide the political project towards social justice in a normative way (Carr & Thésée, 2017; Westheimer, 2015). Its proponents argue that individuals are inscribed within social relations of gender, class, age, and race, and that this limits their democratic participation. They argue that resolving this problem is necessary to ensure a participatory ideal. In critical discourse, social justice is therefore a normative goal that cannot be separated from the democratic project.

A variant of this discourse places more focus on multicultural issues. Proponents of multicultural discourse (5) defend minority groups within societies and prioritize diversity and plurality in the democratic project. They see identity politics as an important goal, and their critique of liberal and deliberative democracy stems from the belief that society benefits from cultural diversity and a more community-based approach. Citizens primarily represent the cultural groups to which they belong, not just themselves (Fraser-Burgess, 2012).

Agonistic democratic discourse (6), advocated by Ernesto Laclau and Chantal Mouffe (2001), proposes a conflict-based approach to the democratic model. In agonistic discourse, democracy is a short-lived agreement that is constantly redefined, and dissent is essential and inherent to the project. The proponents of agonistic discourse assume equal intelligence—that everyone can think and question the established order if they are given the means to do so (Rancière, 1987/2003). In short, political dynamics inevitably exclude certain (dissenting) groups, who then seek to redefine the provisional agreement.

As mentioned above, we add eco-citizenship (7) and care (8) discourses to the ones listed above. These pro-democratic discourses challenge the anthropocentric ideal of Sant's six. For instance, eco-citizenship discourse posits a worldview where humans are no longer the centre of the network of life (Sauvé, 2017). This decentred view challenges the idea that the environment is merely a backdrop for human activity. This perspective on the living world is shared by Indigenous cultures in Quebec (Blanchet-Cohen, 2017) and has been adopted by some eco-citizenship education organizations to promote alternative worldviews and democratic values among young people.

Care ethicists criticize the liberal model and decentre anthropocentrism. They abandon the view of the human being as an independent subject of reason in favour of interdependence between people (Gilligan, 1982/1986) and with the living world (Tronto, 1993/2009). They use the term "care" to encompass the different dimensions of caring relationships, such as caring about, taking care of, care-giving, care-receiving, and caring with (Paperman & Laugier, 2006). Education is one of the most important caring practices (Noddings, 2012) because it involves caring for the living. In turn, caring is part of the democratic ethos (Tronto, 2013) because the fundamental political question behind it is: Who is caring for whom and what, and with which resources? Social democracy depends on people, most often women, to care for younger and older generations and more vulnerable groups. It also depends on institutions, like community organizations, for support. Compassionate organizations that provide vulnerable citizens with a welcoming, inclusive, and supportive environment draw on this approach.

In this section, we identified eight discourses that emphasize the importance of education and the ideal of a democratic society while embracing different views of the world and living things. Although the organizations and facilitation teams we met did not explicitly refer to education, democracy, and these views of the world, we observed them in their practices.

1.2. Youth Citizen Participation in Quebec

A liberal view of democracy puts the focus on institutions, elections, respect for rights and freedoms, and political representation, but creating a democratic society requires much more. Democratic culture is based on civic engagement during and between elections (Blondiaux, 2008). It can take the form of demonstrating, petitioning, joining social movements and local initiatives, and participating in public consultations to influence policymaking (Bherer et al., 2016).

Participatory democracy involves a collective commitment to educating individuals. According to Audric Vitiello (2013, p. 221), understanding participatory democracy means understanding the fundamental, defining aspects of citizens' subjectivity. It is about truly educating citizens to hone their skills, attitudes, socio-political dispositions, and how they express themselves. The idea emphasizes process-based citizenship rather than citizenship by law.

Participatory democracy involves individuals in a subjective, collective, and meaningful project. Young people find this particularly appealing; in Quebec, for example, the student movement for accessible post-secondary education has been one of the most dynamic in the world since the 1960s. More recently, younger students in primary and secondary schools have formed a movement to fight climate change (Dupuis-Déri, 2020a). In 2019, Greta Thunberg travelled to Montreal to march with young Quebecers, the most active members of her global school walkout movement.

Although young people are eager to participate, their enthusiasm does not necessarily result in high voter turnout. In the 2021 federal election, only 66% of 18-to-25-year-olds voted (Élections Canada, 2021). Many have lost faith in institutions (Rosanvallon, 2006) and the political project proposed by politicians, and are angry about the injustices they have experienced (Van de Velde, 2021). They subscribe to the democratic ethos—their state of mind is democratic—but they are trying to redefine their relationship with institutions.

This is why studying the tensions between representative and participatory discourses among Quebec youth is so interesting (Gaudet, 2018). It raises questions about young people's distrust of institutions and the political class's failed attempts to engage them at key political moments like elections.

Representative and participatory democratic practices are complementary; citizens can influence social decisions and participate in democratic culture beyond the occasional election. Participation and civic education initiatives can democratize society and involve citizens in community life and collective decisions, but their success depends on cultivating and sustaining a democratic ethos. Alongside representative democracy, social movements—like the feminist, labour union, and autonomous community movements—have been significant forces in reinforcing Quebec's democratic ideal.

However, the push for participatory democracy can backfire. For example, the state may instrumentalize participatory mechanisms to take power away from citizens (Godbout, 1987) or assign them greater responsibility (Bacqué & Biewener, 2015). If citizens' collective participation does not align with the democratic ideal of social justice, the participatory movement could drift towards de-democratization, which has been observed in certain ethnocentric populist movements. Participation in the democratic ideal and making one's voice heard should not be at odds with what the democratic project requires:

respect for human beings, their integrity, their rights, and the quest for social justice.

Despite these potential aberrations, participating in civic initiatives has been recognized as a form of democratic education for individuals of all ages (Pateman, 1970/1976) and is considered a precursor to political participation (Trudel & Martineau, 2021). In fact, a recent longitudinal study in Quebec shows that young people who participate in civic initiatives are more likely to vote (Groleau & Nanhou, 2022). In the pragmatist tradition, Dewey (1916/1997) believed that the best way to initiate citizens into democratic culture was through collective problem-solving—that is, deliberation, decision-making, and action.

1.3. Citizen Education in Third Places: Learning in a Democracy

1.3.1. Learning to Engage and Engaging to Learn

School is not the only place to learn about democracy. Social settings in everyday life are particularly important for learning a democratic ethos from an early age. Engaging with family, friends, neighbours, and communities that share a social identity, such as a sport or cultural practice, are all ways to learn the democratic ethos. Unlike initiatives that promote learning *about* democracy, youth organizations promote learning *in* a democracy: Instead of learning about institutions and being regarded as citizens in the making, young people participate as members of a democratic ethos.

We call the spaces where this kind of learning occurs third places of democratic citizenship education when they are found outside of school, home, and work. Third places offer young people the opportunity to meet each other and experiment with democracy through experiences facilitated by adults (Gaudet, 2021). These spaces are conducive to putting the democratic ethos into practice.

We borrowed the term "third places" from Ramon Oldenburg and Dennis Brissett (1982), who argue for the importance of social spaces outside the workplace and home, such as cafés and libraries, where individuals can develop a sense of belonging and express their individuality. These places recognize both the social experience of interaction and inclusion, and the aesthetic experience of symbols perceived through our sensibilities.

Studies show that involving young people in making decisions and implementing services for them helps them learn more about political life than they would in school (Akiva et al., 2014). In each of the initiatives we studied, young people learn to engage collectively, with adults playing a crucial role. When these experiences are authentic, meaning that young people get to address and solve real problems they have encountered, they can build communication and leadership skills and become academically motivated (Zeldin et al., 2017).

Young Quebecers have organized several movements, including student strikes and initiatives related to the environmental movement (Dupuis-Déri, 2020b; Simard, 2013). Our research on social and political participation among young people shows that movement organizers often had experience with collective democratic action in youth organizations (Gaudet, 2020b). In organization-led youth initiatives—which this book focuses on—adults play a decisive role. Their ability to act as facilitators often determines how young people feel about their experience.

Adult facilitators help participants share knowledge and ideas, creating an environment that encourages action. Studies over the past decade have begun to examine and understand their potential impact on citizen participation initiatives (Hogan, 2002). Their support can affect how well participants communicate with each other and the success of the initiatives themselves. Despite the growing recognition of facilitators' role in fostering public participation (Bherer et al., 2017), research on their role in citizen participation initiatives for youth specifically is limited. Some studies have noted their ability to build trusting relationships, recognize young people's agency, provide motivation, oversee group interactions and activities, and defend the initiative within the organization (Blanchet-Cohen & Brunson, 2014). In the United States, a substantial body of literature focuses on youth–adult partnerships in youth-focused initiatives and programs. The facilitation teams we observed form similar partnerships with young people regardless of their abilities, age range, or group size. We have observed how important these partnerships are to participants.

1.3.2. A History of Quebec's Third Places

In Quebec, many community, public and para-public organizations welcome people into spaces designed for aesthetic hospitality and social inclusion. Quebec stands out from other Canadian provinces in having the Secrétariat à la jeunesse, a youth secretariat that funds services provided by civil society organizations to engage young people in political and social participation. The result is an ecosystem of youth organizations offering different experiences in citizenship education.

Historically, these third places of youth citizenship education have been run by religious groups. These include the YMCA, the YWCA, Scouts, Young Catholic Students, labour unions, popular education groups, and missionary-led international development groups. Since the 1970s, education and community services have been secularized, but the tradition of investing in youth collectives has remained. The Quebec government created the Secrétariat à la jeunesse in 1983. Its mandate is to coordinate youth initiatives and advise the premier directly. Since the 2000s, a number of philanthropic foundations have joined the cause, subsidizing various initiatives depending on their social missions, including food security, children's physical and mental health, and the social integration of minority groups.

Democratic citizenship is often implicit in youth initiatives, which makes sense given that the very nature of an ethos is to be implicit and informally shared through social interaction. Organizations have limited time and resources to review their discourses on democracy and reflect on their citizenship education practices. Those who participated in our research expressed their need to develop a common language with which to discuss their practices and roles. With this in mind, we studied seven of them and developed a theoretical framework for our observations.

1.4. Types of Initiatives in Third Places

The youth initiatives we observed promote social transformation, empowering young people to act as citizens in groups, neighbourhoods, and society at large. Though they are characterized by different discourses on citizen education, they share a discourse on education in participatory democracy because they engage youth in participatory democracy to varying degrees through deliberation and action.

When we designed our research project, we wanted to observe and compare initiatives involving different forms of democratic participation. In Quebec, some of them have been in place for several decades. Some introduce young people to civic participation and social leadership. Others help young people empower themselves by raising awareness of inequalities and the collective tools available to them. These initiatives are in line with Quebec's community movement history. Still others offer young people the opportunity to experience public action through representative councils at various levels of decision-making, namely student and city councils. Finally, several of them foster democratic participation through the visual and dramatic arts; forum theatres are one example.[2]

Seven organizations opened their doors to us, allowing us to observe and participate in some of their initiatives and to study how they teach democratic citizenship. We provide a detailed analysis of each case study in the second part of the book.

Table 1.1. Type of Participation, Organizational Partners, and Observations

Participation Oriented Towards	Partner Organization	Observations
Democratic Participation	Institut du Nouveau Monde	Participation in the Citizenship Summer School
	Oxfam-Québec	Participation in the World Walk
Social Change	Centre de pédiatrie sociale de Gatineau	Participation on the Children's Rights Committee
	YWCA Montréal	Participation in an Audiovisual Project
	Exeko	Participation in Intellectual and Artistic Mediation
Representative Democracy and Public Action	Commission jeunesse de Gatineau	Participation on a Municipal Youth Council
	Forum jeunesse de l'île de Montréal	Participation in School Board Student Assemblies

1.4.1. Democratic Citizen Participation

Many organizations aim to introduce young people to citizen participation and collective action. We worked with two non-profit organizations that have been part of Quebec's landscape of citizen education third places for several years: Oxfam-Québec and the Institut du Nouveau Monde (INM).

Oxfam-Québec organizes programs and initiatives for young people aged 12 to 35. Our team was interested in studying its annual

World Walk, which began in the early 1970s. In collaboration with Quebec secondary schools, Oxfam-Québec engages teens in a collective walk to raise awareness of social injustices, notably global inequality.

Since it was founded in 2004, the INM has established itself as a key player in democratic citizenship education, engaging youth and adults alike in public consultation and citizen participation processes. Every year, their citizenship Summer School hosts over 300 participants aged 15 to 35. On the syllabus are current social and political issues, which they are encouraged to debate. Through its many partnerships, the school offers a chance to connect participants with Quebec's network of citizen participation organizations.

The events organized by the INM and Oxfam-Québec play a key role in the participatory development of many young people. The Summer School and World Walk introduce a wide audience to political citizenship. Both initiatives echo discourses on liberal democratic education, participatory democracy, and multiculturalism, emphasizing the involvement of young people from a variety of minority and minoritized groups. Oxfam-Québec is more actively involved in eco-citizen and critical education discourses, as the mission of the walk is to raise awareness of inequalities. The INM, on the other hand, leans more towards discourses of deliberative and agonistic democracy. This is because the Summer School is non-partisan—it encourages the expression and deliberation of ideas that may lead to differences of opinion.

1.4.2. Participating in Social Change

The community movement in Quebec has historically produced popular education initiatives aimed at raising people's awareness of their civic rights to empower them as citizens. Organizers understand that certain groups experience oppression, and they promote social citizenship by engaging them in activities where they can build solidarity and a sense of belonging (Ampleman et al., 2012). In so doing, they draw on a range of critical pro-democratic discourses while embracing the discourse of care. The aim of these community initiatives is to support and empower young people to become social and political participants. They challenge youth to address various power dynamics, including inequalities based on age, race, gender, and how these intersect. Organizations typically lead multiple initiatives to meet the diverse needs of young people and neighbourhoods. As part of our research, we collaborated with three organizations: the Centre de pédiatrie sociale de Gatineau[3] (CPSG), YWCA Montréal, and Exeko.

Through their initiatives, they teach young people the history of social struggles to raise their awareness of the collective challenges they face as individuals. Together with the Children's Rights Committee, the CPSG provides support and assistance to vulnerable children (typically ages 10 to 15) who need help learning to make their voices heard; they introduce children to the *Convention on the Rights of the Child* to ensure that they recognize themselves as citizens. In Chapter 6, we see that this initiative draws from liberal, participatory, critical, and care discourses to empower young people who are often at odds with the justice system and the Director of Youth Protection.

Teen-oriented initiatives engage participants more in political reflection. For instance, Exeko collaborates with the *Pathways to Education* program to offer workshops that teach 15-to-17-year-olds about the history of Pointe-Saint-Charles, a neighbourhood in Montreal that is currently being gentrified. YWCA Montréal's *Strong Girls, Strong World* program has a similar approach. The all-female audiovisual initiative introduces 17-to-21-year-olds to intersectional feminism. These initiatives expose young people to different discourses on democratic education, reflecting critical, participatory, multicultural, and care discourses while embracing a pedagogy of hope (Freire, 1970/1974). They also help young people understand inequality issues in context and provide examples of social struggles that have had positive effects on society.

1.4.3. Participating in Representative Democracy and in Public Action

Under Quebec's *Education Act*, secondary schools are required to set up student councils, and many elementary schools encourage classroom teachers to have students elect class representatives. This approach to democratic citizenship education is common, but it receives little attention from Quebec's research community. Researchers who have studied it have identified several challenges to achieving full youth participation (Pache-Hébert et al., 2014). Student school elections are also criticized for promoting popularity and conformity rather than democratic dialogue and social change (Dupuis-Déri, 2006).

In exploring third places of citizenship education, we visited two experimental spaces dedicated to deliberative democracy. These spaces are outside but peripheral to the school setting—peripheral because young people must attend a school to represent it in a public body. We visited with the *Commission jeunesse de Gatineau*[4] (CJG),[5] and observed two school board student assemblies organized by the *Forum jeunesse de l'île de Montréal*[6] as part of its *Prends ta place à l'école*[7] program.[8]

These two organizations represent students through a commission, which helps young people experience representative democracy from a liberal, pro-democratic point of view. By working in committees of citizens and elected representatives, they develop skills related to deliberative and participatory democracy, becoming co-creators of public action. Both initiatives bring together around 20 secondary school students aged 12 to 17.

Participants experience public action differently. Young people involved with school boards struggle more with bureaucracy and adults in positions of power than those working in municipal government. This exposes youth to agonistic discourses of democracy, which is addressed below in more detail.

1.5. A Study in Partnership

During our research, we collaborated with stakeholders from universities, educational institutions, associations, and community groups. Alongside the INM, whose mission is to promote citizen practices that encourage debate and participation, we developed consultative processes to establish the goals and structure of our research. We followed the tradition of public sociology from the Chicago School. In this tradition, sociologists work with civil society to establish connections with public and political institutions. For this reason, our partners were involved throughout the various stages of knowledge production and application (see Gaudet, 2020a).

To identify the most important democratic qualities to teach young people in a collaborative way, we consulted around 30 people with practical, personal, and professional expertise in citizenship education using the Delphi method—a process of reaching a group consensus through rounds of questionnaires. Our online questionnaires identified and prioritized citizen qualities and educational spaces. To ensure our research was relevant, we also gave participants the opportunity to pose their own questions.

We then hosted a symposium for around 50 stakeholders to discuss where they agreed and disagreed in the questionnaires. With the help of the INM, which organized the World Cafés and an open forum, we settled on five projects.⁹ The first was to conduct a multi-site ethnography to compare and understand the diversity of citizenship education initiatives and practices taking place. This would establish a shared language for discussing and identifying the most promising ones.

Ethnography involves observing the practices and discourses of people in a social space by blending in and interacting, rather than observing from a distance. It leads to a better understanding of the culture of an environment and is the most effective way to generate data about the ethos of a group. This approach can give due attention to practices that have previously been overlooked or misunderstood (Beaud & Weber, 1997). Since the social spaces we observed operate in different ways, our observation times varied. For example, we collaborated with a team of seven full-time research assistants for four days to observe the INM Summer School. In contrast, we conducted monthly one-day data collection sessions for over a year to observe the CJG (see Gaudet et al., 2020).

For guidance and to draw comparisons more easily, we used the same observation grid for each case study. We noted (1) the socio-demographic profile of facilitators and youth participants, (2) the nature of the activity and interactions between youth, (3) the pedagogical methods and techniques, (4) the theoretical knowledge transmitted, (5) the practical knowledge transmitted, (6) the soft skills transmitted, (7) the facilitator's educational approach, (8) participants' attitudes towards the activity, and (9) the overall tone. We explain the observation grid in more detail in the Methodological Appendix. We received approval from the University of Ottawa Research Ethics Board and ensured participants remained anonymous by using pseudonyms in the case studies.

Our team of faculty members and students observed and took part in group activities and discussions throughout this ethnographic study. We acquired and analyzed the data in collaboration with our partners, who influenced our understanding of the initiatives throughout the process. These partners also participated in validating the findings, and this book is one of the results of this teamwork. All findings from our research are available (in French only) at: www.educationetdemocratie.ca.

Conclusion

This book presents our research findings. In keeping with the democratic ethos inherent to the initiatives we studied, our goal was to share the knowledge we gained. Despite time constraints, red tape, and a pandemic, we strived to involve our partners—including organizations, facilitators, students, and colleagues—as much as possible throughout the different stages of knowledge production and application. In a way, this book is also a third place for education. It is intended for adults and young people alike who are interested in democratic citizenship education, including its various forms outside the school environment. It gave our team the opportunity to reflect on everyday citizenship and the ways we can recognize and promote youth citizenship.

References

Akiva, T., Cortina, K. S., & Smith, C. (2014). Involving youth in program decision-making: How common and what might it do for youth? *Journal of Youth and Adolescence*, 43(11), 1844–1860. https://doi.org/10.1007/s10964-014-0183-y

Ampleman, G., Denis, L., & Desgagnés, J.-Y. (Eds.). (2012). *Théorie et pratique de conscientisation au Québec*. Presses de l'Université du Québec.

Bacqué, M.-H., & Biewener, C. (2015). *L'empowerment, une pratique émancipatrice ?* La Découverte.

Beaud, S., & Weber, F. (1997). *Guide de l'enquête de terrain : produire et analyser des données ethnographiques*. La Découverte.

Bherer, L., Dufour, P., & Montambeault, F. (2016). The participatory democracy turn: An introduction. *Journal of Civil Society*, 12(3), 225–230. https://doi.org/10.1080/17448689.2016.1216383

Bherer, L., Gauthier, M., & Simard, L. (Eds.). (2017). *The professionalization of public participation*. Routledge.

Biesta, G., De Bie, M., & Wildemeersch, D. (Eds.). (2014). *Civic learning, democratic citizenship and the public sphere*. Springer.

Blanchet-Cohen, N. (2017). Apports des pédagogies autochtones à l'apprentissage de l'écocitoyenneté. In Sauvé, L., Orellana, I., Villemagne, C., & Bader, B. (Eds.), *Éducation, environnement, écocitoyenneté : repères contemporains*, (pp. 67–80). Presses de l'Université du Québec.

Blanchet-Cohen, N., & Brunson, L. (2014). Creating settings for youth empowerment and leadership: An ecological perspective. *Child & Youth Services*, 35(3), 216–236. https://doi.org/10.1080/0145935X.2014.938735

Blondiaux, L. (2008). *Le nouvel esprit de la démocratie : actualité de la démocratie participative*. Seuil.

Carr, P. R., & Thésée, G. (2017). Seeking democracy inside, and outside, of education: Re-conceptualizing perceptions and experiences related to democracy and education. *Democracy and Education, 25*(2), 1–12. https://democracyeducationjournal.org/home/vol25/iss2/4

Dardot, P., & Laval, C. (2010). *La nouvelle raison du monde : essai sur la société néolibérale*. La Découverte.

Dewey, J. (1997). *Democracy and education: An introduction to the philosophy of education*. The Free Press. (Original work published 1916)

Dupuis-Déri, F. (2006). Les élections de Conseils d'élèves : méthode d'endoctrinement au libéralisme politique. *Revue des sciences de l'éducation, 32*(3), 691–709. https://doi.org/10.7202/016282ar

Dupuis-Déri, F. (2020a). Histoire des grèves d'élèves du secondaire au Québec : démocratie et conflictualité. *Revue des sciences de l'éducation, 46*(3), 67–94. https://doi.org/10.7202/1075988ar

Dupuis-Déri, F. (2020b). Mobilisations de la jeunesse pour le climat au Québec : analyse des dynamiques conflictuelles à l'école. *Sociologie et sociétés, 52*(2), 303–325. https://doi.org/10.7202/1088759ar

Élections Canada. (2021). *Nouveaux électeurs – Jeunes*. Centre de ressources. https://www.elections.ca/content.aspx?section=res&dir=rec/part/yth&document=index&lang=f

Fraser-Burgess, S. (2012). Group identity, deliberative democracy and diversity in education. *Educational Philosophy and Theory, 44*(5), 480–499. https://doi.org/10.1111/j.1469-5812.2010.00717.x

Freire, P. (1974). *Pédagogie des opprimés suivi de Conscientisation et Révolution* (L. Lefay & M. Lefay, Trans.). François Maspero. (Original work published 1970)

Gaudet, S. (2018). La société d'acrobates : réflexion critique sur la responsabilité personnelle. In Marchildon, A., & Duhamel, A. (Eds.), *Quels lendemains pour la responsabilité? Perspectives multidisciplinaires* (pp. 51–77). Nota bene.

Gaudet, S. (2020a). Sur le terrain de la sociologie publique : enjeux éthiques d'une recherche collaborative sur les expériences d'éducation citoyenne des jeunes. *SociologieS*. https://doi.org/10.4000/sociologies.15416

Gaudet, S. (2020b). La société d'acrobates : responsabilité, *care* et participation citoyenne des jeunes. *SociologieS*. https://doi.org/10.4000/sociologies.13229

Gaudet, S. (2021). Les initiatives jeunesse au Canada : des tiers-lieux de l'éducation démocratique. *Revue internationale d'éducation de Sèvres, 88*, 93–104. https://doi.org/10.4000/ries.11586

Gaudet, S., Drapeau, É., Marchand, F., & Forest, M. (2020). Repenser le rapport social d'âge sur le terrain : ethnographies de la Commission

Jeunesse de Gatineau et du Comité des droits de l'enfant du Centre de pédiatrie sociale de Gatineau. In Côté, I., Lavoie, K., & Trottier-Cyr, R.-P. (Eds.), *La recherche centrée sur l'enfant : défis éthiques et innovations méthodologiques* (pp. 219–246). Presses de l'Université Laval.

Gilligan, C. (1986). *Une si grande différence* (A. Kwiatek, Trans.). Flammarion. (Original work published 1982)

Godbout, J. T. (1987). *La démocratie des usagers*. Boréal.

Groleau, A., & Nanhou, V. (2022). *Une analyse longitudinale des facteurs associés à la participation électorale des jeunes nés au Québec* (De la naissance à l'âge adulte : Étude longitudinale du développement des enfants du Québec Volume 9, Issue 4). Institut de la statistique du Québec. https://statistique.quebec.ca/fr/fichier/analyse-longitudinale-facteurs-participation-electorale-jeunes-nes-au-quebec.pdf

Hogan, C. (2002). *Understanding facilitation: Theory and principles*. Kogan Page.

Honneth, A. (2015). Education and the democratic public sphere: A neglected chapter of political philosophy (F. Koch, Trans.). In Jakobsen, J., & Lysaker, O. (Eds.), *Recognition and freedom: Axel Honneth's political thought* (pp. 17–32). Brill. (Original work published 2013)

Laclau, E., & Mouffe, C. (2001). *Hegemony and socialist strategy: Towards a radical democratic politics* (2nd ed.). Verso.

Lefrançois, D., & Éthier, M.-A. (2010). Translating the ideal of deliberative democracy into democratic education: Pure utopia? *Educational Philosophy and Theory, 42*(3), 271–292. https://doi.org/10.1111/j.1469-5812.2007.00385.x

Malboeuf-Hurtubise, C., Léger-Goodes, T., Mageau, G. A., Joussemet, M., Herba, C., Chadi, N., Lefrançois, D., Camden, C., Bussières, È.-L., Taylor, G., Éthier, M.-A., & Gagnon, M. (2021). Philosophy for children and mindfulness during COVID-19: Results from a randomized cluster trial and impact on mental health in elementary school students. *Progress in Neuro-Psychopharmacology and Biological Psychiatry, 107*(110260), 1–6. https://doi.org/10.1016/j.pnpbp.2021.110260

Noddings, N. (2012). The language of care ethics. *Knowledge Quest, 40*(5), 52–56.

Oldenburg, R., & Brissett, D. (1982). The third place. *Qualitative Sociology, 5*, 265–284. https://doi.org/10.1007/BF00986754

Pache-Hébert, C., Jutras, F., & Guay, J.-H. (2014). Le comité des élèves dans les écoles primaires et secondaires : une recension des écrits. *Canadian Journal of Education / Revue canadienne de l'éducation, 37*(4), 1–27. https://journals.sfu.ca/cje/index.php/cje-rce/article/view/1723

Paperman, P., & Laugier, S. (Eds.). (2006). *Le souci des autres : éthique et politique du care*. Éditions de l'École des hautes études en sciences sociales.

Pateman, C. (1976). *Participation and democratic theory*. Cambridge University Press. (Original work published 1970)

Rancière, J. (2003). *Le maître ignorant : cinq leçons sur l'émancipation intellectuelle.* Fayard. (Original work published 1987)

Rosanvallon, P. (2006). *La contre-démocratie : la politique à l'âge de la défiance.* Seuil.

Sant, E. (2019). Democratic education: A theoretical review (2006–2017). *Review of Educational Research, 89*(5), 655–696. https://doi.org/10.3102/0034654319862493

Sasseville, M. (Ed.). (2009). *La pratique de la philosophie avec les enfants* (3rd ed.). Presses de l'Université Laval.

Sauvé, L. (2017). L'éducation à l'écocitoyenneté. In Barthes, A., Lange, J.-M., & Tutiaux-Guillon, N. (Eds.), *Dictionnaire critique : des enjeux et concepts des « éducations à »* (pp. 56–65). L'Harmattan.

Simard, M. (2013). *Histoire du mouvement étudiant québécois 1956-2013 : des Trois Braves aux carrés rouges.* Presses de l'Université Laval.

Tronto, J. (2009). *Un monde vulnérable : pour une politique du care* (H. Maury, Trans.). La Découverte. (Original work published 1993)

Tronto, J. C. (2013). *Caring democracy: Markets, equality, and justice.* New York University Press.

Trudel, S., & Martineau, S. (2021). Axel Honneth et l'éducation : entre émancipation, ethnicité démocratique et compétence civique. *Formation et profession : revue scientifique en éducation, 29*(2), 1–11. https://doi.org/10.18162/fp.2021.644

Van de Velde, C. (2021). "Different struggles, the same fight"? A comparative analysis of student movements in Chile (2011), Quebec (2012), and Hong Kong (2014). In Bessant, J., Mejia Mesinas, A., & Pickard, S. (Eds.), *When students protest: Universities in the Global North* (pp. 33–50). Rowman & Littlefield.

Vitiello, A. (2013). L'exercice de la citoyenneté : délibération, participation et éducation démocratiques. *Participations, 5*(1), 201–226. https://doi.org/10.3917/parti.005.0201

Westheimer, J. (2015). *What kind of citizen? Educating our children for the common good.* Teachers College Press.

Westheimer, J., & Kahne, J. (2004). What kind of citizen? The politics of educating for democracy. *American Educational Research Journal, 41*(2), 237–269. https://doi.org/10.3102/00028312041002237

Zeldin, S., Gauley, J., Krauss, S. E., Kornbluh, M., & Collura, J. (2017). Youth–adult partnership and youth civic development: Cross-national analyses for scholars and field professionals. *Youth & Society, 49*(7), 851–878. https://doi.org/10.1177/0044118X15595153

Notes

1. See the *Démocratie* section on the University of Sherbrooke's *Perspective Monde* website (in French only): https://perspective.usherbrooke.ca/bilan/servlet/BMDictionnaire?iddictionnaire=1487.

2. We planned to include forum theatres in our research, but given how precarious they are, the project never got off the ground for financial reasons.

3. Gatineau Social Pediatric Centre.

4. Gatineau Youth Commission.

5. The research report is available (in French only) at https://ruor.uottawa.ca/handle/10393/40305.

6. Montreal Youth Forum.

7. Take Your Place in School.

8. French school boards no longer exist in Quebec as of 2020, but they oversaw groups of secondary and elementary schools by administrative territory. One of the school boards' governing bodies was an elected council of commissioners.

9. At World Cafés, people exchange ideas in small groups around a table, just like at a café.

CHAPTER 2

A Brief Introduction
to Youth Citizenship
in the Social Sciences

Caroline Caron and Stéphanie Gaudet

Abstract

In three parts, this chapter summarizes social science scholarship on youth citizenship. In the first part, we define the concept of citizenship within the transdisciplinary current of citizenship studies. In the second, we address how citizenship differs for children and adolescents with respect to adults. In the third, we discuss youth participation from a children's rights lens as per the *Convention on the Rights of the Child*, highlighting models designed to uphold youth participation rights in practice. Our three-part summary sheds light on the academic and social value of adopting an inclusive understanding of youth citizenship—it permits us to study how young people experience citizenship education initiatives in civil society from their diverse points of view rather than from the perspective of idealized adult norms.

> Children's citizenship is a right to recognition,
> respect and participation.
> Bren Neale

This book is a collection of chapters that detail the participatory experience civil society organizations—and the schools some of them partner with—offer young people in Quebec. Their mission is youth participation: They encourage young people to take part in political action, get involved in their communities, solve social problems, and learn about their rights. They invest time and resources to provide young Quebecers constructive and stimulating opportunities to create media, organize events, discover the history of their neighbourhoods, hold mock elections, and take part in demonstrations and local politics.

Each participatory initiative shapes unique experiences for young people according to its organizational and social context, the time, and the place. This diversity provides rich insights into the *educational role* these organizations play in shaping citizens in Quebec. According to German researcher and theorist Manfred Liebel (2010, p. 176), participation is an enriching experience for individuals and often those around them, which is crucial to the political formation and education of citizens. Participating in initiatives concretizes young people as actors and citizens by providing opportunities to exercise their agency in stimulating settings often tailored to their needs. It also allows them to put their skills into practice and continue improving on them.

But why combine all these initiatives, organizations, young people, and participatory experiences into one book? What do they have in common? How best to interpret the diverse ways in which young people from different age groups, backgrounds, and participatory roles experience these initiatives? Why do we talk about "citizenship education" at all if neither the organizations nor their spokespeople nor youth call it that?

The answer lies in youth citizenship. Over the following pages, this chapter introduces a current of social sciences research that studies youth citizenship from different theoretical and methodological perspectives and under various banners. Accordingly, it offers a rich framework for understanding the diversity of cases in this book.

In the first part of this chapter, we define the concept of citizenship within citizenship studies—the transdisciplinary social science current that emerged in the 1990s. In the second, we address how citizenship differs for children and adolescents with respect to adults. In the third, we discuss youth participation in terms of children's rights as per the *Convention on the Rights of the Child*, highlighting models designed to uphold youth participation rights in practice. This overview sheds light on the value of adopting an inclusive under-standing of youth citizenship in order to study how young people experience the participatory initiatives in this book from their diverse points of view rather than through the lens of idealized adult norms.

2.1. What Is Citizenship?

In its strictest definition, citizenship refers to a legal status that for-malizes our membership in a nation-state and confers us rights, duties, and privileges, like access to a passport. *Le Grand Robert de la langue française* dictionary defines citizenship as possessing the quali-ties of a citizen and being legally recognized by one or more states. It implies that one is devoted to one's country (patriotic) and has a sense of collective duty (civic-mindedness).

In the twentieth century, British sociologist Thomas Humphrey Marshall (1950) argued that the pairing of rights and responsibilities on the one hand, and civil, political, and social citizenship on the other, could lead to a more egalitarian and inclusive society. *Civil citizenship* recognizes all members of the political community as equal and acknowledges their freedoms, including freedom of movement and expression. *Political citizenship* comes with a duty to participate in political life together with political rights, like voting and running for election. *Social citizenship* ensures members have social rights, like access to the social and economic resources they need to exercise political and civil citizenship. Social-democratic states implement social citizenship through policies like free compulsory education for children, universal access to childcare, employment insurance ben-efits, family benefits, and social programs that support low-income households.[1,2,3]

Several critics have pointed out that such a universalistic approach overlooks the barriers minority and marginalized groups like women, racialized persons, young people, the elderly, immi-grants, and undocumented individuals face to participating in civil and political life (Coll, 2010; Yuval-Davis, 2011). In taking issue with Marshall's abstract and universalist view of citizenship, critics intro-duce the ideas of belonging, identity, and participation into the theo-retical debate (Turner, 1997), arguing that, through the lens of participation, we have an opportunity to consider inclusion–exclusion dynamics within the political community and a common social space (Rocher, 2015, p. 140). Feminist and postcolonial female authors have similarly addressed the role identity and recognition play in self-identifying with a political community. They argue that such self-identification is motivated more by concrete opportunities to participate and socialize politically than by obtaining legal status (see Yuval-Davis, 2011).

This debate did not evolve in a vacuum. Governments and public policy workers have interpreted the topic in a variety of ways. In the 1990s, for example, several Western democratic governments responded to a sharp decline in voting and community involvement—particularly among younger generations—by utilizing discourses and government programs centred on active and responsible citizenship (Milner, 2005, 2010; Putnam, 2000). The result was a proliferation of local, national, and international initiatives promoting citizens' duties and responsibilities toward society, with less involvement from the state. Some critics paint the discourse on active and responsible citizenship as prescriptive and paternalistic (Becquet, 2018; Kennelly, 2011). It is mainly directed at youth and often narrowly defines the concept of the "good citizen" within a neoliberal view of society: in terms of individuality and the social sphere. A "good citizen" then would be someone who contributes to society by engaging in their community and who takes responsibility by limiting their demands and criticism of the state. Discourse along these lines is common in academic circles, where volunteer programs only benefit students from privileged social classes (Eliasoph, 2011).

This brief introduction underscores the difficulty of once and for all defining citizenship—a fluid, polysemous and, at times, hotly debated concept. In the social sciences, it refers to a range of theoretical constructs that place legal belonging in tension with belonging to a political community—that is, participating in existing forms of democracy, be they institutionalized or informal. In the political sphere and society at large, it refers to the set of commonly accepted representations, standards, and discourses for what a good citizen could or should be. Our case studies were motivated by a desire to replace theoretical and normative speculation with an empirical and comprehensive understanding of youth citizenship, one that encompasses complexity and tensions in diverse areas of experimentation within civil society.

2.1.1. A Sociological Conception of Citizenship

To understand our diverse findings, we drew from sociological schol-arship[4] on citizenship, a current that emerged within the field of citi-zenship studies in the 1990s and introduced certain social facts into the theoretical discussion.[5] Engin F. Isin and Bryan S. Turner (2007), for example, have pointed out that undocumented individuals, sea-sonal workers, and other groups formally excluded from citizenship are demanding social rights more and more in contemporary Western societies. Through collective mobilization they regard as legitimate, they are demanding better social, economic, political, and legal pro-tection in the name of the "right to have rights,"[6] the right to recogni-tion before the law, and the fundamental principle of equality that governs democratic societies as per the 1948 *Universal Declaration of Human Rights* (Isin, 2009; Isin & Turner, 2007). What these social facts highlight is that the ability of citizenship status to include or exclude people does not prevent them from collectively making demands of the state. Along with understanding the *objective* facts about groups and individuals lacking formal recognition as full citizens, we must also look at how they experience citizenship *subjectively*. What does it mean to them? How do they embody it day to day? In what spaces and modes? And what are the effects?

2.1.2. Empirical Studies on Ordinary Citizenship

The Anglo-Saxon current of citizenship studies introduced the con-cept of "ordinary citizenship" to citizenship research in the social sciences. The term took root in French-language scholarly literature, where scholars advocate investigating social practices that enable individuals to embody their citizenship in their daily lives by (re)creating a sense of belonging to the social and political collectivity through informal social interactions (Breviglieri & Gaudet, 2014; Carrel & Neveu, 2014). The theoretical focus is placed on participants' agency and their lived citizenship, emphasizing citizenship as embodi-ment (Lister, 2003). Through the lens of ordinary citizenship, citizen-ship is a status as well as a social experience; it is invested with meaning from the immediacy of everyday life and from domestic and intimate settings (Neveu, 2015). As a social experience, citizenship also involves a sense of belonging and identity associated with social position and sociopolitical, economic, and cultural social dynamics.

Beyond its theoretical significance, ordinary citizenship calls for an empirical investigation of the interactions, practices, political participation, and democratic ethos shared within groups in formal and informal spaces (Neveu & Vanhoenacker, 2017). In the French-speaking world, researchers take a pragmatic approach, testing participation by examining the challenges and successes of citizen practices in various social spaces (Berger & Charles, 2014), particularly urban spaces, which are fertile grounds for local citizen initiatives (Montambeault et al., 2021). Researchers typically draw from anthropology by using long-term case studies and participant observation to document their lived experiences and practices in ordinary life (Cefaï et al., 2012).

Broadening the definition of citizenship has exposed the dialogic tension between citizenship as a status and citizenship as a sociological concept rooted in social practices and subjectivity. As a status, the focus is on encouraging citizens' agency through institutionalized policies and conditions of participation as defined by the state. As a sociological concept, the focus is on participation in multiple forms, emphasizing the diversity of ways agency can take shape in contemporary societies (Lister, 2003, p. 37). From this point of view, rather than drawing conclusions about citizenship based on observations of political participation focused solely on the *results* of citizen engagement and collective mobilization within a framework restricted to the institutionalized democratic process, the priority is to study citizenship as a *social process—the construction of citizenship by individuals through time, social spaces, and everyday life experiences*?[7]

2.2. How Citizenship Differs for Children Compared to Adults

Marshall (1950, p. 25) laid the foundations for contemporary theories of democratic citizenship by asserting that "children, by definition, cannot be citizens"—rather, "the right of the child to go to school [should be regarded] as the right of the adult citizen to have been educated."[8] This idea has had a lasting impact on citizenship theories. Its implicitly adult-oriented essentialist norms have resulted in either excluding children from citizenship discussions or assigning them the role of "citizens in the making" (Lister, 2007). Consequently, youth agency and lived citizenship are often overlooked by both society and the research community (Prout, 2011).

Public and scientific discourses have long ignored children and adolescents as social actors. According to Émile Durkheim (1922/1973), children are not ready for social life; they are fragile and need to be socialized by the adult world. Pierre Bourdieu viewed the child as a product of the adult world's social reproduction, writing extensively about social reproduction carried out by educational institutions and the transmission of cultural practices within families of different social classes (Bourdieu, 1979; Bourdieu & Passeron, 1970). And developmental psychologists, for their part, have emphasized that young people's cognitive incapacities diminish as they mature into adulthood. Since the 1980s, however, sociologists and citizenship studies researchers have challenged this essentialist view of childhood to emphasize children's agency, whereby the child is no longer seen as just a product of socialization but as an active partner in the socializing process (Sirota, 2005).

The tension between the adult and child worlds, and the particularities of child and adolescent agency, are at the heart of sociological discussions and debates on childhood (see Gaudet, 2018). The debates vary from one social context to another, demonstrating just how much influence culture can have on defining childhood. It is thus not surprising that their tenor differs greatly between French, Quebec, American, and British sociology, respectively.

In the last decade, British research in childhood studies has probably been the most dynamic. According to Pascale Garnier (2015), it is dominated by four scientific discourses. The first focuses on children's agency based on their ability to make choices and take action, even though their skills differ from adults'. The second discourse addresses young people's ability to make an impact in their world, emphasizing the importance of horizontal, peer-to-peer social relationships. The third recognizes children as a minority social group with rights, including the right to participate and to have their point of view considered in decisions that concern them. The fourth discourse focuses more strictly on the dynamic relationship of agency between children and adults, including diverse, evolving partnerships in which each individual's abilities are taken into account (see Figure 2.1).

The exclusion of children and adolescents from political life resonated loudly with the feminist movement. Historically, women were excluded from the political sphere by virtue of arguments like those used to justify children's partial citizenship—namely, their relegation to the private sphere, legal guardianship assignments, the presumption of inferiority and incompetence, and the perception of disqualifying differences that set them apart from the norm of the adult male citizen with a full-time job (Lister, 2003). Since the 1980s, the synergy between the feminist movement, an influential and dynamic international children's rights movement, and a "new sociology of childhood" has allowed scholars to challenge these prejudices and make them a subject of study, theorization, and social and political advocacy (Lister, 2007).

The breakthrough made way for a new perception of childhood: Instead of being viewed as incomplete, immature, dependent, irrational, and passive objects under the control of adults and social institutions, children could be seen as *different* social subjects capable of participating in society according to their abilities and aptitudes (Caron, 2018; Gaudet, 2018; Hart, 1992; Kallio et al., 2020; Liebel, 2010; Lister, 2007; Moosa-Mitha, 2005; Weller, 2007). Ruth Lister sums it up best:

> "The contemporary sociology of childhood's construction of children as social actors with agency and varying degrees of competence opens up possibilities for the recognition of children as active citizens in a way that a construction of them as passive objects of adult policies and practices did not" (2007, p. 697).

In scholarly writings on international development—echoed in the discourse of international organizations—the definition of youth citizenship has been marked out by two interdependent themes: children's rights on the one hand, and recognizing, defending, and promoting their participation in how societies function and develop on the other (see Hart, 1992; Liebel, 2010). These themes have evolved in tandem with a differentiated, inclusive view of citizenship that rejects adult norms and takes young people's position in society into account, emphasizing that their psychosocial development gradually increases their cognitive abilities and autonomy. Indeed, during adolescence and early adulthood, some individuals start to challenge adult-held stereotypes and norms. Some even become activists and protest their social subordination and the injustices they experience as young people (Liebel, 2010; Moosa-Mitha, 2005; Roche, 1999).

2.3. Participation as an Exercise in Citizenship

The case studies in this book cohere under the theme of youth participation. Research recognizes participation as a vital force for societal development, despite it being often questioned in public discourse. Public institutions understand this, which is why they implement mechanisms to structure youth participation (see Becquet & Stuppia, 2021). Understanding youth participation in all its complexity and the vital role adults and institutions have in it is thus crucial, and the reason we embarked on researching the organizations in this book.

The view of youth participation adopted by these organizations is inherent to citizenship as an inclusive concept that goes beyond idealized, adult norms and recognizes young people as full citizens in the present moment, regardless of their age or social standing (see Caron, 2018). None of the organizations we worked with refer much, if at all, to ordinary citizenship, citizenship studies, or other theoretical vocabulary used to discuss citizenship in academic circles. Yet, in their mandates, missions, and youth initiatives, they all prioritize youth participation above all else. They de facto *enact* inclusive citizenship by offering young people opportunities to experience it in practice—a lived citizenship—allowing them to develop a sense of belonging to their community and recognize themselves in certain social identities. It is clear that a lot remains to be researched in Quebec's fertile environment.

The broad range of cases included in this book led us to examine youth citizenship as a social process. Our in-depth study is based on a comprehensive rather than normative or evaluative approach and enriched by several examples that reveal the diverse but also unique roles that civil society organizations play in practical citizenship education.

2.3.1. Youth Participation as a Right

Since the 1990s, many people—including scholars, international organization workers, social movement organizers, and professionals in social work, law, and international development—have made participation an object of research, analysis, and advocacy. The catalyst was the UN's adoption of the *Convention on the Rights of the Child* in 1989. Several articles in the Convention lay out the rights related to youth participation in all its forms. This includes the child's:[9]

- Right to exercise their rights (Article 5);
- Right to express their views and be heard in all matters that affect them (Article 12);
- Right to freedom of expression (Article 13);
- Right to freedom of thought, conscience, and religion (Article 14);
- Right to freedom of association and peaceful assembly (Article 15);

- Right to access information aimed at promoting their social, spiritual, and moral well-being, as well as physical and mental health (Article 17).

According to Jeremy Roche (1999), adopting the Convention marked a turning point. Theories on citizenship began to challenge the subordinate position assigned to children in contemporary societies. Talk of rights sparked a social shift that began to respect and value children's unique contribution to society and challenge the hierarchy typical in adult–child power dynamics. As the Convention repeatedly emphasizes, the goal has become to recognize that minors are different yet equal, and that we ought to take account of their many diverse skills. Indeed, being *different* than adults does not mean that children and adolescents lack qualities, skills, the ability to reason, or the desire to engage (Moosa-Mitha, 2005).

The innovative shift informed by children's rights invites adults to be less patronizing toward youth and to commit to listening—to taking their views seriously and including them in decisions that affect them in order to develop the kind of institutional and organizational policies that can offer them participatory experiences suited to their needs and expectations (Roche, 1999). Participation thus gains a new set of requirements.

2.3.2. What Is Youth Participation?

A lot has been written about what youth participation should look like to align with the rights in the Convention. It provides community organizations, researchers, and international development workers with an impressive number of definitions, classifications, conceptual schemas, and guidelines. Liebel (2010, p. 175) highlights the research community's agreement that youth participation should not be defined exclusively by traditional politics:

> "In the research on [youth] participation today, there is a consensus that it should not be interpreted only in the formal sense as membership or participation in certain institutions, but also as active participation on all possible occasions and in all social spheres, be they public, private, individual, and collective."

Tim Corney et al. (2020, p. 5) define participation as "the inclusion of young people in decisions that affect them" and as being "actively involved in something," reflecting how widely the concept is disseminated across different professions and fields of research. For Liebel (2010) and Roger Hart (2007), there are three dimensions to participation: it can be a means to (1) exercise one's rights; (2) realize one's potential (personal interest); and (3) advocate for change around one social and collective scope. Although this third aspect tends to stand out in our case studies, the chapters that follow show how all three dimensions are intertwined.

Hart, a pioneer in developing models for implementing children's participation rights, proposed a model that has had a lasting impact on the field. His Ladder of Participation consists of eight ascending rungs, each of which symbolizes a different level of decision-making power that youth truly exercise in participatory initiatives. It invites us to critically consider whether the adults in charge are living up to, or failing to live up to, the ideal reflected in the Convention. Figure 2.1 illustrates the difference between instrumentalizing youth and offering them genuine opportunities to participate.

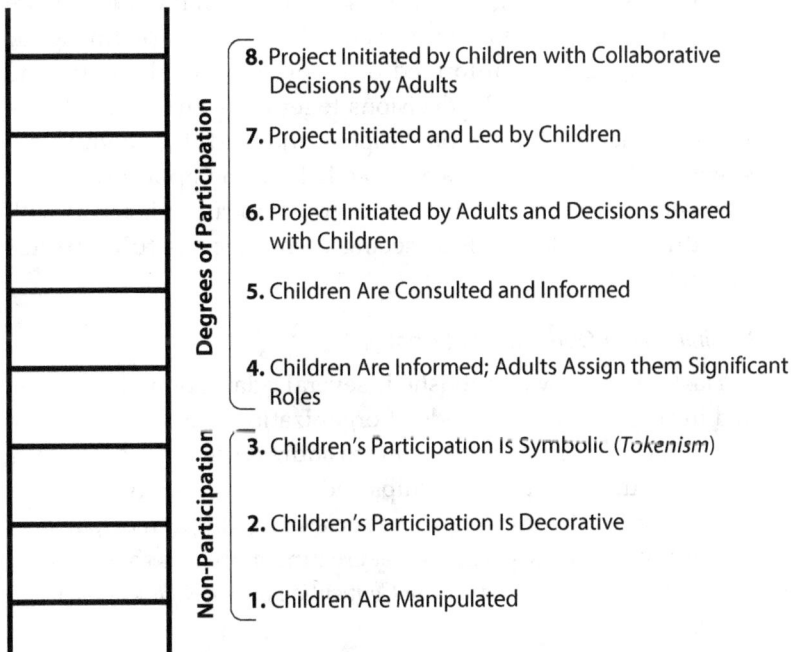

Degrees of Participation

8. Project Initiated by Children with Collaborative Decisions by Adults

7. Project Initiated and Led by Children

6. Project Initiated by Adults and Decisions Shared with Children

5. Children Are Consulted and Informed

4. Children Are Informed; Adults Assign them Significant Roles

Non-Participation

3. Children's Participation Is Symbolic (*Tokenism*)

2. Children's Participation Is Decorative

1. Children Are Manipulated

FIGURE 2.1. Hart's Ladder of Participation (1992).
Source: Adapted from Hart (1992).

According to Harry Shier (2001), one of Hart's most valuable contributions was to raise awareness about the risk of instrumentalizing young people's voices and participation through youth initiatives, the majority of which are designed and run by adults. While this is a sure sign of their dedication and support for children's participation rights, adults often have difficulty letting young people take charge (see Liebel, 2010; Shier, 2001). The first three rungs of Hart's ladder characterize what happens when adults appropriate young people's voices and participation: Young people limited to a passive role may end up being manipulated (first rung), used to make the organization look good (second rung), and reduced to a token presence with no actual say (third rung). Studies carried out in several countries confirm how frustrating these relatively common experiences are to young people (see Hart, 2007).

Genuine participation starts on Hart's ladder when adults respect children as partners and at the very least inform them before involving them in an initiative or taking action on their behalf (Liebel, 2010, p. 184). The first level of genuine participation happens when adults assign young people a task and inform them of the aim (fourth rung). It increases as adults consult young people during the initiative, keeping them informed of its progress (fifth rung), and offer them chances to make decisions together (sixth rung). At the top of the ladder, young people propose and lead their own initiatives, with help from adults when needed and no appropriation of their power (seventh rung), and invite adults to run initiatives with them, with all people involved seeing themselves as full partners (eighth rung).

2.3.3. Minimum or Optimum Participation?

Since Hart's ladder was published, several adaptations have been created in response to the needs of organizations involved in youth advocacy. Each different version aims to address the power dynamics inherent to youth–adult relationships and, as advocated in the sociology of childhood, the importance of socializing children as partners of the adult world. This suggests that creating a process that respects both the spirit and the letter of the *Convention on the Rights of the Child* is possible.

Table 2.1 compares three other frequently cited models of youth participation, illustrating five ubiquitous trends: participation levels differ according to (1) the type of participation young people are assigned (consultation, participation, or leadership), (2) the role they are assigned (guest, participant, or leader), (3) how adults share responsibility with youth—meaning to what extent young people are involved in making decisions or lead and implement projects themselves, (4) who initiates the process; some initiatives are *initiated and led by adults*, others are *initiated by adults and led at least in part by young people*, and (5) how youth share power with adults in projects primarily *initiated and led by young people*, sometimes with adults as decision-making partners.

Table 2.1. Youth–Adult Partnerships: Three Models

	Lansdown (2001)	Shier (2001)	Treseder (1997)
Minimal level of Participation	1. Adults consult children	1. Adults listen to children	1. Adults initiate but inform children
		2. Adults encourage children to express themselves	2. Adults initiate but consult and inform children
	2. Children Participate	3. Children's perspectives are taken into account	3. Adults initiate but take decisions with children
Optimal level of Participation		4. Children are involved in decisions	4. Children initiate and lead but benefit from the support of adults when necessary
	3. Children lead and decide	5. Children share responsibility and take decisions with adults	5. Children initiate and lead but consult with adults and take decisions together

Source: Lansdown (2001), Shier (2001), and Treseder (1997).

These models were created in the spirit of providing organizations and the adults who run them with tools to optimize their alignment with the *Convention on the Rights of the Child.* Shier's model (2001) invites organizations to re-evaluate their mission, objectives, available resources, internal policies, and decision-making processes to clearly and realistically understand how much staff, money, time, and space they are willing to commit. He insists that only initiatives founded on integrating young people into decision-making processes meet the minimum participation requirements specified in the Convention—that means including young people before initiatives are conceived so they can help define them. At a time when initiatives are proudly labelled "by and for young people," these methods give organizations useful benchmarks for thinking critically about how they welcome, support, and promote youth participation.

Over the past 25 years, discussions on youth participation have advanced in academic and institutional settings. Nowadays, political apathy among young people, which dominated discussions in the 1990s and 2000s, shares the stage with more encouraging and less accusatory perspectives (Corney et al., 2020; Gaudet, 2018). Building on youth participation models, other conceptual tools have been developed to encourage constructive youth-adult relations and provide young people with genuine decision-making power over initiatives (see Blanchet-Cohen & Brunson, 2014; Kallio et al., 2020; Zeldin et al., 2017). We address these themes in different ways in each chapter and in the book's conclusion, where we review the case studies as a whole.

Conclusion

The organizations in this book strive to give young people opportunities to participate in initiatives, in what should be seen as an embodiment of citizenship on their own terms rather than under prescribed models. As both a status and social practice, this kind of citizenship rejects adult norms by dissolving the boundaries by which minors were historically viewed as "citizens in the making"—in the name of a prejudice that presumed their age limited their intellect and autonomy (see Caron, 2018). Civil society, however, can offer unique and tailored opportunities for young people to participate as full members of society, recognizing their true abilities and aptitude for learning (Kallio et al., 2020). In the following chapters, we examine young people's lived experiences of citizenship. We aim to shed light on how experiments in collective participation contribute to citizenship education while taking into account the unique situations, interests, skills, and social standing of the young people involved.

References

Becquet, V. (2018). Comprendre l'instrumentation des questions de citoyenneté dans les politiques d'éducation et de jeunesse : une typologie des dispositifs d'action publique. *Lien social et Politiques, 80*, 15–33. https://doi.org/10.7202/1044107ar

Becquet, V., & Stuppia, P. (2021). *Géopolitique de la jeunesse : engagement et (dé)mobilisations*. Le Cavalier Bleu.

Berger, M., & Charles, J. (2014). *Persona non grata*. Au seuil de la participation. *Participations, 9*(2), 5–36. https://doi.org/10.3917/parti.009.0005

Blanchet-Cohen, N., & Brunson, L. (2014). Creating settings for youth empowerment and leadership: An ecological perspective. *Child & Youth Services, 35*(3), 216–236. https://doi.org/10.1080/0145935X.2014.938735

Bourdieu, P. (1979). *La distinction : critique sociale du jugement*. Les Éditions de Minuit.

Bourdieu, P., & Passeron, J.-C. (1970). *La reproduction : éléments pour une théorie du système d'enseignement*. Les Éditions de Minuit.

Breviglieri, M., & Gaudet, S. (2014). Présentation : les arrières-scènes participatives et le lien ordinaire au politique. *Lien social et Politiques, 71*, 3–9. https://doi.org/10.7202/1024735ar

Caron, C. (2018). La citoyenneté des adolescents du 21e siècle dans une perspective de justice sociale : pourquoi et comment ? *Lien social et Politiques, 80*, 52–68. https://doi.org/10.7202/1044109ar

Carrel, M., & Neveu, C. (Eds.). (2014). *Citoyennetés ordinaires : pour une approche renouvelée des pratiques citoyennes*. Karthala.

Cefaï, D., Carrel, M., Talpin, J., Eliasoph, N., & Lichterman, P. (2012). Ethnographies de la participation. *Participations, 4*(3), 7–48. https://doi.org/10.3917/parti.004.0005

Coll, K. M. (2010). *Remaking citizenship: Latina immigrants and new American politics*. Stanford University Press.

Corney, T., Williamson, H., Holdsworth, R., Broadbent, R., Ellis, K., Shier, H., & Cooper, T. (2020). *Approaches to youth participation in youth and community work practice: A critical dialogue*. Youth Workers Association.

Durkheim, É. (1973). *Éducation et sociologie* (2nd ed. of new edition). Presses universitaires de France. (Original work published 1922)

Eliasoph, N. (2011). *Making volunteers: Civic life after welfare's end*. Princeton University Press.

Garnier, P. (2015). L'"agency" des enfants : projet scientifique et politique des "childhood studies." *Éducation et sociétés, 36*(2), 159–173. https://doi.org/10.3917/es.036.0159

Gaudet, S. (2018). Introduction : citoyenneté des enfants et des adolescents. *Lien social et Politiques, 80*, 4–14. https://doi.org/10.7202/1044106ar

Hart, J. (2007). Empowerment or frustration? Participatory programming with young Palestinians. *Children, Youth and Environments, 17*(3), 1–23. https://www.jstor.org/stable/10.7721/chilyoutenvi.17.3.0001

Hart, R. A. (1992). *Children's participation: From tokenism to citizenship.* UNICEF, International Child Development Centre. https://www.unicef-irc.org/publications/100-childrens-participation-from-tokenism-to-citizenship.html

Isin, E. F. (2009). Citizenship in flux: The figure of the activist citizen. *Subjectivity, 29*(1), 367–388. https://doi.org/10.1057/sub.2009.25

Isin, E. F., & Turner, B. S. (2002a). Citizenship studies: An introduction. In Isin, E. F. & Turner, B. S. (Eds.), *Handbook of citizenship studies* (pp. 1–11). Sage.

Isin, E. F., & Turner, B. S. (Eds.). (2002b). *Handbook of citizenship studies.* Sage.

Isin, E. F., & Turner, B. S. (2007). Investigating citizenship: An agenda for citizenship studies. *Citizenship Studies, 11*(1), 5–17. https://doi.org/10.1080/13621020601099773

Kallio, K. P., Wood, B. E., & Häkli, J. (2020). Lived citizenship: Conceptualising an emerging field. *Citizenship Studies, 24*(6), 713–729. https://doi.org/10.1080/13621025.2020.1739227

Kennelly, J. (2011). *Citizen youth: Culture, activism, and agency in a neoliberal era.* Palgrave Macmillan.

Lansdown, G. (2001). *Promoting children's participation in democratic decision-making.* UNICEF Innocenti Research Centre.

Le Robert. (n.d.). Citoyenneté. In *Le Grand Robert de la langue française.* Retrieved Month Day, 2022, from https://grandrobert.lerobert.com/

Le Robert. (n.d.). Civisme. In *Le Grand Robert de la langue française.* Retrieved Month Day, 2022, https://grandrobert.lerobert.com/

Liebel, M. (2010). *Enfants, droits et citoyenneté : faire émerger la perspective des enfants sur leurs droits* (in collaboration with P. Robin & I. Saadi). L'Harmattan.

Lister, R. (2003). *Citizenship: Feminist perspectives* (2nd ed.). Palgrave Macmillan.

Lister, R. (2007). Why citizenship: Where, when and how children? *Theoretical Inquiries in Law, 8*(2), 693–718. https://doi.org/10.2202/1565-3404.1165

Marshall, T. H. (1950). *Citizenship and social class and other essays.* Cambridge University Press.

Milner, H. (2005). Are young Canadians becoming political dropouts? A comparative perspective. *IRPP Choices, 11*(3). https://irpp.org/wp-content/uploads/assets/vol11no3.pdf

Milner, H. (2010). *The internet generation: Engaged citizens or political dropouts.* University Press of New England.

Montambeault, F., Bherer, L., & Cloutier, G. (2021). *L'engagement pousse là où on le sème : le Carré Casgrain, de jardin ouvert à collectif citoyen.* Écosociété.

Moosa-Mitha, M. (2005). A difference-centred alternative to theorization of children's citizenship rights. *Citizenship Studies, 9*(4), 369–388. https://doi.org/10.1080/13621020500211354

Neale, B. (Ed.). (2004). *Young children's citizenship: Ideas into practice* (in collaboration with C. Willow, R. Marchant & P. Kirby). Joseph Rowntree Foundation.

Neveu, C. (2015). Of ordinariness and citizenship processes. *Citizenship Studies, 19*(2), 141–154. https://doi.org/10.1080/13621025.2015.1005944

Neveu, C., & Vanhoenacker, M. (2017). La participation buissonnière, ou le secret dans l'ordinaire de la citoyenneté. *Participations, 19*(3), 7–22. https://doi.org/10.3917/parti.019.0007

Prout, A. (2011). Taking a step away from modernity: Reconsidering the new sociology of childhood. *Global Studies of Childhood, 1*(1), 4–14. https://doi.org/10.2304/gsch.2011.1.1.4

Putnam, R. D. (2000). *Bowling alone: The collapse and revival of American community.* Simon & Schuster.

Roche, J. (1999). Children: Rights, participation and citizenship. *Childhood, 6*(4), 475–493. https://doi.org/10.1177/0907568299006004006

Rocher, F. (2015). Sur les dimensions constitutives de la citoyenneté : perspective des minorités ethnoculturelles et religieuses dans un Québec à l'identité incertaine. *Recherches sociographiques, 56*(1), 139–170. https://doi.org/10.7202/1030276ar

Shier, H. (2001). Pathways to participation: Openings, opportunities, and obligations. *Children & Society, 15*(2), 107–117. https://doi.org/10.1002/chi.617

Sirota, R. (2005). L'enfant acteur ou sujet dans la sociologie de l'enfance : évolution des positions théoriques au travers du prisme de la socialisation. In Bergonnier-Dupuy, G. (Ed.), *L'enfant, acteur et/ou sujet au sein de la famille* (pp. 33–41). Érès. https://doi.org/10.3917/eres.bergo.2005.01.0033

Treseder, P. (1997). *Empowering children and young people: Promoting involvement in decision-making.* Save the Children.

Turner, B. S. (1997). Citizenship studies: A general theory. *Citizenship Studies, 1*(1), 5–18. https://doi.org/10.1080/13621029708420644

Weller, S. (2007). *Teenager's citizenship: Experiences and education.* Routledge.

Yuval-Davis, N. (2011). *The politics of belonging: Intersectional contestations.* Sage.

Zeldin, S., Gauley, J., Krauss, S. E., Kornbluh, M., & Collura, J. (2017). Youth–adult partnership and youth civic development: Cross-national analyses for scholars and field professionals. *Youth & Society, 49*(7), 851–878. https://doi.org/10.1177/0044118X15595153

Notes

1. For more on social rights in Canada, see this *Canadian Encyclopedia* article on the welfare state: https://www.thecanadianencyclopedia.ca/en/article/welfare-state

2. In his seminal work, Marshall (1950) argued that modern citizenship is the result of the historical development of three types of rights. Civil rights

were established in Europe during the seventeenth and eighteenth centuries and were institutionalized in civil law. Political rights were endorsed and implemented by parliamentary democracies in Europe and North America during the nineteenth and twentieth centuries. Social rights are a product of the twentieth century and the welfare state. See Isin and Turner (2007) for an overview. It is important to note that feminist perspectives challenge the sequential development of these three types of rights, claiming they only apply to male citizens belonging to certain social classes, such as landowners and workers (see Lister, 2003).

3. Some authors suggest adding participation rights as a fourth category. Various social groups and international organizations have successfully introduced topics such as sexual rights, minority rights, and environmental rights into public discourse and national and international political arenas. For an overview, see Isin and Turner (2002a, 2002b).

4. A sociological approach to citizenship focuses on how citizenship is theorized and studied as a social phenomenon in academic disciplines and interdisciplinary fields. The definition of citizenship thus extends beyond legal status and encompasses its tangible manifestations in society. This is why sociological studies of citizenship rely on empirical research and descriptive or explanatory analyses.

5. Several publications appeared in the English-speaking world during this period. Notably, the acclaimed international journal *Citizenship Studies* was founded in 1997.

6. The origin of this expression is attributed to the philosopher Hannah Arendt.

7. For this reason, citizenship studies explores topics beyond the scope of collective action through institutionalized democratic processes such as lobbying parliamentarians, influencing public policy and legislation, and making changes to how political and government bodies work.

8. "The right to education is a genuine social right of citizenship, because the aim of education during childhood is to shape the future adult. Fundamentally it should be regarded, not as the right of the child to go to school, but as the right of the adult citizen to have been educated" (Marshall, 1950, p. 25).

9. The three categories of rights as per the *Convention on the Rights of the Child* are commonly referred to as "the three Ps": the right to *protection* (from physical and psychological harm), to *provision* (like access to resources, care, and security), and to *participation* (including civil liberties and the right to act on one's own behalf in one's own interest). The Convention is the result of the sustained work of an internationalist movement that has promoted the interests and rights of children throughout the twentieth century. For more information, see Liebel (2010) and the United Nations website: https://www.ohchr.org/en/instruments-mechanisms/instruments/convention-rights-child.

PART II

CASE STUDIES

A) Experiences in Citizenship Education Based on Participatory Democracy

CHAPTER 3

A Friendly Introduction to Civic Participation: The Institut du Nouveau Monde Summer School

Emilie Drapeau and Stéphanie Gaudet

Abstract

This chapter presents the 2017 Institut du Nouveau Monde (INM) Summer School. Every year, hundreds of adolescents and young adults gather in Montreal for an eclectic four-day program. Participants get to customize their schedule based on their interests and work directly with around 50 adults taking part as mentors, speakers, and facilitators. Through concrete scenarios, they are introduced to different ways of interpreting citizenship and engagement, broadening their horizons and social networks in the process. Because of the number and diversity of people behind it, the school is a gateway to an entire ecosystem of youth organizations. It offers young people a unique form of citizenship education based on participatory democracy.

Wednesday, August 9, 2017. It's 6 p.m. A group of Summer School students is lining up to register at the welcome booth in the entrance hall. A few of them start chatting and I [Emilie] take the opportunity to introduce myself to the ones near me. A volunteer hands us bingo cards, explaining that they're for an icebreaker. Instead of numbers, each card lists activities like biking, composting, and playing a musical instrument. After we register, the volunteer invites us into the adjacent room, where we gather around the cocktail tables laid out. Once all 300 of us have arrived, the icebreaker begins. The goal is to check off the activities on our card with the initials of new acquaintances who enjoy doing them. Participants wander from group to group, alone or in small delegations. As we network, the initial awkwardness gives way to excitement. People around me are warm and welcoming. One of the facilitators invites us to wrap up the activity with a symbolic act: write the impact we want to have on the world on the card and fold it into an airplane. Together, we launch our planes into the air and pick up the one that lands at our feet.

So began the INM Summer School of 2017. The program took place in Montreal from August 9 to August 12, at the National School of Public Administration and the Conservatoire de musique et d'art dramatique du Québec.[1] Over 350 young people and around 50 partners from the public, private, community, and labour union sectors came together to *make an impact*—the theme of the school that year—through actions, goals, ideas, innovation, advocacy, and art (*Guide to participation*, p. 12). Each student had access to networking events, talks, roundtables, and workshops in addition to one of seven citizen engagement courses running simultaneously that they selected at registration: art, communication, entrepreneurship, exploration, innovation, participatory leadership, and mobilization.

The INM is a non-profit and non-partisan organization. Since 2004 when it was created, it has been instrumental in teaching young people about democratic citizenship and, more generally, about participatory democracy in Quebec (see Gaudet, 2021).[2] By actively and continuously maintaining a space for public participation and dialogue on sociopolitical issues, the organization has been playing an important role in civil society (see Mailhot et al., 2021).

The Summer School is at the heart of an ecosystem of organizations that has been dedicated to getting young Quebecers civically engaged every year for almost 20 years. The school is a microcosm of the year's headlining social issues—during elections, the school invites political figures to answer participant questions and organizes debates on the environment, the inclusion of minority groups, intersectional feminism, and degrowth.

It is a meeting place for young people from diverse backgrounds and organizations with equally diverse goals and mandates. The INM has developed inclusive practices to accommodate this diversity; the warm and caring space is a third place for citizenship education. We attended hoping to find out what citizenship education means at the school and how young people feel about their experience there.

To document our findings, our research assistants—supervised by two professors—did participant observation in the seven courses. Here is a summary of some of the ethnographic data we collected.[3]

3.1. Citizenship Summer School

In the participant guide, the Summer School is described as a "space of engagement" for working on collective projects, deliberating on social issues, and reflecting on innovative proposals (*Guide de participation*, p. 10). It is a complex social space where individuals, groups, and institutions come together to discuss different views on citizenship and democratic citizenship education. Several adults participate as speakers, facilitate the courses and workshops, and mentor participants by sharing their experiences. Though most of them do not work for the INM, they embrace and embody different views on citizen participation as well as the organization's pragmatic position on education: that it should recognize young people's citizenship and agency.

The Summer School is open to individuals between the ages of 15 and 35, but from our observations, most participants are between 18 and 23. We also noticed a high proportion of young women, immigrants, and people from racialized groups. The school schedule alternates between activities open to everyone and citizen engagement courses reserved for registered participants (see Table 3.1). The courses draw from a variety of citizen participation practices and, in keeping with the INM's ideal, strive to empower participants politically beyond simply getting them to vote. They offer young people an opportunity to debate specific issues and make decisions together with 30 to 50 of their peers.

3.2. How Young People Experience Citizenship Education

What makes the Summer School unique is how many kinds of citizenship emerge across its courses and activities, even if participatory citizenship is dominant. Each course invites participants to work on a project and present it at a closing celebration. In the entrepreneur-ship course, they prepare a social entrepreneurship project; in the mobilization course, a social advertising campaign. In the commu-nication course, they write newspaper articles to learn about the role of journalism in a democracy. The other courses place even more emphasis on public expression. In the participatory leadership course, participants develop a project that calls on their collective intelligence. In the art course, they put on an "emancipating" play. In the innova-tion course, they discuss issues related to digital democracy and write a collective open letter "to the citizens of today and tomorrow." The exploration course is designed specifically for younger participants between the ages of 15 and 17. They explore Montreal and learn about the contribution of different cultural communities to Montreal's his-tory and development.

3.2.1. Participatory and Deliberative Citizenship through Experiential Learning

Making an Impact, the theme of the 2017 Summer School, invokes the idea of an engaged, participatory citizen. The seven experiential citi-zen engagement courses are based on a pragmatic pedagogical approach inspired by the work of John Dewey (1916/1997, 1927). According to Dewey, education should train citizens to think criti-cally, reason, and act to solve collective problems. It is rooted in the political experience of the *demos*—that is, shared decision-making to achieve a common goal.

In the courses, facilitators share their knowledge and skills with participants to help them plan and complete their projects. Youth have a chance to mobilize tools and experiment with discussion and teamwork, which helps develop their competencies.

In the space of a single workshop, we'd receive information and be introduced to a new tool, then get to experiment with putting an approach into practice. [...] A typical workshop starts with a roundtable discussion where we can share our experiences and knowledge on a topic. A mentor would offer a particular tool, approach, or piece of experiential knowledge. We'd then break out into smaller teams to discuss how to apply the tool or approach to our project. After a while, we'd present our progress to the broader group and discuss any improvements that needed to be made. (Entrepreneurship course)

This description of a typical workshop in the entrepreneurship course shows us that young people are learning by participating in collective projects but also, through roundtable discussions, getting the opportunity to put theory into practice and receive constructive feedback that encourages them to self-correct—a marker of deliberative citizenship.[4]

They receive a wealth of knowledge in each of the courses, which empowers them to not only learn as individuals but also acquire "collective know-how" as a team, where they can develop their interpersonal skills. For one of the first times in their lives, young people from their teens to their thirties come together outside the school environment to talk about values, social cohesion, and working together.

In workshops across all the citizen engagement courses, participants are organized into small groups of four to five so everyone has a chance to express themselves. This is when they come up against the relational and emotional challenges of working toward a consensus as a group:

> *One participant assumes the role of group leader. She makes decisions and is clear about what she does and doesn't like. Another, younger participant contributes lots of ideas enthusiastically, often qualifying them with, "Does that make sense? It makes sense in my head." The group leader addresses him pedagogically, suggesting alternative ways to frame his ideas. Generally speaking, ideas are not discarded, only reformulated. We always proceed by consensus. The person who yields to others doesn't appear offended and recognizes that the group's decision is the right one.* (Communication course)

In most of the small groups we observed, one person usually takes the lead, moderating discussions, managing workflows, and acting as spokesperson for the group. Participants have different leadership styles; some put more focus on participation and consensus, others on the tasks, others still on giving everyone a chance to talk. It is not unusual for tensions to arise because not everyone's ideas are heard and reflected within the group:

> *There's a bit of tension in two of the groups. When the group leaders presented the groups' ideas, I observed non-verbal signs that some participants weren't onboard. Some people were excluded and the same people*

almost always took the lead. Many participants had strong personalities and needed to express their opinions, which may have caused some friction and awkwardness. But generally speaking, discussions were respectful. (Mobilization course)

Tension and awkwardness are part and parcel of the collective experience of learning how to deliberate and participate. Young people learn to live with the discomfort of disagreeing with someone and how to navigate imperfect power dynamics when sharing the floor and making decisions with others. This was particularly the case in the mobilization course, where many of the participants were from visible minority and racialized groups and often felt marginalized and voiceless in the public arena. This gave rise to discussions on cultural diversity that highlighted a multicultural conception of citizenship (see Sant, 2019).

At times, we observed tensions rising between the adult facilitators and youth participants, where participants would question the facilitators' instructions or advice. This was the case in a workshop in the communication course when a facilitator asked participants to add information to an article they were writing to make it more "objective":

The tone of the discussions is pretty tense, and there's clearly a disagreement between the young people and the facilitator, which I gather from the reactions of one of my teammates. In a low voice, she tells me she finds the idea of objectivity "really old-fashioned" and "old school." She says we'll add the missing information and see about the rest—implying that we may not do everything the facilitator asked. She and I are willing to try and make the article more objective, but the other two don't see the point. It doesn't seem important to them. (Communication course)

In several of the courses, technical skills such as writing articles and leading awareness campaigns or entrepreneurial projects are presented to young people as neutral means to ends like objectivity and equality, which are sometimes treated as self-evident. Facilitators will sometimes "take off their facilitator hat" to express their own point of view or step in to "resolve" a dispute or redirect a discussion if questions are getting too heated and opinions too polarizing. Actions like these can shut down discussion and reveal how easy it is in concrete situations to overstep the very values the organization seeks to promote. As observed in other initiatives, values are some-times taken for granted and thus absent from critical self-reflection. Young people seem particularly sensitive to a perceived lack of neu-trality on the part of the adults in charge, highlighting how much youth participation experiences depend on good facilitation. These situations provide valuable opportunities for (self) reflection, even though their fleeting nature makes this quite difficult.

Experiential learning has many advantages, but it also poses challenges. Developing a project and presenting it at the closing event can be an engaging form of learning, but it puts pressure on partici-pants and facilitation teams. Sometimes, facilitators are forced to cut short questions and debates because of time constraints. This hap-pened, for example, in the entrepreneurship course, where a debate on the differences between social entrepreneurship and the social economy was halted. It also happened in the exploration course, where participants could not fully discuss their different interpreta-tions of a mural for lack of time. These examples show what a critical resource time is in the day-to-day of a democracy and the difficulty organizations face in managing it effectively.

3.2.2. Liberal, Critical, and Agonistic Citizenship

During our observations, we also identified liberal democratic dis-course. In the liberal democratic model, individuals have a duty to understand how institutions work in order to benefit from the free-doms associated with them (Sant, 2019). Their participation in activi-ties and in society depends on their ability to learn and respect the rules. The Summer School's participation guide includes a code of conduct that delineates the behaviours expected of a "good" partici-pant and, by extension, a "good" citizen:

> Keep it short and to the point. Express yourself as clearly and succinctly as possible to leave time for others. Attack ideas, not people! Listen respectfully to what others have to say. If you dis-agree, you have the right to say so politely. Dare to speak out and be open to diversity. You share responsibility for how successful the activities are. Be ready to act when asked, and be open-minded enough to hear ideas different than your own. When your comments are relevant, share them with the whole group! Avoid chatting with your neighbours as it prevents you from listening to guests. Be on time for the activities you've chosen.

If you arrive late, be discreet. Don't wander between rooms while
activities are in session. (*Guide de participation*, p. 122)[5]

This excerpt reflects the ethic of discussion implicit in democratic
societies, where everyone's right to speak is respected and citizens
share a sense of togetherness (Blondiaux, 2008; Habermas, 1991/2013).

The idea of how a "good" citizen should behave does not just
appear in the participation guide. Mentors at the Summer School use
storytelling—a communication technique to share their deep convic-
tions—to encourage participants to be virtuous and moral. Course
facilitators teach participants kindness, openness, empathy, respect,
and listening. They frequently address participants as members of a
generation that can make a difference. The school encourages them
to take responsibility by growing their personal skills for the good
of the community. In the school's opening panel, one of the facilitators explores the idea of individual responsibility:

*The facilitator talks about the theme of making an impact. He defines
impact as influence—a way of leaving our mark on the world and influencing society through individual and collective action. He challenges us to
consider how far-reaching our impact should be with a series of questions
he invites us to answer by a show of hands. "Should we change ourselves?"
Several hands shoot up. "Or someone else?" Slightly fewer hands go up this
time.* (Opening panel)

To the panelists, making an impact means different things:
being a role model; working on ourselves, but not only ourselves;
starting small, like persuading one person; finding our issue; being
wary of extremes; and getting involved by starting with something
that bothers us and that we want to change.

As we leave the room, several participants are discussing what
we just heard. Some feel the ideas and values promoted by the panelists are too consensus-oriented and reformist and that it is "necessary
to rattle the cage." The panelist who captured their attention most
was Abenaki filmmaker Alanis Obomsawin. She had spoken about
her struggle to gain recognition for Indigenous culture and history.
Participants admired her for fearlessly challenging the established
order. One of them confided, "I liked her the most because she's a
rebel." In contrast to the other panelists, her contribution reflects an

agonistic approach to democracy, whereby it is important to not only denounce power relations but also resist them (Sant, 2019).

The Summer School's organizing committee seems to have intentionally invited guest speakers with very different views on what participation and social change should entail. The concept of critical democratic citizenship—which calls into question power dynamics built into the structure of society—slips into many discussions, presentations, and workshops, even if the INM never spells it out explicitly. For example, social inequalities are often discussed due to the presence of unions, which are partners of the school. But, as an apolitical and non-partisan organization, the INM avoids steering participants in any one political direction in discussions on justice and equality. Instead, they offer them an opportunity to debate and consider different possibilities. As the participation guide mentions, situating its efforts within a perspective of justice and social inclusion is characteristic of the INM's approach:

> We face a lot of complex challenges: climate change, living as a community, the refugee crisis, growing social inequalities—all set against a backdrop of a revolution in technology and media that's noticeably impacting how we get information, communicate, and live democratically. What are the best strategies for creating social change and mobilizing as many people as possible to be agents of change? [...] To make an impact, young people have to occupy public spaces, make their voices heard, be able to think critically, and act in response. (*Guide de participation*, p. 10)[6]

The summer school provides ample opportunities for participants to learn about and question the causes of various social justice issues as diverse as the environment, gender parity, and the inequalities experienced by Indigenous people. For instance, one of the participatory workshops aims to raise awareness of the issues facing Indigenous youth:

> *The facilitator asks us to stand in a circle. The circle, he explains, is important in Indigenous culture. He invites us to introduce ourselves, share what we know about the Indigenous community, and take turns by passing around the proverbial torch—a feather. Many say they know very little about what life is like for Indigenous people. We return to our seats and the facilitator hands out a brochure on the myths and realities of Indigenous*

communities. He explains some of the myths that history teaches us about Quebec's Indigenous population. After showing us a series of short films, he asks us to share what we think about the stereotypes and historical relations between Indigenous Peoples and Caucasians. (Participatory leadership workshop: "Beyond Prejudice: A Cinematic Foray into First Nations Realities")

3.3. Adult–Youth Collaboration

The success of participatory democratic citizenship education is determined by how well youth and adults get along (Zeldin et al., 2013). The quality of their relationship hinges on the collaborative rapport created through collective action and teamwork. The adults are required to mentor groups and facilitate interactions (Blanchet-Cohen & Brunson, 2014) by creating opportunities for young people to be heard and participate actively and genuinely in deliberations (Zeldin et al., 2013). Much depends on establishing a fair balance of power. It was interesting to observe this dynamic play out in the courses, where facilitation teams helped participants with their final projects over a three-day period. Throughout the Summer School, we observed adult mentors, facilitators, and guest speakers listening to participants with genuine interest and encouraging them to express themselves:

All in all, the atmosphere in the workshop is friendly and laid-back as well as polite and engaging. The two facilitators are as warm and welcoming as before. They encourage people to share their thoughts, make sure everyone has a chance to speak, and take the time to reword ideas so that everyone gets the message. One of them helps participants develop their ideas by posing lots of questions. (Entrepreneurship course)

Real youth–adult collaboration starts when facilitators and participants work together on the final projects. The role of facilitators is not just to invite participants to express themselves. It is also important that they listen and welcome differing points of view, even those between adults and youth. Unlike in school, this gives participants a chance to interact with adults without being evaluated. In the mobilization course, participants debate with the facilitator—a marketing expert—supervising their creative advertising project:

During the workshop, the facilitator takes us through the technical skills we need to create a good ad. He then invites us to discuss a series of ads and analyze their target audience, objectives, slogan, and efficacy. Afterwards, he talks to us about the creative process in advertising. When someone is presenting, he asks them questions to help them develop their idea further. For the first time, the whole group is engaged; everyone has something to say. In fact, small debates about the ads start popping up. Some participants say why they disagree with the facilitator's interpretation. He doubles down and keeps trying to convince the group. All in all, participants seem to really appreciate the chance to discuss and debate their ideas together. (Mobilization course)

A true sign of collaboration is when youth and adults share decision-making power. Facilitators make efforts to recognize participants' skills and leave room for them to make decisions. We observed this in the innovation course where, when adults called on them to develop a project, participants took the lead and determined how it would be organized:

In the third workshop, participants negotiated their time management and work groups with the facilitator. They drafted proposals for how their group project would be completed and carried out most of the work themselves. One participant suggested the format—a letter—and the youth chose the recipient and what to write. (Innovation course)

The facilitators at the Summer School are less directive than the adult authority figures in young people's daily lives, which turns the typical power dynamic on its head. In their interactions, facilitators display qualities that foster a sense of closeness, as indicated by participants themselves, who have described them as cheerful, approachable, friendly, and charismatic. Their more hands-off approach seems to help blur the lines between different age groups, roles, and social statuses. Adults do have authority, but they manage to create a horizontal and informal environment where everyone feels equal. As one research assistant notes in the leadership course, it felt like the facilitation team "was inviting us to try certain things, rather than telling us to." While the adults set the terms of the mentorship relationship in some cases, in others the adults and youth decide together using mutual consent and acknowledging each other's points of view:

The facilitators and participants are equal partners. The environment is really one of sharing and co-construction. No one is the authority figure. Even if the facilitation team and guest speakers are experts in their field, they don't make us feel that way. They help guide our thinking without imposing a particular worldview. The facilitators don't explicitly ask anything of us. Just the opposite: they say their goal is to help us take ownership of what we learn from the presentations and activities and make up our own minds. As we work on our performance, no one is thinking about being evaluated. At the closing event, we will be our only judges. (Art course)

The facilitation teams play a support role with the youth in addition to structuring the social environments to ensure they are respectful and inclusive. During the art course, participants are encouraged to invite other attendees at the school to join their performance. As one observer noted, "The facilitators stand back so we can fully enjoy the activity, reminding us from time to time, 'I'll just be at the back,' or 'I won't be far.'"

Introducing several hundred young people to several dozen members of civil society in a short span of time seems to be a key feature of the Summer School. Mentorship is also very important. Several participants said they registered for the communication and entrepreneurship courses because they wanted to pursue a career in journalism or entrepreneurship. Accordingly, facilitators have an opportunity to teach and mentor demonstrably grateful individuals who may well grow up to work in the same fields. Indeed, attending the Summer School is a special learning opportunity offering knowledge that is distinct from what youth are used to in schools.

3.4. What Have Young People and Communities Gained from the Experience?

For many participants, the Summer School is a powerful and emotional learning experience, both individually and collectively. Based on our observations, its contributions to participatory democratic citizenship education are threefold: (1) it provides youth with the opportunity to develop a sense of belonging in an inclusive space within a social network of like-minded individuals; (2) it introduces them to inspiring people who can serve as role models; and (3) it teaches them practical and social skills.

3.4.1. A Sense of Belonging in an Inclusive Space

What sets the Summer School apart is the energy the team puts into caring for participants. The school creates a welcoming, inclusive, and kind environment. The team uses several techniques to help youth express themselves and create a welcoming space. This begins with how the adults position themselves vis-à-vis the youth (horizontally and informally), the physical organization of the spaces (that encourage interaction), and the choice of activities (which are stimulating and enjoyable). The two excerpts below highlight the effort the school invests in creating an inclusive and caring space where participants feel they are heard and belong:

The facilitation team emphasizes the importance of listening and respect. They start the course by reminding us to follow the "code of conduct" in discussions and workshops to ensure we're respectful and get along with each other. They highlight that discussions should revolve more around ideas than people. "The key word is kindness," one facilitator states as he concludes his speech. (Entrepreneurship course)

At the very start of the course, the facilitator presents the "rules of the game": listening, caring, questioning, and having fun. The activities unfold in an air of respect for these values. [...] The atmosphere is friendly, respectful, and polite. Discussions are generally very uplifting and participants are very receptive to others' ideas, even when opinions differ, and listen attentively when someone is speaking. The atmosphere becomes even warmer with time, and by the last session, participants seem very at ease in their groups, joking and laughing at times. (Innovation course)

The organization's dedication to creating a welcoming atmosphere was evident throughout the four-day event. Adults devoted time and attention to participants so that even the shyest ones interacted, built relationships, and developed a sense of belonging within the group.

I'm talking to a young girl at the conference. She says she feels inspired here and happy to meet people that are socially engaged. There aren't a lot of opportunities to do this where she's from, she tells me. She says she sometimes lacks self-confidence, and she does seem pretty shy and talks quietly. She tells me she's happy to be out of her comfort zone. Her mother had insisted she come, and she doesn't regret it. I ask her if she'd like me to introduce her to other people. She laughs and says no, and that she prefers to stay in the background for now. Later, as the activity unfolds, I see her talking to other people and integrating into small groups. (Opening activity on International Youth Day)

By the third session, participants were forming ties and exchanging contact information. I knew almost everyone in the group. The small size was perfect for creating a sense of bonding. (Exploration course)

In addition to the first icebreaker marking the school's launch and described in the introduction, the team uses fun techniques to encourage all participants to express themselves during the event. There is a friendly atmosphere in several of the courses, and participants seem very grateful for the opportunity to express themselves. Several activities in the innovation course encourage discussion. On the first day, for example, facilitators asked three questions about democracy that participants had to answer and discuss for one to two minutes while facing a partner. In each session of the entrepreneurship course, they could take the floor and share their impressions and takeaways from the program in roundtable discussions. The only course that did not incorporate icebreakers or take steps to promote group discussions was the exploration course.

The art and participatory leadership courses, which by nature are based on collective intelligence and group strength, include many icebreaker activities that encourage participants to be themselves. They create comfortable and inclusive spaces for young people to discuss and share ideas.

Because our group was small, we were able to create a safe space where a few participants felt comfortable sharing more personal information. Everyone was committed to nurturing a warm, open atmosphere. We even decided to keep in touch afterward. (Art course)

In the art course, one participant on the autism spectrum told us how much he enjoys being at the school and learning so much in such a short time. He likes observing and interacting with the others. "I feel comfortable expressing myself here," he says. "I usually keep to myself."

3.4.2. Meeting Inspiring Role Models

Our observations show that participants also benefit from meeting young people and adults they identify with and consider role models. The stories adults share at mentoring sessions and conferences are often emotionally charged and inspiring. For example, in one of the activities, a young man with reduced mobility shared his poignant story:

He has trouble expressing himself and jokes a lot. He tells us he was hit by a car at 14 and had to learn everything all over again. He jokes that he is "not bad, though," garnering laughs from the audience. Everyone appears to listen to him closely and laughs heartily at his jokes. He's here to raise awareness of the challenges of living with disability and reduced mobility. He tells us the main point is to keep going. "It's better to screw up and start over than waste your life doing nothing." You have to "go for it and never look back." The audience applauds warmly again. Some of them rise to their feet for a standing ovation. (Lightning round)

First-hand testimonials are a lot more interesting than traditional lectures, and participants really seem to enjoy learning this way: They listen attentively, applaud warmly, and even show great empathy. The school offers a wide range of mentors they can identify with, who share their practical knowledge and life experiences. Some are symbols of resilience and determination, some stand out for their far-reaching achievements, and others model dissent and resistance to the established order.

3.4.3. Acquiring Practical Skills

The Summer School is also the perfect place to learn practical skills through experiential learning. While our observations on knowledge transmission reveal the many practical and soft skills acquired, participants themselves often say they feel better prepared afterward to engage in society as citizens. In the communication course, for example, they learn journalism skills by creating content:

Some see the workshop as an opportunity to try something new, like conducting an interview, creating a photo essay, or writing a newspaper article for the first time. They seem to enjoy it a lot. A few participants tell me they learned a lot about writing, working under pressure, what it's like in a newsroom, etc., suggesting they've picked up quite a few technical skills. (Communication course)

Young people value gaining skills that can serve them in future commitments, especially practical and technical skills, which they consider to be more useful. They appreciate the citizen involvement courses for the opportunities, including to: experiment with management techniques like pitching and using the Impact Gap Canvas analysis tool (entrepreneurship course); learn how to recognize an effective advertisement and create an awareness campaign (mobilization course); explore new artistic mediums (art course); develop journalism skills like using particular equipment and software, social media, and producing articles, interviews, reports, and podcasts (communication course).

Conclusion

We attended the Summer School hoping to find out what citizenship education means there and how young people feel about their experiences as participants in the program. Based on our participant observations, we can say that the school and many of its stakeholders see democratic citizenship education as being centred on youth participation, specifically the collective experience of speaking up and taking concrete action. This is evident in the warm welcome the youth received at the start of the four-day intensive and the caring and inclusive techniques facilitators used throughout the event. Our observations confirm that the Summer School provides a citizen education experience that participants enjoy thanks in large part to adults' success in forming bonds with them (Zeldin et al., 2013). As we have highlighted in this chapter, the adults involved in this initiative recognize young people's agency, offer them support in their projects, and ensure that everyone remains respectful. The success of the program can be attributed to the INM's longstanding record of experience and well-honed methods of organization and facilitation.

While the school emphasizes deliberation and action in preparing young people for participatory democratic citizenship, it would be inaccurate to say this is the only form of citizenship at play during the event. In discussions, facilitation techniques, and social interactions, we also witnessed some of the democratic citizenship education discourses classified by Edda Sant (2019), such as liberal, critical, multicultural, and agonistic.7 Exposing young people to a diversity of discourses helps them discover themselves, which is how the Summer School may pave the way for a diverse range of journeys in citizen engagement and participation.

References

Blanchet-Cohen, N., & Brunson, L. (2014). Creating settings for youth empowerment and leadership: An ecological perspective. *Child & Youth Services, 35*(3), 216–236. https://doi.org/10.1080/0145935X.2014.938735

Blondiaux, L. (2008). *Le nouvel esprit de la démocratie : actualité de la démocratie participative.* Seuil.

Dewey, J. (1927). *The public and its problems.* Holt Publishers.

Dewey, J. (1997). *Democracy and education: An introduction to the philosophy of education.* The Free Press. (Original work published 1916)

Fournel, A. (2016). Doute et autocorrection dans une communauté de recherche philosophique. *Recherches en éducation, 24.* https://doi.org/10.4000/ree.5448

Gaudet, S. (2021). Les initiatives jeunesse au Canada : des tiers-lieux de l'éducation démocratique. *Revue internationale d'éducation de Sèvres, 88,* 93–104. https://doi.org/10.4000/ries.11586

Habermas, J. (2013) *De l'éthique de la discussion* (M. Hunyadi, Trans.). Flammarion. (Original work published 1991)

Institut du Nouveau Monde. (2017). *Guide de participation. Génération d'impact : École d'été 2017 de l'Institut du Nouveau Monde.*

Mailhot, C., Gaudet, S., Drapeau, É., & Fuca, J. (2021). Éduquer à la citoyenneté démocratique par l'innovation sociale : l'idéal de l'entrepreneuriat social remis en question. *Canadian Journal of Nonprofit and Social Economy Research / Revue canadienne de recherche sur les OSBL et l'économie sociale, 12*(2), 58–73. https://doi.org/10.29173/cjnser.2021v12n2a381

Sant, E. (2019). Democratic education: A theoretical review (2006–2017). *Review of Educational Research, 89*(5), 655–696. https://doi.org/10.3102/00346543 19862493

Zeldin, S., Christens, B. D., & Powers, J. L. (2013). The psychology and practice of youth-adult partnership: Bridging generations for youth development and community change. *American Journal of Community Psychology, 51*(3–4), 385–397. https://doi.org/10.1007/s10464-012-9558-y

Table 3.1. List of Activities at the INM Summer School

Date	Time	Activity
Wednesday 9 August 2017	6 – 7:30 pm	Welcome – Networking Session
	7:30 – 9 pm	Welcome and Opening Panel – "Generation Impact"
Thursday 10 August 2017	8:30 – 9 am	Welcome
	9 am – 12:30 pm	Profiles of Citizenship Involvement – Day 1
	12:30 – 2:15 pm	Lunch
	2:30 – 4:30 pm	Choice of Participatory Workshops –Women at the heart of solutions to climate change –Powerful women of the 21st century –From Dream to Reality –Advocacy and Leadership at Oxfam-Québec –Influence, consultation et transformation of the city by, for and with Young People –Cover exercise: Discovering the history of indigenous peoples –Youtubers – the new opinion leaders –From the Individual to the Collective: Ricochet of impact from intellectual mediation –Communicating with Impact: Advice for developing a clear vision in messaging –Beyond Prejudice – Cinematic View on the Reality of the First Nations –Listening to the electoral silence of young people: What to make of it?
	5 pm	"5 à 7" – Networking and Meeting
Friday 11 August 2017	8:30 – 9:15 am	Welcome
	9:15 – 10:45 am	Choice of Activities – Block 1 –Citizenship meeting with Alexandre Jardin –Conversation: Ten years after the Bouchard-Taylor Commission – Where does Quebec stand now? –Round table: Information under pressure
	11 – 12:30 pm	Choice of Activities – Block 2 –Round table: The Trump effect – Redefining international relations –Environmental struggles or how to save the planet –Round table: Are the arts too white? Action and Reaction –Round table: Economic experimentation or the future of the economy
	12:30 – 2 pm	Lunch
	2 – 2:15 pm	Break / Yoga Session
	2:15 – 5:30 pm	Citizenship Involvement Profiles – Day 2

Date	Time	Activity
Saturday 12 August 2017	9 – 9:30 am	Welcome
	9:30 – 10:15 am	Opening of International Children's Day
	10:20 –11:30 am	Flash Conferences
	11:30 – 1:30 pm	Lunch / Foire de l'engagement
	1:45 – 4:30 pm	Citizenship Involvement Profiles – Day 3
	4:30 – 6:30 pm	Dinner
	6:30 pm	Summer School Closing Events (Youth Forum and Festive Evening)

Source: *Guide de participation de l'École d'été de l'INM* (2017).

Notes

1. Quebec Conservatory of Music and Dramatic Art.

2. For more on participatory democratic citizenship education, see Chapter 1.

3. For more details, see the Methodological Appendix.

4. Self-correction is the ability to evaluate and question one's own opinions. See Fournel (2016).

5. English translation is ours. Original: "Soyez bref et direct. Exprimez votre opinion le plus clairement et succinctement possible afin que d'autres puissent avoir le temps de s'exprimer. Attaquez les idées et non les personnes ! Écoutez respectueusement l'opinion des autres. Si vous n'êtes pas d'accord, vous avez le droit de le dire tout en étant poli. Osez prendre la parole et soyez ouvert à la diversité. Vous avez une part de responsabilité dans le succès des activités. Réagissez quand on vous le demande et ayez l'ouverture d'esprit nécessaire pour entendre des idées qui ne sont pas les vôtres. Quand les commentaires sont pertinents, partagez-les avec l'ensemble du groupe ! Évitez les discussions ou les commentaires avec vos voisins, car cela nuit à l'écoute des invités. Soyez ponctuel et respectez vos choix d'activité. Rendez-vous à l'heure aux activités que vous avez choisies. Si vous arrivez en retard, soyez discret. Ne vous promenez pas d'une salle à l'autre pendant une même plage horaire." (*Guide de participation*, p. 122)

6. English translation is ours. Original: "Les défis à relever sont nombreux et complexes : changements climatiques, vivre ensemble, crise des réfugié-es, accroissement des inégalités sociales […] Le tout avec pour toile de fond, des révolutions technologiques et médiatiques aux conséquences déjà bien senties sur la façon de s'informer, de communiquer et de vivre notre démocratie. Quelles sont les meilleures stratégies pour une transformation sociale, pour mobiliser un maximum de personnes, pour devenir un acteur de

changement ? [...] Générer de l'impact demande aux jeunes d'occuper l'espace public, de faire entendre leurs voix, de pouvoir s'interroger sur ces enjeux et d'y répondre. [...]"

7. In some workshops, for example. We present a more detailed discussion of the differences between these concepts in Chapter 1.

CHAPTER 4

Oxfam-Québec's World Walk: A Critical and Participatory Citizenship Experience for Secondary School Students

Brieg Capitaine and Hérold Constant

Abstract

This chapter presents two editions of Oxfam-Québec's World Walk initiative in a secondary school in the Laurentides region of Quebec. The annual walk and the preparatory activities that precede it throughout the school year allow young people to learn and develop a critical consciousness about a variety of issues, and then mobilize to raise awareness in society. Our case study shows that Oxfam-Québec uses a popular education approach to provide young people with a space where they can socialize and feel empowered, and where the most committed of them learn to challenge school norms and knowledge hierarchies. The World Walk offers young people a unique form of citizenship education based on participatory democracy.

*I*t's 7:30 a.m. on May 11, 2018, and a dozen school buses are parked in front of the secondary school, ready to take hundreds of 12-to-17-year-olds to Montreal. We recognize Alexis, Julie, Isabelle, Clara, and Olivier—they've been the most involved in the preparations. They're in their last year, so this will be their last World Walk. The youngest students seem a bit lost in the hustle and bustle of the unique situation and the older ones step up to direct *them to their respective buses. There are a lot more people than at the meet-ings. "You'll see," says Guillaume, the school's Spiritual Care and Guidance and Community Involvement Service (SCGCIS) counsellor. "When our school arrives at the World Walk, we get noticed!" Throughout the school year, a core group of around 60 students from various committees attend the lunch-time and afterschool meetings. They're easy to spot this morning: they're carrying banners, helping each other out, and handing out little blue and yellow flags to students who are joining them today for the first time. Guillaume is also helping direct students to their buses, calling out their first names. A few of them seem lightly dressed. "Did you pack rain gear?" he asks. "You should have worn other shoes; we'll be walking a long time." To represent their school, two students have prepared a sign with the school name that will hang from a four-metre mast and are trying to fit it through the bus door. Students from the Amnesty International committee have built a tree—a symbol of their commitment to climate justice. They are having trouble fitting their creation through the bus door as the unenthused bus driver looks on. Finally, the tree is stored in the luggage compartment and the buses head off. Even though it's early, it's party time. Flags are waving all over the bus. Some students start to chant: "So-, so-, so, solidarity!" An hour later, the buses pull up near La Fontaine Park in Montreal and hundreds of students pile out. Alexis, Clara, and Isabelle seem cheerful and skip to the middle of the park. Young women from Oxfam-Québec in green vests greet us with site maps and Oxfam stickers, posters, and temporary tattoos. "Hi gang! We're counting on you!" they offer encouragingly. Music is blaring from loudspeakers on a stage. A dozen tents have been set up around it, each raising awareness about the refugee crisis and the various programs Oxfam-Québec runs to help women and youth in developing countries. The 2018 World Walk will start in an hour—just enough time for students to visit the tents.*

Oxfam-Québec's World Walk initiative is a public demonstration that mobilizes citizens on global issues like poverty, healthcare, and the environment. It has been organized annually since 1970 and aims to raise awareness and encourage action among young people. In cities where Oxfam is present, like Montreal, hundreds of young people march in the streets for kilometres to protest and denounce violence, injustice, and poverty and demand a just, inclusive, and equal world. Each year, Oxfam-Québec's World Walk initiative invites 12-to-17-year-old secondary school students to make their voices heard together around a theme. In 2018, students raised awareness of gender injustices and racism under the theme *À égalité!*[1] In 2019, they protested young people's lack of representation in and access to governance systems under the theme *Une place pour nous.*[2] For several years, Oxfam-Québec has also used the slogan *Nos voix comptent* to empower young people to make an impact.[3] Their World Walk initiative is also an opportunity to raise funds in support of vulnerable populations around the world.

Throughout the year, around 60 students on various[4] committees at the secondary school[5] where we carried out our ethnographic study meet to prepare for the walk. They discuss the values they want to defend, raise money, and raise awareness among their peers about poverty, exclusion, the environment, mental health, children's rights, and LGBTQ2+ communities. They meet to make banners, signs, and flags to raise awareness at the school during the year and to hand out to the 200 to 300 students that will join them on the day of the walk. While they work, they discuss their values and brainstorm solutions to global issues.

Based on Joel Westheimer and Joseph Kahne's (2004) citizenship education models (see Chapter 1), our research shows that the students who are most involved in Oxfam-Québec's school-based initiatives come to question educational organizations and knowledge hierarchies as they build their careers in participatory citizenship.

This chapter is structured in four parts. In the first, we present Oxfam-Québec's mission and values and the secondary school helping implement its citizenship education initiatives. In the second, we present our observations at two walks and the preparatory meetings leading up to them. We identify multiple citizenship discourses and discuss how they sometimes clash with the educational institution and its culture. In the third part, we discuss the crucial role of the facilitator in helping students make the initiative their own and how the activities reflect different citizenship types. In the last part, we share what students themselves have said they learned from the World Walk.

4.1. Oxfam-Québec's Partnership with Secondary Schools

Part of our case study took place at a public secondary school in the Laurentides region of Quebec. The school can accommodate up to one thousand students. Its goal is to provide a comprehensive education that enables students to achieve their full potential. A range of extra-curricular activities are provided, including two community-focused initiatives in partnership with Oxfam-Québec: the *Magasin du Monde*, which promotes social entrepreneurship and fair trade, and the World Walk.[6] Across both, Oxfam-Québec uses a popular education approach anchored in agency, raising awareness, and collective mobilization.

Oxfam-Québec is a regional branch of Oxfam Canada that became independent in 1973. It defines itself as a non-profit, non-partisan, and secular international charity. According to its official website, Oxfam-Québec is affiliated with the Oxfam International confederation.[7] It shares the international organization's vision of "a just world without poverty." Slogans like *The Power of People Against Poverty* and values like respect, tolerance, solidarity, equity, responsibility, innovation, and sharing knowledge are at the heart of the citizen initiatives it backs. Its main mission is to help create sustainable solutions to poverty and injustice, particularly in developing countries. To this end, Oxfam-Québec works with local, international, government, and non-government stakeholders on issues related to the following: human rights; humanitarian aid; climate, economic, and gender justice; agriculture and food security; women's reproductive health; sustainable development; youth and citizen education; conflict intervention and mediation; access to social services and advocacy; and lobbying.

The school's SCGCIS counsellor, Guillaume, has been coordinating these initiatives for over 20 years. The students involved on the committees are often enrolled in the school's International Education Program (IEP). Volunteering is a mandatory part of their program—but that is not why they get involved with Oxfam-Québec. As Guillaume points out, "Students can volunteer elsewhere if they want to." While IEP classes are evenly split between boys and girls, the vast majority of committee members are female—close to 8 out of 10. We observed this secondary school, which sends a lot of youth to the World Walk each year, as part of our case study to learn about the kind of citizenship education Oxfam-Québec promotes, how youth feel about their experience, and how they relate to the adults in charge.

4.2. The World Walk

It's 10 a.m. on May 10, 2019. It's 12 degrees and pouring rain in Montreal. The students are barely off the buses before they take off across a muddy La

Fontaine Park toward the Oxfam "village"—the meeting place and starting point for the walk. Youth from the school have already arrived at "Zone 2.0," which Oxfam has set up in the middle of the park. According to their event guide, the NGO has set up tents as "experiential spaces." Inside, some Oxfam employees are presenting economic development initiatives in the Democratic Republic of Congo; others are discussing initiatives to combat systemic inequalities that impact women in developed and developing countries. Some students line up to visit a tent on the refugee crisis. Some take advantage of materials the organization has provided to make signs. Others walk around with green Oxfam tattoos on their cheeks, holding the signs and banners they have made during the year. Every year, a jury of influential individuals—from the labour union, government, community, and private sectors—evaluates them as part of a competition and awards a prize to the school with the most impactful and eco-friendly props. Each school committee has made its own: the Magasin du Monde *built huge fair-trade chocolate bars from cardboard; the* Amnesty International *committee sewed a quilt featuring a tree; and members of the environment committee are wearing flower pots around their necks that they've planted seeds inside. Some of the props, like the huge mast that bears the school's emblem, make an appearance every year.*

The students are gathered far from the stage where the bands are playing. They barely pay attention to the two facilitators enthusiastically shouting "Looking good, folks!" and "Today, we're going to change the world!" at them. They chat, impatiently waiting for the walk to start, protecting their signs from the rain ahead of the judging. Finally, it's 10:30 a.m. Les 3 Doums—an orchestra troupe from Louis-Riel secondary school—kicks off the march with a loud cacophony of drums, including djembes and tambours. Other Louis-Riel students walk behind them. Oxfam volunteers in green vests are around for security purposes and to help set the energy with musical numbers and signs that read "Make some noise!", "Do the wave!", and "Say 'hurrah'!" Students are holding up signs with slogans and statistics to raise awareness around poverty, gender inequality, and homophobia, among other issues.

After walking for 30 minutes, we're almost at the overpass that overlooks the highway—students in their last year know that this means it's competition time. They start preparing the younger students—"We're coming up to the overpass! Hold on to the tree! Exactly! Go more to the left!"—who stop to comply then continue chanting. Even though it's raining, there's a renewed energy in the air as the pressure of the competition mounts. It has to go just right; winning is like a badge of honour. The Amnesty International committee's diversity tree quilt is starting to tear. It's completely soaked and probably three times as heavy. "We'll keep it out until we get to the overpass and then pack it away," their group leader announces, resigned. The 101 committee's A place for LGBTQ2+ fabric banner has already breathed its last breath. Two students have wrapped it around its long, wooden handles and are carrying it over their shoulders. The procession stops just in front of the overpass as students shout and wave their remaining signs in unison to impress the judges watching from atop it. On the climb back to the park, fatigue sets in. Two Oxfam facilitators on a tandem bike are playing R & B from loudspeakers—Shakira, it sounds like. They chant slogans, getting others to join in. Suddenly, we come to a halt. We are in the "silent zone." According to organizers from Oxfam, this is an opportunity to take a break from our fast-paced lives and observe a moment of silence in solidarity with those around the world who don't have the right to speak. Silence settles over us as Oxfam employees wave "Silence" signs. The moment is "for those who don't have a voice," a younger student tells us. All the students are familiar with this part. Some have put small x-shaped Oxfam stickers over their mouths. Passers-by take photos and film us in the rain. We keep holding the silence. Suddenly, a noise erupts from the front of the procession and makes its way to us as the whole crowd breaks the silence and starts the next phase of the walk: the fiesta zone. After an emotional moment of silence, it's time to let loose in a big party and celebrate our citizen power in colour and creativity—to paraphrase an information sheet on the walk. The music starts up again, the dancers dance on the street corner, and the walk continues. Half an hour later, we're back at La Fontaine Park. A ceremonial host of Oxfam volunteers greets us with signs. "You're amazing!", "Your voices matter!" they call out. This is the appreciation zone. It's 12:30 p.m. Drenched from the rain, many of the students run back to the buses. Unlike last year, they won't be eating lunch in the shade with their friends. In fact, only about thirty of them stick around. From the stage, a facilitator tells them how pleased he is with how the day went: "You've influenced thousands of people," he tells them. "They're talking about you on social media." Some students are waiting for the award ceremony, their signs and banners soggy and torn, paint running. As soon as the verdict is in, they run back to their buses in high spirits and visibly proud of their achievement.

The World Walk combines participatory and critical citizenship education. Students have an opportunity to participate in an initiative run by Oxfam and its volunteers where adults teach them about different initiatives and social and economic injustices, and they get to ask questions and discuss ideas. Oxfam's aim to raise awareness among youth about social injustices highlights the critical approach. It comes across in the slogans at "Zone 2.0" of the walk, which are aimed not only at passers-by in general but also at other youth. And unlike conventional social movements, the World Walk is designed to build skills, promote action, and raise awareness about global citizenship. Organizers see the slogans and information as a way of inspiring action and future mobilizations.

The dominant form of citizenship at play in the World Walk is participatory, where "to solve social problems and improve society, citizens must actively participate and take leadership positions" (Westheimer & Kahne, 2004, p. 240). In fact, the World Walk serves as an experiential learning space where young people can acquire the leadership and activism skills they need to mobilize collectively. They develop what Lilian Mathieu (2004) calls "protest skills." Political and practical in nature, they span from making signs and banners to crafting slogans to wearing appropriate clothes and shoes for the weather. Here, "protest" refers to acts that aim to raise awareness, change social dynamics, and make a difference in the world. Students perform many of these acts throughout the initiative, including during the minute of silence and the subsequent celebration, and while chanting slogans, dancing, and displaying their tattoos. Reflecting on her experience, one student from the *Magasin du Monde* committee shared, "Maybe I'm reading the situation wrong, but in my head, [in] a normal protest, you're supposed to denounce injustice, raise awareness, and that's it. Whereas in the World Walk, [we] do so much more: we denounce injustice, raise awareness, and encourage others to engage." As they acquire these skills, young people feel their impact on the world. "There are cameras a lot of the time," the student says. "We're on TV. I say to myself, 'Okay, this really influences people, and it can change the way society thinks about young people.' People come out of their apartments. Daycares take the kids outside. People bang on pots and pans and cheer us on."

Rather than reductively examining just the event itself, we also observed the preparations surrounding the World Walk during our ethnographic study. We spent 15 days at the school between April 2018 and October 2019, which helped us understand the amount of work students put into making key preparations for the walk, including by participating in committees and attending Oxfam's awareness workshops. During breaks and between classes, we observed students interacting with each other and with adults. We also observed interactions among adults.[8] From January to May each year, students on various committees create facilitation tools for the walk, such as banners and signs, which they carry by bus to Montreal for the event. Their reflection on the choice of messages, shapes, colours and art techniques, and their productive action, seemed to embody the values and principles promoted by Oxfam through everyday interactions and ordinary gestures, while also anticipating future social participation.

4.3. Youth–Adult Partnerships at School

While facilitating Oxfam-Québec's initiatives, Guillaume helps students at the school bond. For example, he organizes a 24-hour sleepover to integrate the youngest members into the *Magasin du Monde* committee. On a Friday in October, around 15 students stay overnight at the school to brainstorm ideas and participate in ice-breakers, like taking turns putting themselves in embarrassing situations to become less sensitive to judgment. They sleep in the auditorium and, late into the night, play the annual hide-and-seek game in their pyjamas through the school halls and classrooms. The next day, older members of the committee hold a training session for younger ones. For 24 hours, the school becomes their playground. But to make it happen, every year, Guillaume fights with the administration, which threatens to restrict access to the building for safety, insurance, and relevance reasons. The bond that develops between students after the team-building sleepover is visible, especially compared to the other committees. For example, in April, when the committees were making their banners and props, the youngest and oldest members of the *Magasin du Monde* committee worked together on the large cardboard box they were painting. In contrast, younger and older students worked separately on the Amnesty International committee:

> *Two younger students, clearly intimidated by the older ones, are standing in a corner of the room. Guillaume takes more of a leadership role, handing them paint and brushes and giving them instructions. The younger students get to work in the corner without interacting with the older ones.*

The fact that Guillaume can be involved to a greater or lesser degree in leading the meetings shows that students have different citizenship education experiences in different committees. Guillaume is there throughout the students' time at the school and while they prepare for the World Walk. He also mentors three or four CEGEP students. He is constantly moving from one committee to another, sometimes reminding students to respect the timetable, other times observing or encouraging discussions between committee members. His presence guarantees students' autonomy. When we talk about his approach, Guillaume insists that when adults want to make decisions for young people, it does not work. He believes what works best is letting young people take the initiative and following their lead. Young people like Alexandra appreciate his approach:

> Guillaume is an extraordinary coach to have. He leads and provides advice, but he's not there to manage us. [...] He's excellent at putting young people first. He'll tell us something like, "Don't hold back with your ideas. Just make them realistic and then go for it," whereas leaders of other community initiatives will tell us to "settle down," "watch how it's done," and follow suit.

In his office, Guillaume keeps large binders with information on everything you need to know about Oxfam initiatives. These detail the organization's values, how to run the *Magasin du Monde* and train personnel, and the knowledge to be transmitted to the students, who adapt it to produce their own training tools.

The latter is not surprising, since both Oxfam and Guillaume seek to empower students. The notion of empowerment here refers to a process of subjectivation and search for self and authenticity, in contrast to the socialization and interiorization of norms and school values based on hierarchy and compliance.

The various initiatives are designed to offer young people an opportunity to make their voices heard, feel empowered, and learn leadership skills. Partnerships between youth and adults tend to be horizontal, which has a significant impact on their experience, boosting their self-confidence and sense of pride. When students are invited to take part in these initiatives, they become partners whose ideas and opinions count in the decision-making process. On the Amnesty International committee and the *Magasin du Monde*'s board of directors, it is the students who decide what actions need to be taken. In Elena's words:

> We're really like a youth business. We run the *Magasin* with Guillaume's help. It's not like he manages us and we help out. It's just the opposite! [...] He gives us tips, advice, and reminders, like "Oh! Maybe you should try this," or "Try to wrap up as soon as possible," or "Oh! The World Walk is [coming up]—we need to get moving!" We also have a Facebook group with him where we write to each other.

According to one of the students we interviewed, the horizontal nature of the youth–adult partnerships challenges the common perception that young people spend "all their time on their phones." For her, young people can also be actors of change. Guillaume often shares encouraging messages with the students. "They forget they have so many skills," he says. "They know about social issues, about organizing a board of directors, [about the role of] a leader. Not all young people are like that. It's great to have young people like them. They're amazing to watch. It's awesome seeing young people get involved." Every year, Guillaume organizes a recognition gala to raise the profile of the students' achievements.

4.4. Youth Experiences: "There's Room to Be Yourself"

We have looked at Oxfam-Québec, its mission, and how it runs. But how do young people feel about the World Walk and their year-round involvement in Oxfam's citizen education initiatives?

The World Walk is mainly an educational experience in participatory citizenship. Students cultivate practical skills throughout the year and during the event by fundraising, helping mobilize their peers, participating in awareness-raising activities in the classroom, and petitioning for signatures. These are skills they apply in their communities, for example when floods hit the Laurentides region in 2019. Isabelle tells us:

> It seems like nothing is impossible anymore. We wanted to help [during the floods]; it was happening right next door, impacting

people we know, so we decided to mobilize. It didn't start all at once. It started with little things, like painting continents. Then it was painting a chocolate bar. Then it was just setting up a little booth downstairs. We know we can do it.

The CEGEP interns are grateful for the personal and professional guidance they receive. They say the activities give them an opportunity to discover themselves. As one intern puts it: "We already have it in us; we're just given the means to bring it out. I don't think I would have done [social work] otherwise."

The initiative's critical dimension is not immediately apparent, except in the youth discourse. However, when young people refer to this critical aspect, they focus less on knowledge or progressive ideas than on concrete practices. Students seem most interested in the issue of subjectivation, in authenticity in the context of educational institutions focused on instilling social norms, and in incorporating social norms. They achieve subjectivation by appropriating the school space, for example, by creating murals on school premises and through crafts and games. Some students, often the older ones, help raise critical consciousness of the systemic nature of poverty. However, students do not just acquire information; they produce and pass on critical knowledge during their craft workshops. This includes the work of the 101 committee, which supports LGBTQ2+ rights:

> As they do every lunchtime in April leading up to the World Walk, seven girls and one boy from the 101 committee meet in a classroom. They're talking about a school trip. The committee lobbied the school to make the rooms mixed-gender, but not everyone was in favour and the school refused. "We need to finish the signs," says Camille. Each sign represents a flag from the LGBTQ2+ community and displays the words "Human being." The theme of this year's walk is Une place pour nous. "We wanted to fight labels," Audrey explains. "We're all human." Later, Chanelle tells me that the committee wanted to dress up as drag queens. "We were told it could be misconstrued as a show whereas the World Walk is about defending rights."

Here, the school sets limits on how young people can critique homophobia in their efforts to bring about social change. Conflicts with school administration typically revolve around the use of time and school space. This is not surprising since time and space are central to institutions of socialization (Foucault, 1975/2014), and schools are no exception (Sayad, 2014). Upon our arrival, Guillaume shared the daily challenges he faces. He encounters resistance from teaching staff who view student involvement as a waste of time and are hesitant to open their classrooms to committees wanting to raise awareness on democratic issues among students. He also needs to negotiate with the administration to secure permission for students to remain on school premises after hours, in addition to locating available rooms for committee meetings and ensuring they are promptly vacated. Citizen education is often undervalued in comparison to more prestigious disciplines such as math, science, and French.

Despite these difficulties, the school remains a prefigurative space where students can enact a different kind of social structure (Pleyers & Capitaine, 2016). Citizen engagement transforms the school into a place of solidarity and collective belonging in contrast to deinstitutionalization and competition (Dubet, 2002). Reflecting on why the *Magasin du Monde* has been such an enriching experience for her, Camille puts this into her own words:

> We're like a family. Life can be a bit of a roller coaster, you know? We're always worried about this or that and trying to keep up with our hectic schedules. And then there's the "How's it going?" item at the board meeting. You could say "Oh, that's kind of stupid," but it feels good to know everyone is there for you. We listen to each other and help each other out, so [...] I've never regretted my choice. Ever. There's room to be yourself.

Empowerment develops through teamwork and creating a sense of solidarity at school. "When I first started [at the *Magasin du Monde*], I was really self-conscious," Laura confides in us. "But I can say that I feel much more at ease now [...] I've really come out of my shell—out of my little comfort zone—and I'm really [...] glad I was able to do that." "I was able to manage my stress," Camille also reflects in retrospect.

Students are nevertheless aware of social norms and the logic of institutions; many of them enroll in the IEP and join the World Walk as a way to take "good" classes and better position themselves in the job market when they graduate. Justine disapproves of the trend, but she does not blame the students. She says it is up to those in charge:

> It's just the way things are. There are people higher up—the school board, the government. It even looks like the IEP is drift-ing from what we signed up for. One of the reasons I stay in the *Magasin du Monde* is because it feels like some light has gone out everywhere else. At the *Magasin,* I feel like it never will.

Justine's critical remarks show that for students, getting involved in Oxfam initiatives can be a concrete reaction to and form of resis-tance against a world they perceive as becoming disengaged (see Ion, 2012).

Conclusion

Throughout the year, right up to the day of the World Walk, students organize into committees and debate the issues they want to defend that year. They create banners and props, raise funds, and occupy a public space, gathering in Montreal in the thousands in early May to raise awareness about social injustice, poverty, fair trade, discrimi-nation, and climate change. Here, young people are seen as empow-ered agents who are able to think and participate in the major decisions that affect their community. The World Walk aims to pro-mote a set of social justice values among secondary school students and offers them a space to interact with their peers and exercise agency. Teaching students values while simultaneously giving them an opportunity to experience action as individuals is at the heart of Oxfam-Québec's education approach. Through workshops on gender equity, the solidarity economy, climate justice, and other activities at the school, the organization first raises awareness among students so they can in turn raise awareness among others. Oxfam-Québec's approach is unique in that it fosters critical consciousness among young people through social justice initiatives and the World Walk itself. Critical citizenship is reflected in how the students experience subjectivation as the initiative progresses. The most committed among them cultivate their autonomy, coming to challenge school norms through both their words and their actions, highlighting how the World Walk—a citizenship education initiative based on participatory democracy—brings to life a vision of transformative education that instills in young people an appetite for citizen engagement (see Brodeur Gélinas & Vanasse, 2021).

Reference List

Brodeur Gélinas, M., & Vanasse, G.-G. (2021, March 5). *Une éducation transformatrice : pour des jeunes au pouvoir citoyen émancipateur*. Le Réseau ÉdCan. https://www.edcan.ca/articles/une-education-transformatrice-pour-des-jeunes-au-pouvoir-citoyen-emancipateur/?lang=fr

Dubet, F. (2002). *Le déclin de l'institution*. Seuil.

Foucault, M. (2014). *Surveiller et punir : naissance de la prison*. Gallimard. (Original work published 1975)

Ion, J. (2012). *S'engager dans une société d'individus*. Armand Colin.

Mathieu, L. (2004). *Comment lutter ? Sociologie et mouvements sociaux*. Textuel.

Pleyers, G., & Capitaine, B. (Eds.). (2016). *Mouvements sociaux : quand le sujet devient acteur*. Éditions de la Maison des sciences de l'homme. https://doi.org/10.4000/books.editionsmsh.9891

Sayad, A. (2014). *L'école et les enfants de l'immigration : essais critiques* (texts collected by B. Falaize et S. Laacher). Seuil.

Westheimer, J., & Kahne, J. (2004). What kind of citizen? The politics of educating for democracy. *American Educational Research Journal, 41*(2), 237–269. https://doi.org/10.3102/00028312041002237

Notes

1. On Equal Terms.
2. A Place for Us.
3. Our Voices Matter.
4. Like many Quebec secondary schools, this one has many committees. The committees we observed because of their large involvement in the march were: *Magasin du Monde*, Amnesty International, the 101 committee, the environment committee, and Les Amis de la Saint-Camille.
5. For ethical reasons, we did not name the school and we used pseudonyms to identify participants. We warmly thank the students for their involvement and curiosity in our research, and the school's SCGCIS counsellor for opening the doors to his job for us during our case study. Thank you, as well, to Geneviève-Gaël Vanasse of Oxfam-Québec for her suggestions and comments on a preliminary version of the text, and to the founder of

the World Walk, Jean-Pierre Denis of Oxfam-Québec, for his advice on the first phases of the project.

6. World Shop.

7. For more information, visit oxfam.qc.ca/en/

8. Several adults are involved in the initiative. Guillaume, the SCGCIS counsellor, has a crucial role. He is assisted by three or four young CEGEP student interns whom he hosts and trains each year. In some cases, they are former students of the school who are involved in committees and in organizing the walk on their own time. The other adults are part of the teaching and administrative staff.

B) Experiences in Citizenship Education Based on Creating Social Change

CHAPTER 5

A Feminist Approach to Citizenship at YWCA Montréal: *Strong Girls, Strong World*

Sophie Théwissen-LeBlanc, Caroline Caron,
and Stéphanie Gaudet

Abstract

This chapter presents the feminist organization YWCA Montréal and its *Strong Girls, Strong World* program. Over several months, we observed the making of the documentary *IntersectionnELLES,*[1] which highlights the ethnic, cultural, and religious diversity of women in Montréal. Our research shows that the program enables young people to experiment with collective action, learn about multiple relationships to feminism, and develop a feminist and critical conception of citizenship. Under the supervision of two skilled facilitators, participants gain a feminist perspective and a sense of belonging in a setting that fosters empowerment and commitment to making a change in society. The *Strong Girls, Strong World* program represents a unique form of citizenship education based on social change.

O n a beautiful Saturday afternoon in November, four young women gather at YWCA Montréal. Along with the two facilitators running the Strong Girls, Strong World *program, they're preparing the landmark project of the year: a feminist documentary composed of interview segments with women from Montreal, highlighting their ethnic, cultural, and religious diversity. The goal is to represent women through media in a positive light to counterbalance the stereotypes and devaluing discourses circulating in Quebec's media and public sphere. The premiere is scheduled for the program's annual International Women's Day event in March. As the group brainstorms ideas for the outline, their enthusiasm shines throughout their dynamic conversations. After pinning down the objectives and themes of the documentary, they discuss what they'd like to ask the interviewees. One participant suggests asking them about their experience of "everyday feminism." Inspired by the suggestion, another takes the opportunity to share a personal experience with sexism—one of many interludes of the meeting. When the group turns their attention back to the documentary, they debate whether asking each interviewee the same questions is the right approach. One of the facilitators suggests they adapt the questions a little before each interview, reminding them that "the goal of the documentary is not for every woman to say the same thing," but for each to have the opportunity to share her unique experience.*

This chapter discusses how several aspects of the *Strong Girls, Strong World* youth program contribute to participants' democratic learning experience in the context of a collective project informed by a feminist perspective. Our findings are based on an ethnographic study that took place from November 2017 to May 2018 at YWCA Montréal (Théwissen-LeBlanc, 2020). We describe some of the features of the feminist perspective on citizenship that the program offered 15 girls and young women from the ages of 17 to 21. Support from the organization, the non-hierarchical decision-making structure, and the quality of the relationships they formed with Donia and Julie, the group facilitators, are just some of the reasons the volunteer, empowerment-focused program has such an astonishingly high retention rate.[2]

5.1. YWCA Montréal and the *Strong Girls, Strong World* Program

YWCA Montréal is a community organization located in downtown Montreal founded in 1875.[3] Its mission today is "working together to build a better future for girls, women and their families" (YWCA Montréal, n. d. b). The organization offers housing, employability, youth, and community services, mainly to low-income immigrant clients.

Strong Girls, Strong World focuses on community action and leadership development. It is one of the many programs offered through the organization's youth services. Since its launch in the fall of 2015, it has focused on giving girls and young women—mainly between the ages of 16 and 19—"the means to become agents for change and make a difference in their communities" (YWCA Montréal, n. d. a). The program includes a recruitment and kick-off camp, self-defence training, presentations and activities on topics related to feminism and social causes, workshops on feminism and gender equality issues led by secondary school students, an annual open mic event for International Women's Day, and a photography project about 12 inspiring women.[4] Around 30 teenagers took part in the kick-off and roughly 20 intermittently participated in the rest of the activities. In its first two years, the program was funded by the Canada-wide edition of the *Strong Girls, Strong World* program—a collaboration between Plan International Canada, YWCA Canada, YMCA Canada, and Status of Women Canada.[5] When public and national funding dried up in the spring of 2017, YWCA Montréal kept *Strong Girls, Strong World* in its youth programming because of how many participants wanted to stay involved for another year.

5.2. The *IntersectionnELLES* Documentary: Long-Term Voluntary Participation

At the end of summer 2017, the participants and facilitators met to discuss what kind of project they wanted to work on in the coming months. One of the participants, Carla, sums up how they landed on making a documentary:

> We talked as a group about what we wanted to do... and we said Hey! [we did] an open mic event and a photo exhibit. For the next step, it would be cool to make a documentary with basically the same goals [as the other projects], which was to seek out the opinions of engaged women [...] and highlight what they are doing in the community [...] And just share what we have to say among women, to advance the cause.

Their feminist documentary *IntersectionnELLES* features interviews with eight women from various ethnic, cultural, and religious communities in the Montreal area. The production took place over five months and required several prep meetings, interview filming sessions, complex video editing, and organizing a public screening. How does such a demanding list of tasks get done on a voluntary basis?

Almost all the participants joined the program when it first launched and have stayed on over the years. Participants were 17 to 21 years old when they participated in the project. Nearly half of them are young women from racialized communities and the majority are first- or second-generation immigrants. They live in Montreal, most of them in boroughs close to the community centre. Almost all of them attend CEGEP or university and balance this with work and family commitments. However, they get to choose how much time they dedicate to the program, and it is precisely this flexibility that makes it all possible. Participants are free to join activities when they are available. "*Strong Girls* is voluntary," a participant named Gal tells us. "You don't have to come to every meeting. The fact is, if you're here, it's because you want to be. You chose this over spending time with your family, studying, or watching Netflix."

Unsurprisingly, attendance is inconsistent—some participants attend almost every meeting while others only come once or twice over the course of the whole project. In line with the organization's philosophy on developing young women's autonomy and respecting their individual time constraints, arriving late and leaving early is tolerated. The facilitators, Donia and Julie, are in their twenties and work for YWCA Montréal. They supervise the group and provide support throughout the project.

The group meets 15 times to plan and produce the documentary. They update the schedule as they go depending on participant and equipment availability, taking care to complete the major stages of the project within the set timeframe. They often use digital tools to coordinate schedule changes. For example, Donia and Julie post surveys on the group's private Facebook page to determine when the most participants will be available. With no recurring schedule, meetings vary: they may take place during weekdays or weekends; fall in the morning, afternoon, or evening; and last from two to five hours. The meeting place also changes frequently—the community centre, different filming locations like the homes, schools, and workplaces of the women being interviewed, and an editing room at the CEGEP one of the participants attends.

Besides being flexible, voluntary, and conducive to building friendships over the years, the program is successful at engaging participants because they get to exercise decision-making power at every stage of the production. Before filming begins, they devote a few team meetings to deciding on the themes of the documentary, outlining the concept—including the style, content, and length—selecting the interviewees, and writing the interview questions. The group deliberates and makes each decision together. To help them reach decisions faster and move the project along, Julie and Donia organize the meetings and topics to address ahead of time.

In January 2018, preparations are behind them and filming begins. This is when participants enjoy even more autonomy. Even though filming is rigorous, and punctuality becomes a factor, the shoots are flexible because there are no predetermined roles. The group negotiates who is doing what on the spot. By taking charge of the decision-marking process, participants develop a sense of control over the project and get to feel empowered. This is in no small part thanks to the logistical support Donia and Julie provide behind the scenes. Besides guiding the group in the early stages in meetings, discussions, and collective decision-making, they provide invaluable assistance on several essential tasks, like identifying and contacting potential interviewees, arranging appointments, and organizing transportation to filming locations. The following excerpt from our observations illustrates one of the moments where empowerment took place:

Galadrielle (Gal) and Kamila are setting up their tripods in the living room of one of the women featured in the documentary. It's nearly 2 p.m. on a sunny afternoon in mid-January. Preparations for the fourth shoot are underway. Gal is the team lead since she has the most experience directing. Only one of the facilitators, Donia, has already arrived; Julie is en route with one of the participants. The woman being interviewed is friendly. She's prepared snacks and laid them out on a table nearby. She helps the group move furniture for the shoot. Gal politely asks if it's possible to open the blinds to let in the daylight. Shannon and Gal, after some discussion, decide they'd like to interview their host jointly. Gal asks who's recording the sound and Galadrielle tells her that Chloé, who's running late, "really wants to do it." They continue setting up. Shannon helps Gal and Kamila position their cameras. The atmosphere is friendly, with people making light chit-chat as they work. Finally, they invite their host to take a seat on the couch. Gal and Shannon remind her of the general outline of the documentary. Donia jumps in every now and then with her two cents. About ten minutes later, Julie and Chloé arrive. After some friendly greetings and a short chat, Chloé takes over the sound recorder; the others had saved that role for her. Gal helps her configure the settings and Gal gives her a hand with the placement, offering some technical tips along the way. Once they're ready to start filming, Gal checks that everyone has set their phone to silent. The cameras start rolling and Shannon asks the first question: "Why did you agree to be in our documentary?"

The excerpt above illustrates how the program recognizes participants' technical skills—from photography direction and lighting to sound recording and editing—and encourages them to apply them. Filming and editing sessions are also opportunities for participants to share some of their knowledge with the rest of the group and the facilitators. Along the way, they build several skills for working individually and on a team as they organize, deliberate, make decisions, and bring a collaborative project to completion. A big part of the participants' dedication and engagement has to do with growing their skills and feeling proud of themselves. Reflecting on her experience, Carla shares what she gained from the team accomplishment:

> You meet inspiring people who've made an impact on society and inspire you to do the same. You develop more technical skills, too: audiovisual skills, time and project management skills—because you have to organize everything from A to Z—communication skills. [...] You have to think about so many things and [you end up with] a concrete final project you can share with anyone.

The 25-minute documentary features excerpts from interviews with the eight women the group selected.[6] It covers a wide range of topics, including feminism, discrimination, media representation, pride, and women's solidarity. With the help of the facilitators and the support of the organization, the program participants organized a screening attended by over 100 people on March 8, 2018. The project they had started a few months earlier came to a close that night as the audience warmly congratulated the group of young feminists on their achievement.

5.3. An Introduction to Collective Action from a Feminist Approach to Citizenship

The feminist, women-only nature of *Strong Girls, Strong World* affects the group dynamics and tone of the activities. As Julie remarks:

> We're a feminist program, which is very different [compared to
> other youth programs]. It's something that brings us together.
> Everyone who takes part in our discussions and debates around
> the table calls themselves a feminist. It definitely impacts our
> goals and what we do.

The workshops, presentations, events, and year-long projects that
make up the *Strong Girls, Strong World* program introduce participants
to YWCA Montréal and to collective feminist struggles—that is, to
the movement demanding women's rights and promoting social
change (see Lister, 2003; Maillé, 2000). Participants get opportunities
to learn about intersectional feminism and how it can be applied
methodologically to social problems. Instead of engaging in univer-
sity-style feminist theory, the point is to raise awareness of the social
barriers that impact women, including gender, age, race, language,
physical ability, sexual orientation, religion, and citizenship status
(see Hamrouni & Maillé, 2015). The program includes activities on
sexism, racism, the history and living conditions of Indigenous communities in Canada, the status of immigrants, Islamophobia, mental
health issues, disability, and the struggle for LGBTQ2+ rights—topics
that expand participants' understanding of social problems and social
marginalization from a structural point of view, rather than from the
perspective of neoliberalism and individual responsibility.

The *IntersectionnELLES* shows participants' desire to apply and
grow their understanding of intersectionality—a concept in feminist
theory that refers to the interconnected nature of social relationships
(Hamrouni & Maillé, 2015). Their eagerness to learn about the many
forms of women's oppression is sometimes at odds with the views
the women they are interviewing share at the shoots. Contrary to
their expectations, not everyone considers herself a committed feminist, or even a feminist at all, and not everyone talks openly about
sexual and racial discrimination or sees the world through the group's
lens of intersectional feminism.

The facilitators seize tense moments like this to help the group
navigate their discomfort and uphold the very values they claim to
stand for—inclusion and valuing women's diversity. The shoots
become a wider learning opportunity for participants to understand,
as young feminists, what attitude to adopt with people who do not
share their views or know as much about feminism. Carla, one of the
participants, shares that the group members became aware they

needed to respect different opinions and perspectives, including those
of women who distanced themselves from the movement. "We realize
that not all women have the same definition of feminism as we do,"
she says, "and that not all women call themselves feminists." Donia
echoes her sentiment:

> The best part of my job was helping them navigate the situation
> and hearing their reactions [to what the women interviewed had
> to say]. I think it helped them confront their feminism and their
> ideas overall. They let themselves be challenged by other people's
> stories. [They chose] eight women from diverse backgrounds
> [who] weren't going to have the same points of view whether they
> liked it or not. Even if the participants consider them all outstand-
> ing feminists in their fields, they don't have to share the same
> point of view and that's okay. We need different perspectives.

The following excerpt illustrates a learning opportunity that took
place after an interview:

> *While waiting for the bus after a shoot, the participants are discussing
> the interviews they held so far. They're a bit disappointed—they weren't
> expecting some of the answers they got to the questions they'd prepared.
> They discuss some of the surprising remarks that downplayed the importance
> of female solidarity—a very important value for the group. Donia, the facili-
> tator, interprets their experience in a positive light and explains the benefits
> of confronting ideas that contradict our own. The group is a microcosm, she
> says, where participants interact with women who have already embraced
> feminist values and have had lots of opportunities to learn about and reflect
> on the movement. "It's true that we hang out a lot with like-minded people,"
> Shannon agrees. The discussion continues. Many participants are surprised
> that one of the women they interviewed downplayed the seriousness of hav-
> ing been subjected to discrimination. Donia points out how this illustrates
> the subtlety of microaggressions, which frequently go unnoticed.*

Participants sometimes learn from other participants new ways
to relate to feminism as it is not uncommon for group members to
have different opinions. As their friendship grows over time, defending ideas they are passionate about at all costs takes a backseat to
being mindful of each other's feelings in debates and preserving the
bonds created between them.

This suggests that when it comes to democratic education, the journey is more important than the destination—even though it, too, is valuable. *Strong Girls, Strong World* encourages participants to form feminist identities and learn practical skills, like organization, listening, deliberation, feminist analysis, and coordinated action. While technical skills are a big part of what they gained from producing the documentary, the months-long process also left them with newly developed (democratic) attitudes, lessons learned, and critical thinking abilities—including self-reflection. As Iris Marion Young (2000) points out, democratic citizenship requires listening, communicating your ideas, being open to others, being respectful, and being able to compromise.

The type of citizenship that *Strong Girls, Strong World* promotes corresponds to the social justice–oriented citizenship in Joel Westheimer's model (2015). More specifically, the program mobilizes a feminist conception of citizenship in which activism is rooted in a structural analysis of the inequalities and oppression women experience (Young, 2000). The documentary's intersectional feminist framework is apparent from the title itself; with *IntersectionELLES*, participants wanted to portray women from Montreal's minority ethnic, cultural, and religious communities onscreen in a positive light. By applying what they learned in the program, they were able to conceptualize a project and make a series of editorial decisions. These included conducting interviews to amplify minority voices, interviewing women who represent diversity and inclusion in different ways, portraying women onscreen outside the framework of dominant discourses and stereotypes, and preparing interview questions that shine a spotlight on women's lived experiences of discrimination and the social dynamics behind them.

The program's pedagogical approach is a departure from the common neoliberal approach applied across many social and community programs for girls and young women in North America and industrialized countries (Harris, 2003). Many programs emphasize individual responsibility over critically analyzing social inequalities, taking part in protest movements, and defending rights (Westheimer, 2015). *Strong Girls, Strong World* focuses on feminism as a means to engage in collective struggle. It provides participants with a unique space to socialize, engage in activism, develop and embody a confident feminist identity, grow their self-esteem, and gain a sense of belonging to a community and social movement.

5.4. Reciprocity and Collaboration:
Building Trust in Youth–Adult Partnerships

In no small part, the program's high retention rate is due to the partnerships facilitators were able to foster with the group. Two key ingredients played a decisive role: reciprocity and collaboration. As Julie puts it:

> We're not teachers [giving] a lecture in an amphitheatre to a silent audience. It's not like that at all. In fact, it's the opposite! [...] In our workshops, we talk and share ideas. We encourage everyone to participate and always try to create an environment where young people feel comfortable expressing themselves. We try to express ourselves too and we challenge the group with questions rather than giving them the answers.

This excerpt refers to several facilitation techniques that, according to research, help establish horizontal youth–adult partnerships in community organizations (Blanchet-Cohen & Brunson, 2014; Zeldin et al., 2014). Because the facilitators take a collaborative approach as opposed to a supervisory or authoritative one, they are able to create a bond with participants that is rooted in trust and reciprocity. This keeps the group interested and motivated. Donia and Julie also ensure participants needs are met by providing constant encouragement to the group as a whole and personalized support to individual participants. They create a framework of activities and interactions through which everyone can develop a sense of belonging.

Above all, they help participants develop leadership skills by encouraging, rather than dominating, the creative process over the course of the documentary project. Using a variety of techniques, they motivate participants to get involved and ensure that every voice is heard, that everyone feels included, and that the group reaches decisions by consensus. "I think it empowers them," Julie tells us. "It's motivating to feel like we're talking to each other as equals. No idea is better than another. They're all welcome and they all get the same level of attention." Several participants confirmed that this was, in fact, their experience. "I feel like my opinion has a place there," Gal tells us. "If I raised my hand to disagree with something, she'd listen to what I had to say," shares Éléonore about one of the facilitators. "They pretty much always [...] try to include as many people as possible," Mia corroborates.

Facilitators thus take on a more helpful than supervisory role. "They didn't impose anything on us," says Isabelle in a personal account of her experience. "They gave us tools and were there to guide us. They taught us a bit about how to do things and supported us [...]. It helped create the feeling that we were equal." Donia and Julie's facilitation techniques are focused on building informal inter-personal relationships, which contributes to the strong bonds they end up forming with participants. In fact, during our case study, they said they developed lasting friendships with some of the group members—echoing what the group had to say about them. Looking back on our case study, it is clear that the feminist youth group of *Strong Girls* had accepted Donia and Julia as one of their own.

Donia and Julie also ensured that participants were included in decisions about the program, not just the projects. At the participants' request, *Strong Girls, Strong World* would run for another year despite a lack of external funding. "We ran out of money, but the girls really wanted to keep the group going," Donia tells us. She urged the organization to allocate funds internally so the program could stay open. The strategy worked, reflecting another winning practice according to research—namely involving community organizations in the allocation of financial, material, and human resources to youth programs and practices (Blanchet-Cohen & Brunson, 2014).

In May 2018, the facilitators once again invited the group to share their thoughts on the project and future possibilities. What did they take away from the experience? What did they learn? What worked well? What could be improved? Do they want to keep working on projects together? The following excerpt is a glimpse into this discussion, illustrating the collaborative and reciprocal nature of the youth–adult partnerships in the program, which helped build trust:

"We want to give the next generation everything this project has given us," says Sasha, piggybacking on Carla's suggestion to start a new feminist group that mentors adolescents. Two months after the documentary screening, eight members of the group are discussing their experience with Donia and Julie around a large picnic table in a green space next to YWCA Montréal. The facilitators had asked them to share their thoughts and make suggestions to improve the program. Sasha suggests sharing what they've learned; she wants to widen their circle. Carla agrees, saying she wants to

"share the knowledge" they gained throughout the program, and Donia notes down their suggestions. Kiana says they need to promote girls' leadership, and Sasha proposes creating a "mini Strong Girls" group for younger participants. Donia asks what they think about inviting new participants their own age into the group; a few young women had expressed an interest after the public screening of the documentary. Carla suggests that initiating them into the group or organizing a "Strong Girls Summit" would be a good way to explore this idea. The discussion continues. Participants spontaneously jump in to comment on an idea or share a new one. Gal would like to attend practical workshops—for example on managing a budget—so that the group can eventually take on more responsibility for the Strong Girls, Strong World *program. One participant suggests organizing an activity in a chalet. Donia thinks these are both good ideas but adds that the organization still hasn't heard back about external funding. Sasha asks the facilitators their thoughts on next steps, and Julie says that "the idea of the chalet comes from you," which makes it an interesting avenue to explore.*

Ultimately, it is not just the approach to citizenship that is feminist in the *Strong Girls, Strong World* program; the collaborative and reciprocal youth-adult partnerships, established by the facilitators and agreed to by the participants, are implicitly part of a feminist philosophy on pedagogy (see Amboulé-Abath et al., 2018; Manicom, 1992). Indeed, the traditional youth-adult/teacher-student hierarchy is flattened, and relationships and knowledge circulation tend to be horizontal and collective in nature. At meetings, Donia and Julie realized they knew less about the technical aspects of making a documentary than some of the participants, so they had those individuals lead the filming and editing process. This type of reciprocal relationship is common in feminist approaches seen in other community organizations and youth programs where adults take on the role of guides or facilitators (see Blum-Ross, 2015).

5.5. An Authentic Collective Learning Experience Rooted in the Real World

The *Strong Girls, Strong World* program offers participants an authentic group engagement experience where hands-on learning is possible. Reflecting on what she gained from the documentary project, Isabelle shares:

> I find it's not only one of the best ways to learn but also the best way to really understand their situation and do a project. Because if you do a project without being in the field [...] you're much less connected to what's going on [...]. I find it's also amazing having the person right in front of you. It's such a part of the experience. It's crucial and so important for me.

For her part, Gal reflects on what she learned about democratic participation in the program:

> I think being a good citizen is something you learn from experience. You don't learn it by taking a class and writing a test. You learn from your own experiences and the people you meet. And I think a program like Strong Girls allows you to do that, but times a thousand because you meet new people and hear different opinions. You talk about things that you wouldn't necessarily talk about at dinner with your parents.

Throughout the project, participants got to meet various inspiring women working in local government, psychoeducation, chemical engineering, social work, and the arts. Several of them are pioneers in traditionally male-dominated sectors: the first Black woman to graduate from the École nationale de l'humour (Quebec comedy school), the first Asian woman to work for the Service de police de la Ville de Montreal, the first female chair of the Montréal city council, and the first Hasidic Jewish woman elected to political office in Quebec.[7]

"I think meeting inspiring women enables us to see how they [respond] to negative opinions on feminist issues," shares Gal. Like many of her colleagues, she emphasizes how positively these encounters have impacted her. "We can draw inspiration from their responses when we come up against similar situations in our own lives."

According to many of the participants, the central role of feminism in the program was a key factor in learning lessons that are both valuable and unique. "We don't talk about [feminism] much or at all at school," says Éléonore. "When I got involved in the project, I didn't know much about gender equality or feminism," adds Carla. "Or should I say, the different kinds of feminism, because there are several." Others report having changed their minds about feminism because of the program. Kiana, for example, says that before she joined Strong Girls, Strong World, she did not even like the word, believing that the reference to women (*fem*-inism) "meant that women wanted to dominate men." When we interviewed them, several participants also told us about the many opportunities they got to meet other feminists through the program. Mia emphasizes how much the fact that everyone was there voluntarily added to the experience. "The fact that we could take part on [a] voluntary basis meant that everyone who showed up wanted to be there," she says. "[It meant we wanted] to talk about feminism and be involved in the project. [...] It created such a positive and pleasant atmosphere."

The *Strong Girls, Strong World* program encourages participants to strengthen their relationship to feminism. The feminist identity they ultimately embraced is rooted in a collective, intersectional movement that champions women's rights and equality. Some participants said the program helped them learn about the history and foundations of feminism and how to incorporate their own feminist values into their daily lives. This is Éléonore's most important take-away from the program: "It's considering myself a feminist," she says. "I think that's really it. It's part of my everyday life."

Participants develop skills and abilities that apply to their lived citizenship—that is, to how they live the everyday aspects of a democratic society (Kallio et al., 2020). It is a feminist citizenship, a way of engaging that is evident in how they act and interact, think and feel, and exercise their autonomy. Many take the lessons they have learned beyond the activities of *Strong Girls, Strong World*. They report feeling more comfortable expressing their opinions, asserting themselves in discussions, and raising awareness about equality and women's rights beyond their inner circle. It's important "when an opportunity presents itself [...] to make certain people conscious of certain issues or situations that women [or others] may be facing," says Mia. Similarly, Gal notes that even today "not everyone agrees with the idea of feminism." She is happy to have learned how to "defend the opinions of a minority part of society" by defending her own feminist point of view when others do not share it.

Conclusion

The *Strong Girls, Strong World* youth volunteer program promotes social change by introducing participants to feminist action. Its role in citizenship education is to fill the gaps schools leave, including content on women's citizenship and the history of feminism, and encouragement to get involved in social and protest movements (see Brunet, 2017; Kennelly & Llewellyn, 2011). The program also teaches participants how to think critically by analyzing gender relations and how they intersect with other differentiating social factors. Participants learn about feminism and become skilled at applying concepts like intersectionality as an analytical lens to discern the inequalities women face. In the community setting, program participants learn the lessons that schools are reluctant to teach: that social inequalities have structural causes and that social movements are essential drivers of change. In order to create change in civil society, however, individuals need to know how to come together and organize their action around concrete goals rooted in values like equality and justice. It is precisely this democratic practice that they learn in the *Strong Girls, Strong World* program.

References

Amboulé-Abath, A., Campbell, M.-È., & Pagé, G. (2018). La pédagogie féministe : sens et mise en action pédagogique. *Recherches féministes, 31*(1), 23–43. https://doi.org/10.7202/1050652ar

Blanchet-Cohen, N., & Brunson, L. (2014). Creating settings for youth empowerment and leadership: An ecological perspective. *Child & Youth Services, 35*(3), 216–236. https://doi.org/10.1080/0145935X.2014.938735

Blum-Ross, A. (2015). Filmmakers/educators/facilitators? Understanding the role of adult intermediaries in youth media production in the UK and the USA. *Journal of Children and Media, 9*(3), 308–324. https://doi.org/10.1080/17482798.2015.1058280

Brunet, M.-H. (2017). Des histoires du passé : le féminisme dans les manuels d'histoire et d'éducation à la citoyenneté selon des élèves québécois de quatrième secondaire. *McGill Journal of Education / Revue des sciences de l'éducation de McGill, 52*(2), 409–431. https://doi.org/10.7202/1044473ar

Hamrouni, N., & Maillé, C. (Eds.). (2015). *Le sujet du féminisme est-il blanc ? Femmes racisées et recherche féministe.* Éditions du remue-ménage.

Harris, A. (2003). *Future girl: Young women in the twenty-first century.* Routledge.

Kallio, K. P., Wood, B. E., & Häkli, J. (2020). Lived citizenship: Conceptualising an emerging field. *Citizenship Studies, 24*(6), 713–729. https://doi.org/10.1080/13621025.2020.1739227

Kennelly, J., & Llewellyn, K. R. (2011). Educating for active compliance: Discursive constructions in citizenship education. *Citizenship Studies, 15*(6–7), 897–914. https://doi.org/10.1080/13621025.2011.600103

Lister, R. (2003). *Citizenship: Feminist perspectives* (2ⁿᵈ ed.). Palgrave Macmillan.

Maillé, C. (2000). Féminisme et mouvement des femmes au Québec : un bilan complexe. *Globe, 3*(2), 87–105. https://doi.org/10.7202/1000583ar

Manicom, A. (1992). Feminist pedagogy: Transformations, standpoints, and politics. *Canadian Journal of Education / Revue canadienne de l'éducation, 17*(3), 365–389. https://doi.org/10.2307/1495301

Théwissen-LeBlanc, S. (2020). *L'éducation à la citoyenneté dans un programme jeunesse féministe non-mixte : le cas de* Force des filles, force du monde [Master's thesis, University of Ottawa]. https://ruor.uottawa.ca/handle/10393/40724

Westheimer, J. (2015). *What kind of citizen? Educating our children for the common good.* Teachers College Press.

YWCA Montréal (n. d. a). *Strong Girls, Strong World.* https://www.ydesfemmesmtl.org/en/youth-services/youthprograms/strong-girls-strong-world/

YWCA Montréal (n. d. b). *Mission, vision & values.* https://www.ydesfemmesmtl.org/en/about-us/mission-vision-values/

Young, I. M. (2002). *Inclusion and democracy.* Oxford University Press.

Zeldin, S., Krauss, S. E., Collura, J., Lucchesi, M., & Sulaiman, A. H. (2014). Conceptualizing and measuring youth-adult partnership in community programs: A cross national study. *American Journal of Community Psychology, 54*(3–4), 337–347. https://doi.org/10.1007/s10464-014-9676-9

Notes

1. A play on the French words for "intersectional" and "she."
2. All first names are pseudonyms.
3. https://www.ydesfemmesmtl.org/.
4. The name of the initiative is *Des femmes et des ~~maux~~ mots* (Women and ~~Pain~~ Words). In French, "pain" and "words" are homonyms.
5. Even though the Montreal program is offered in French under the translated name *Force des filles, force du monde*, participants and facilitators prefer using the English name *Strong Girls, Strong World*—or *Strong Girls* for short.
6. The documentary is available on YouTube in French only: https://youtu.be/ffI_41COKTI.
7. The Montreal Police Department.

CHAPTER 6

Between Justice and Care: The CPSG Children's Rights Committee

Stéphanie Gaudet and François Marchand

Abstract

This chapter presents the Children's Rights Committee of the Centre de pédiatrie sociale de Gatineau.[1] At the recommendation of the nursing staff, young people between 10 and 15 years of age are invited to take part in the committee to learn about their rights and how to amplify their voices. To commemorate the adoption of the *Convention on the Rights of the Child*, they prepare an annual march through a series of activities under the supervision of a lawyer and a social worker. Our research shows that in addition to learning about the Convention and how it applies to their daily lives, children who participate in the committee gain a positive experience of being part of a group and making an impact. This program offers them a unique form of citizenship education based on creating social change.

*I*t's November 19, 2019—the eve of the march that the CPSG Children's Rights Committee organizes every year in honour of World Children's Day.[2] The team is busy finalizing the last details. Some of the children are washing dishes and cleaning as Josée, the committee's co-facilitator and lawyer, plans the evening's events. She has divided the group into three. The first group is in a corner painting large wing-shaped cardboard boxes that illustrate the theme of the march: "Rights give you wings." The second group *is working on slogans and signs, while the third consists of children who will speak at the march. The atmosphere is somewhat chaotic. I move from group to group and offer to help design the signs. Some are almost done. The slogans include: "We have the right to eat, live, and have fun"; "The right to appropriate clothes for the season"; and "I have the right to a roof over my head!" Josée asks the group of young people speaking at the march what they want to say. She offers ideas and takes notes. From time to time, she reads back what they've brainstormed. Some of the children will be speaking in front of an audience for the first time.*

The Children's Rights Committee is dedicated to amplifying the voices of children who receive services at the CPSG. This initiative drew our attention because it represents a "third place" for children's democratic citizenship education—it is a space outside the school and home where young people can share ideas and learn about democratic citizenship. The organization's educational approach is informal—there is no curriculum or precise learning objective to be evaluated. A key feature is that the leaders' care for young people takes the form of empowering them by teaching them about their rights.

The committee draws on several kinds of democratic citizenship (Sant, 2019): liberal, through its emphasis on individual rights; participatory and critical, through its focus on social justice and community (Westheimer & Kahne, 2004); and feminist, through its focus on the ethics of care and healing (Tronto, 1993/2009). The CPSG uses the *Convention on the Rights of the Child* in its medical and psycho-social interventions, which is uncommon among youth organizations and services. As per the Convention, the adults who facilitate the organization's activities have to balance citizenship education, on the one hand, and care ethics and practices, on the other. Although the committee prioritizes emotional support for vulnerable children, they are considered full-fledged citizens in the decision-making process.

6.1. The Children's Rights Committee

Dr. Gilles Julien founded the CPSG in 2009 in collaboration with the organization Les Centres jeunesse de l'Outaouais, to offer the most vulnerable children in the Vieux-Gatineau community services that were better adapted to their needs.[3] A second branch opened in Hull in 2015. The CPSG's mission is to take in children who are sick or have been neglected or abandoned, help restore their health, and empower them. During our case study, the CPSG consisted of about 15 health and social services professionals, including physicians, social workers, psychoeducators, and special education teachers.

It is part of a network of over 40 Quebec organizations that offer children and their families community-based social pediatric care. This comprehensive, holistic, and multidisciplinary approach to healthcare views children's health in the broader context of their social, school, and family environment and takes account of the physical, mental, and social dimensions of their health and development (Spencer et al., 2005, p. 106).

When it was founded, the CPSG put the Children's Rights Committee into motion to offer children an emotionally safe environment where they could express themselves and learn to advocate on their own behalf. The committee holds around 10 meetings a year to teach children about their rights and prepare an annual march in honour of World Children's Day. The meetings are held at the CPSG and last about two hours. They generally start in the winter and end on November 20—the day of the annual march.

During our year-long case study, we observed around 10 young people ranging in age from 10 to 15; a core group of half a dozen 10-to-13-year-olds, plus a few older participants who, being very attached to the group, would join from time to time. The committee provides them an opportunity to attend events that expand their understanding of the world of justice. They organize court visits, observe public consultations, and take part in projects like the Children's Rights Trail, during which they created signs on the seven principles of the *Convention on the Rights of the Child* to install at the centre. Committee members are responsible for planning, attending, and running meetings and activities.

The committee is headed *pro bono* by Josée, a lawyer, as part of CPSG's Alliance Droit Médecine Sociale program, which aims to help children and their families access justice and improve social pediatric care in the community (Angba et al., 2016).[4] Along with heading the committee, Josée acts as the liaison between children and families and the legal system, in addition to playing an essential role in creating a stimulating learning environment. Her co-facilitator Julianne, a CPSG social worker, provides psychosocial support to the children so they can learn in a safe group environment.

Most participants are invited to join the committee by the care team, which consists of the clinical director, staff members, and the committee facilitators. They select participants based on three main criteria: that they can integrate into a group, that they may have difficulty speaking on their own behalf, and that they want to join the committee.

Our research team first contacted the Children's Rights Committee in the fall of 2018. The participant observation in this field consisted of filling out a logbook during meetings and helping out during activities. François Marchand recorded observations as part of his doctoral thesis and assisted with activities. His approach was hands-off—he was still the adult, but he intervened as little as possible (Gaudet et al., 2020). In the winter of 2020, the committee was put on hold due to the COVID-19 pandemic. We had around 10 observation notes by that time.

6.2. Citizenship Education Based on Justice and Care

Since the committee's approach is based on understanding individual rights, it adopts a liberal citizenship perspective, but is not limited to this. In fact, the CPSG and activities of the Children's Rights Committee are in line with Quebec's tradition of community action, which emerged in the second half of the twentieth century in working-class urban environments and feminist movements (Lamoureux et al., 2002). The latter accorded particular importance to popular education, solidarity, democracy, the defence of social rights, and collective action to tackle social issues. As part of this community movement, the CPSG thus also promotes critical citizenship, because it seeks to raise collective awareness of structural problems to promote a more just society.

6.2.1. Educating for Liberal Citizenship

Western liberal democracies are founded on the principle of equal individual rights (Sant, 2019). The Children's Rights Committee's meetings are informal learning spaces where children can familiarize themselves with the principles and articles of the *Convention on the Rights of the Child* and apply them in their daily lives. Through the lens of the Convention, committee activities offer children a chance to better understand their own lives and the social rights inherent in our society. They learn what they are entitled to expect from their family, school, community, and adults in general. During our case study, we observed an activity in which committee participants considered the differences between needs, rights, and wants to gain awareness of the language of rights and justice.

At Josée's request, the children partner up. Each team of two receives around 20 stickers with images like a house, a bicycle, a glass of water, or a music player. They have 10 minutes to classify each sticker as a "right," a "need," or a "want." The room goes quiet as participants concentrate on their task. Here and there, adults offer a hand or pose prompting questions. When everyone has finished, the group as a whole discusses the meaning of each sticker and how it relates to children's rights. Debates break out every now and then, but there's no sense of competition. There are no right or wrong answers—instead, the co-facilitators' goal is to get participants thinking.

As a lexical tool, the Convention offers participants an alternative to the individualizing and stigmatizing terminology of diagnoses (attention deficit disorder, behavioural problems, etc.) and the technical language of youth centres and social services they are often subjected to. This process helps them avoid the labels of biomedical discourse and develop a positive perspective on their citizenship. This new lexicon also helps them reflect constructively on their situation and legitimize their fundamental needs, which are also rights—protection from violence, access to education, the right to have a family, and to play and participate.

Josée's role is to provide context and explain why citizens should know the language of rights. "Why is knowing our rights so important?" she asked the group during one of the workshops. When one child replied, "So we know when there's bullying going on," Josée took the opportunity to explain the meaning of bullying to the group. She posed a few more questions and returned to the children's answers, emphasizing the importance of learning to use our rights to defend ourselves.

6.2.2. Fostering Participatory and Critical Citizenship

By familiarizing themselves with the rights set out in the Convention and talking about them together, children on the committee can better understand their shared experience as well as the social injustices that shape their lives yet fall outside their individual responsibility. The committee's activities empower them to take action by raising their awareness about the social and shared nature of their experiences, and by inviting them to participate, share their ideas, and make a difference in their local communities as active citizens.

Since the Children's Rights Committee was set up in 2009, it has focused on two main projects: the Children's Rights Trail and the annual march for children's rights. The trail project was coming to an end as our case study was starting. With the help of the committee's co-facilitators, the children had learned about the seven principles of the *Convention on the Rights of the Child* by illustrating them on plaques that would be installed in front of the CPSG building. In keeping with its participatory and collaborative philosophy, the centre developed the project in partnership with seven community organizations that could and would manifest one of the principles in the community. The collaborative Children's Rights Trail project was primarily led by the committee's facilitators, and the children shared responsibility for the content of the plaques. The initiative made it possible to co-construct a consciousness-raising process and share knowledge about the Convention. It exemplifies a participatory approach to citizenship education, because it involved young people in decision-making and encouraged them to take concrete action in their community. The committee's second main project is the annual march in honour of World Children's Day. On November 20, after a year of preparations, the committee participants see citizen mobilization in action—most of them for the first time—as they raise awareness of children's rights alongside adults and other children from the CPSG and local schools. They are joined by elected officials, the media, and members of the CPSG's management team, whose presence legitimizes their citizenship and civic agency in the eyes of society. Here is a glimpse into the festive, rallying atmosphere of the annual march:

On November 20, 2019, nearly 200 children from several schools in the Outaouais region gather at Fontaine Park in Gatineau as part of World Children's Day. They are joined by teachers, school and community workers, a few parents, municipal councillors, representatives of provincial and federal parliamentarians, and the mayor. Everyone is marching with signs in hand— We are the future; I have the right to health, play, and respect; We have the right to express ourselves; Freedom of choice! *they read. The atmosphere is festive. The two-kilometre walk ends at the Maison du Citoyen with a buffet and programming.[5] The children take their seats at the 10 large tables set up around the room. Josée, four children from the committee, the CPSG's clinical manager, and dignitaries including the mayor and town councillors take turns addressing everyone from a stage for about 12 minutes. They all emphasize the importance of further recognizing and actualizing children's rights. After the presentations, the children take part in fun workshops led by a magician. Committee members take the opportunity to unveil a large pair of multicoloured wings suspended above the room—a work of art symbolizing how rights give them wings.*

Beyond fostering children's liberal citizenship, the committee's two projects support critical citizenship education based on social justice. The aim of the CPSG is not just to defend individual rights, but to inform the group and mobilize it around a political vision for a fairer and more inclusive society that provides children and their families with the resources they need to live better and participate actively in it. In line with Quebec's tradition of community action and Joel Westheimer and Joseph Kahne's (2004) model of critical citizenship, the march represents the educational practice aimed at collectively creating a more just society.

6.2.3. Fostering a Feminist View of Citizenship Based on Care

Feminist care-based theories developed in the 1980s in opposition to liberal moral theories, which view society through the lens of universal justice and the concept of independent, rational human beings (Gilligan, 1982/1986; Tronto, 1993/2009). Carol Gilligan and Joan Tronto, instead, propose the notion of a society based on caring in which human beings are interdependent. They emphasize the importance of context, emotions, and sensitivity, advocating for a view of justice that recognizes particularities. These views of human beings inevitably influence the model of democratic citizenship associated with them, namely liberal and care-based approaches. Today, care theorists recognize that both go hand in hand (Pulcini, 2013) and, indeed, we observed that the CPSG's Children's Rights Committee is already putting theory into practice by implementing a citizenship education approach based as much on justice as on caring.

That the CPSG prioritizes young people's well-being is evident from its welcoming atmosphere and focus on personal connections. In fact, while the care and specialized services rooms are accessed through an inconspicuous corridor at the back, the centre's bright, colourful, open-plan kitchen and living room feels more like a family home than a clinic. The social space has games and is constantly abuzz with adults paying attention to the kids (doing ponytails and chatting with them) as they go about household tasks like cleaning, preparing food, and sweeping the floors. Support is provided during the activities and not necessarily formally. The following vignette depicts the diverse ways in which social life is cultivated in the space.

As the children spread out to focus on an activity—illustrating one of the principles of the Convention—Julianne circulates the room offering ideas, posing questions, and encouraging them to keep working. She speaks with one of the children going through a difficult time in his family. He and his mother are moving to another region, so this will be his last day at the CPSG. Elsewhere in the room, Violine—a special education trainee—is doing a few of the girls' hair. I overhear a conversation about Harry Potter. The atmosphere is relaxed. Later, one of the children vents to Julianne about how her teacher kicked her out of class today. She's clearly frustrated and Julianne listens patiently, asking questions to better understand and offering suggestions on how to handle the situation.

Before activities begin, committee members usually enjoy each other's company over dinner in the kitchen. Josée and Julianne also plan for free time in the program. This gives them an opportunity to chat with the children in a friendly environment. It also gives children the space to express opinions, converse, and vent about any challenges they are going through. Hospitality, together with the care taken to welcome and include people, fosters positive social interactions, which is essential when working with children in vulnerable situations.

The CPSG's focus on creating a friendly space aligns with the thinking of feminist care ethicists, who see providing support for the maintenance of life as a collective practice rooted in attentive thought, a concern for others, the provision of care, and an awareness of our impact on the person we are caring for. The approach is usually considered feminist given that women are culturally more likely to take on the kind of responsibility it comes with. This is the case at the CPSG, which mainly relies on the day-to-day work of women.

In concrete terms, care ethics are put into practice through interventions that allow young people to better integrate socially, participate, and thus enact their citizenship. The role of the adults, then, is to create a caring space for everyone. For example, the co-facilitator and psychosocial worker watches for signs of anxiety, distress, and disruptive behaviour, all of which may indicate that a child may need more support. Interventions are often carried out preventively in such a way that includes children with potentially disruptive behaviours within the group so they do not become withdrawn. The following excerpt from our ethnographic notes shows the value Josée and Julianne place on creating a welcoming and inclusive space for caring for children in vulnerable situations:

> We're seated around the table, sharing a pizza before the workshop begins. Xavier, one of the more rambunctious children, has taken over the conversation. He seems to enjoy provoking the others with controversial topics, which is raising the tension in the room. Julianne subtly takes the seat next to him and engages with him several times during the meal. As the meeting progresses, Xavier starts contributing more and more thoughtfully to the group's conversations. In one of the activities, Julianne assigns him an active role by suggesting that he write down the group's answers on the board. I would later learn that he had witnessed a family tragedy in his home a few months earlier.

The excerpt above highlights how important it is to intervene when children exhibit disruptive behaviour in order to protect the positive dynamic of the group and help the child avoid a social fall-out. It also shines a light on the crucial role of emotional support, which can help a child assume responsibilities and a role within a group. Xavier's positive outcome may not have been possible without Julianne's sensitivity and the concern she expressed for the complexity of his emotional experience.

6.3. Adult–Youth Collaboration

The care practices we observed at the CPSG help Josée and Julianne establish trust and respect with the children in the committee, which in turn allows them to provide the care they need. Only then can they gradually start working with them on empowering projects that amplify their voices. Agency in children depends in large part on strong youth-adult partnerships (Blanchet-Cohen & Brunson, 2014). Collective action led by community organizations that encourage youth-adult partnerships rooted in reciprocity, learning together, and sharing power is recognized as the most promising form of citizenship education for young people and communities (Zeldin et al., 2017). While research on youth-adult partnerships focuses on teenagers, the CPSG uniquely works with vulnerable children ages 12 and under, which necessarily impacts the extent to which they can collaborate.

Many of the children in the committee live in vulnerable situations, and the CPSG strives to provide them a safe space where they can express themselves and experience success. Co-facilitation by a lawyer and a social worker acknowledges them as citizens while respecting their emotional and cognitive limits and their vulnerabilities as young people in socially precarious situations. Indeed, legitimizing their citizenship involves acknowledging their daily practices while respecting their differences. At the CPSG, they are full citizens, just without the right to vote.

Involving young people in strategic decisions commits adults to "sharing" their power and creating a less hierarchical partnership. For the past several years, the co-facilitators have invited committee members to evaluate the annual march in honour of World Children's Day. The year before our case study, the children reported feeling they were not involved enough in organizing and running the 2017 march. In response, Josée proposed that the committee meet with the CPSG board of directors to discuss the matter, creating a bridge between the children and the administration to support the process. The committee nominated delegates to present their requests to the board and, by the following year, almost all had been accepted and implemented.

Inviting feedback and offering children a framework for influencing decisions that affect them powerfully acknowledges youth agency and provides for richer, more authentic youth-adult partnerships. According to Roger Hart's Ladder of Participation (1997), children convincing adults to collaborate with them on projects they would like to undertake is the highest level of youth engagement.[6]

6.4. What Do Children and Communities Gain from the Experience?

Besides fostering liberal, participatory, critical, and care-based democratic citizenship, organizing the annual march helps committee members develop skills in collective action and deliberation: In committee meetings they discuss shared issues and how they relate to the Convention, and in workshops they reflect on the messages they want to share, whom they want to share them with, and how. It is all part of the process of becoming more aware and learning how to raise awareness and consciousness in society and mobilize people.

Committee members get a chance to create slogans and brainstorm how to express themselves collectively in front of dignitaries and people in positions of power. Participating in the committee allows them to learn about the Convention and how it applies to their daily lives, and to experiment with creating social change as a collective. We interviewed former committee members between the ages of 15 and 18 who told us that the experience helped them develop a lasting sense of self-confidence and belonging to the group:

> When I ask the four teenagers what they took away from their experience with the Children's Rights Committee, they are unanimous: a "great group," "meeting great people," "good memories we'll have for a long time," and "having a space to talk about ourselves, our happiness, our sadness, our joys and our pains, without feeling judged."

The co-facilitators' participatory approach allows young people to express themselves freely and experience the benefits of being part of a group in an emotionally safe space. This is often a first for committee members, most of whom have tense situations at home and in school. The committee provides them with a third place where they can make their voices heard, discuss shared issues, and brainstorm ways of exercising their agency. As noted by the clinic director and one of the facilitators, it is a crucial learning experience for building self-confidence:

> They both tell me about a boy who was so shy when he first joined the committee that he would sometimes hide under the table during meetings. He became increasingly more secure with time until, amazingly, he was even the "jury foreperson" in a mock trial the committee had organized while preparing for a courtroom visit.

Observing the group over a year and half allowed us to witness the progress of another child who initially had low self-confidence and difficulty expressing himself. A year after joining the committee, he volunteered to speak at the annual march. Josée and Julianne told us how proud parents of committee members are to see their children's growing confidence.

Many children feel that being on the committee gave them an opportunity to make a real difference in their community's transformation, echoing the participatory and critical approach behind the educational initiative:

I ask one of the children if she thought the committee had an impact on her community. She tells me about how the committee helped with the installation of play structures at her school. As part of their participation in revitalizing the Notre-Dame/Vieux-Gatineau neighbourhood, the committee recorded a video on "the right to play" to call attention to the lack of play structures in her schoolyard. The video was presented at a neighbourhood event attended by community development stakeholders and the mayor, and the school has since installed play structures. She's convinced the video had a lot to do with it and is very proud.

Involving children in concrete projects helps them discover their agency and the role they can play as citizens. In the excerpt above, a young girl was able to express herself, put her knowledge of the Convention into practice, understand how the consultative process works, and, above all, be recognized as a citizen by her peers, family, neighbourhood, and adults in positions of power. Youth civic participation depends in large part on recognition from such adults (Augsberger et al., 2018). It can have a ripple effect, empowering parents and other young people to get involved in their community.

Conclusion

The CPSG Children's Rights Committee helps us understand how a friendly, welcoming social space can become a third place for teaching children in socially vulnerable situations about democratic citizenship. In keeping with Quebec's tradition of community action, the committee draws from the *Convention on the Rights of the Child* to emphasize society's responsibility toward children as well as their right to freedom of participation (Article 12), expression (Article 13), and thought (Article 14). The committee's activities and the annual march on World Children's Day in particular are an opportunity for young people to mobilize, speak up, and raise awareness to create a society that is fairer to children.

The committee successfully combines complementary conceptions of democratic citizenship—liberal through their focus on rights, participatory and critical through their focus on mobilization and raising awareness, and care-based. The co-facilitation arrangement between a lawyer and social worker combines two normative paradigms: the liberal ethics of law, in which the understanding and implementation of rights are considered fundamental conditions for justice, and the ethics of care and vulnerability, in which justice is viewed through the lens of human relationships and emotions. The spotlight feminist care ethicists shine on the political dimension of emotions strikes us as a promising way to understand mechanisms of citizenship education. The CPSG's Children's Rights Committee allowed us to deepen our understanding of the sociological issues connected with emotional support in efforts aimed at children's emancipation.

References

Angba, L., Tremblay-Perron, D., & Fauser, R. (2016). *Mettre en place un comité des droits des enfants dans un centre de pédiatrie sociale en communauté : démarches et conseils.* Fondation Dr Julien.

Augsberger, A., Collins, M. E., & Gecker, W. (2018). Engaging youth in municipal government: Moving toward a youth-centric practice. *Journal of Community Practice, 26*(1), 41–62. https://doi.org/10.1080/10705422.2017.1413023

Blanchet-Cohen, N., & Brunson, L. (2014). Creating settings for youth empowerment and leadership: An ecological perspective. *Child & Youth Services, 35*(3), 216–236. https://doi.org/10.1080/0145935X.2014.938735

Gaudet, S., Drapeau, É. Marchand, F., & Forest, M. (2020). Repenser le rapport social d'âge sur le terrain : ethnographies de la Commission Jeunesse Gatineau et du Comité des droits de l'enfant du Centre de pédiatrie sociale de Gatineau. In Côté, I., Lavoie, K., & Trottier-Cyr, R.-P. (Eds.), *La recherche centrée sur l'enfant : défis éthiques et innovations méthodologiques* (pp. 219–246). Presses de l'Université Laval.

Gilligan, C. (1986). *Une si grande différence* (A. Kwiatek, Trans.). Flammarion. (Original work published 1982)

Hart, R. A. (1997). *Children's participation: The theory and practice of involving young citizens in community development and environmental care.* Routledge. https://doi.org/10.4324/9781315070728

Lamoureux, H., Lavoie, J., Mayer, R., & Panet-Raymond, J. (2002). *La pratique de l'action communautaire* (2ⁿᵈ ed., rev. & augm.). Presses de l'Université du Québec.

Pulcini, E. (2013). *Care of the world: Fear, responsibility and justice in the global age* (K. Whittle, Trans.). Springer.

Sant, E. (2019). Democratic education: A theoretical review (2006–2017). *Review of Educational Research, 89*(5), 655–696. https://doi.org/10.3102/00346543 19862493

Spencer, N., Colomer, C., Alperstein, G., Bouvier, P., Colomer, J., Duperrex, O., Gokcay, G., Julien, G., Kohler, L., Lindström, B., Macfarlane, A., Mercer, R., Panagiotopoulos, T., & Schulpen, T. (2005). Social paediatrics. *Journal of Epidemiology & Community Health, 59*(2), 106–108. https://doi.org/10.1136/jech.2003.017681

Tronto, J. (2009). *Un monde vulnérable : pour une politique du care* (H. Maury, Trans.). La Découverte. (Original work published 1993)

Westheimer, J., & Kahne, J. (2004). What kind of citizen? The politics of educating for democracy. *American Educational Research Journal, 41*(2), 237–269. https://doi.org/10.3102/00028312041002237

Zeldin, S., Gauley, J., Krauss, S. E., Kornbluh, M., & Collura, J. (2017). Youth-adult partnership and youth civic development: Cross-national analyses for scholars and field professionals. *Youth & Society, 49*(7), 851–878. https://doi.org/10.1177/0044118X15595153

Notes

1. Gatineau Social Pediatrics Centre.
2. The UN has declared November 20 World Children's Day. This date commemorates the adoption of the *Declaration of the Rights of the Child* (1959) and the United Nations' *Convention on the Rights of the Child* (1989). See: https://www.un.org/fr/observances/world-childrens-day.
3. Outaouais Youth Centres.
4. Law and Social Medicine Alliance.
5. Citizen's House.
6. In Chapter 2, we presented Roger Hart's (1997) Ladder of Participation and other models.

CHAPTER 7

Exeko's Cultural and Intellectual Mediation Approach: Introducing Teens to Their Neighbourhood's Activist Tradition

Maxime Goulet-Langlois and Emilie Drapeau

Abstract

This chapter presents the *Pathways to Education* program offered to secondary school students by the organization Exeko and the Pointe-Saint-Charles YMCA in Montreal. It consists of five workshops on the neighbourhood's activist history. Through meetings with residents engaged in a variety of practices, the students discover this history and participate in an ecosystem where diverse concepts of citizenship exist side by side. These otherwise unlikely exchanges are an occasion for young people to find their place in the local tradition of solidarity and activism. The program constitutes a unique form of citizenship education based on social change.

*T*he workshop is held in the heart of Pointe-Saint-Charles, a former working-class neighbourhood in the Sud-Ouest bordered by the immense Canadian National (CN) rail yard to the southeast and the Lachine Canal to the north. Many families of Irish origin settled here during the nineteenth century. Long one of the poorest neighbourhoods of Montreal, it has been gradually gentrifying over the past several years, bringing significant socio-economic disparities to light. We are in Bâtiment 7, a two-storey, industrial *red brick building that once belonged to CN. Kirianne, Zoé, and Cilia, three adolescents around 16 years of age, enter a large room with a high ceiling and dusty brick walls. Through the huge, steel-grid windows, we see that night has already fallen on this Friday, November 2019 evening. Two women around 30 years of age are moving heavy-looking tools. They are wearing used work coats that contrast with the school uniforms worn by the teens. Cilia calls out to them: "Hi! Could we ask you some questions?" adding timidly, "If it's no bother?" A bit surprised to see the three young girls, one holding a recorder, one of the women answers hesitantly: "Well, OK, what are you doing?"*

"We're from the YMCA Pathways to Education program," explains Zoé. "Today we're doing a workshop with Exeko to learn more about the neighbourhood, about how people get involved. We decided to do a vox pop here in Bâtiment 7, but the recording is just between us, to reflect on activism." After a brief question-and-answer exchange on the two women's forms of engagement, Cilia asks: "Where do you see youth in the future of the neighbourhood?"

"Wow! That's a big question." one of them answers. "I think they should continue being involved. When we see you here, whether in an artist's workshop or some other community organization, we hope you'll want to get involved and make it something that is more about you and what's happening now. For example, the Press Start arcade was created by the neighbourhood youth.[1] They said, 'There's a need and the existing organizations aren't meeting it.'" The other woman adds: "You shouldn't be shy to join existing organizations and bring your own voices to make change where you see a need..." Kirianne, with a timid voice but very lively eyes replies: "Thank you. That was our last question, but I have another question..." Everyone laughs. "Is it hard to run a metal sculpture workshop?" The conversation continues on the history of the workshop and their reasons for starting it.

This chapter describes a citizenship education experience that grew out of a collaboration between Exeko and the Pointe-Saint-Charles YMCA *Pathways to Education* program. It includes excerpts from an ethnographic participant-observation study carried out by the two authors of this chapter, who adopted the roles of participant observer/mediator and non-participant observer respectively. The project consisted of a series of five workshops in which youth learned, asked questions, and took positions on their neighbourhood's activist past and present.

During this vox pop activity, students equipped with a crash course in journalism were asked to visit Bâtiment 7 and reach out to engaged citizens in their neighbourhood. Today, as at the start of all the other workshops, a group of 12 high school students aged 15 to 17 has gathered in a large room of the Pointe-Saint-Charles YMCA. Three quarters of them are young women from immigrant and visible minority families (primarily African Canadian, Maghrebi, Indian, and Asian).[2] *The youth take their seats at five large round tables set up in the space. They are greeted by Maude and Maxime,*[3] *who are the mediators from Exeko, and Vivianne, a facilitator*[4] *from the* Pathways to Education *school perseverance program. Large photographs of the sites visited during the previous Friday's guided neighbourhood tour are laid out on the tables, and the youth are encouraged to talk about what touched them the most. We hear them speaking in both French and English about the Alexandra Hospital for tuberculosis that was converted to social housing after citizen protests; the Black Rock monument commemorating the deaths of thousands of Irish immigrants and the harsh living and working conditions they faced during the construction of the Victoria Bridge; Le Ber Park, where workers lit fires in trash cans on Victoria Day to protest the legacy of British rule; the Sebastopol embankment, where a group of residents mobilized to block casino and baseball stadium development projects; and Bâtiment 7, transformed by a group of residents, much to the dismay of real estate developers, into a self-managed community space offering a multitude of services to local residents: a grocery store, a bistro, an arcade, and cooperatives specializing in bike repair, metalwork, carpentry, ceramics, photography, and silkscreen printing.*

This citizenship education project is interesting because it connects youth not only to their neighbourhood's activist tradition but also to a diverse cross-section of engaged citizens. Through experiential and relational workshops tied to places, social relations, and local memory, youth discover tangible initiatives for social change. The following pages illustrate how equal youth–adult cooperation contributes to the quality of the learning experience. While participating in various activities, youth develop an understanding of social justice–oriented citizenship at their own pace, based on what they have learned from the mediation team and some of the activists. The workshops foster exchange between youth and adults who would probably never have met otherwise. This allows youth to perceive and position themselves as essential actors in continuing the neighbourhood's local tradition of solidarity and activism.

7.1. From Ideas to Action: Raising Youth Citizenship Awareness about Local Civic Issues

Exeko is a charity organization based in Montreal that develops projects at the crossroads of popular education, collective mobilization, and cultural mediation. The organization's mission is to use artistic and intellectual creativity to foster inclusive and liberating social change. Founded in 2006, the organization today has 13 employees and around 20 mediators from a wide range of backgrounds such as circus arts, theatre, visual arts, literature, and philosophy. The Pointe-Saint-Charles project is part of *idAction*, a program primarily aimed at youth who are marginalized or at risk of exclusion. This program engages critical thinking, social analysis, and civic action using experiential teaching methods (e.g., theatre, debates, exploring cities) to stimulate collective reflection. Outcomes include the co-creation of products like zines, podcasts, and films.

Exeko collaborates with other organizations for most of its projects. This chapter presents their work with the Pointe-Saint-Charles YMCA *Pathways to Education* program. Originating in the Toronto area over 20 years ago, the *Pathways* program now operates in more than 20 Canadian communities with elevated school dropout rates. Offered to secondary school students to help them overcome systemic barriers to graduating, the program is based on four pillars: personalized, academic, financial, and social support. Exeko's workshops fall within the fourth category, specifically, within the framework of citizenship engagement activities addressed to youth.

Over a sequence of five workshops, youth participating in the program explore activism and social change in a forum theatre exercise (Workshop 1), visit key sites of social struggle in their neighbourhood during a guided tour led by an activist from Action-Gardien (Workshop 2), prepare and conduct vox pop interviews with engaged residents in Bâtiment 7 (Workshop 3), collaborate on messages that allow them to express their vision of social engagement (Workshop 4), and learn silkscreen basics so they can print their messages on shirts and wear them with pride (Workshop 5). This progression clearly illustrates how the *idAction* program is based on generating ideas and translating them into action. The youth gain theoretical and experiential knowledge by learning about the history of activism, participating in group discussions, and interviewing people in the neighbourhood. They then translate this knowledge into action with their silkscreen creations.

By taking part in this citizenship education program, youth become acquainted with their neighbourhood and its activist history, while also developing social ties, competencies, and interests that prepare them to play an active role. According to the *Pathways* program's coordinator:

> Assuming your role as a citizen, forging your own opinion— these things don't happen overnight; it is a gradual process. This is where Exeko comes in. For us, it is important that the youth get to know their neighbourhood. [...] For them, civic engagement seems very distant, and getting them to act and reflect on issues in their neighbourhood was possible thanks to the workshops, which were very creative.

In keeping with the *Pathways* program approach, the workshops help young people acquire a sense of citizenship that is very situated and tangible. In a complementary manner, Exeko promotes a vision of citizenship oriented towards social justice. Over the course of the workshops, youth develop their ability to think and act through a critical learning experience that reveals the structures and power dynamics in which they live. The theme of social change, presented to the youth as the guiding principle of the workshop series, is defined as follows by the mediator: "Social change is when people who share an unjust situation come together to make something happen, to change things." Consistent with the practice of cultural and intellectual mediation (Goulet-Langlois, 2017), the workshops place youth in situations of collective reflection and peer-to-peer exchange that encourage individual expression and debate. Inspired by the pedagogical principle of equal intelligence (Beauchemin et al., 2015), Exeko's mediators seek to create spaces in which all are considered valuable interlocutors who can reflect on political and philosophical issues—setting aside prejudices and social distinctions based on title, status, or expertise. The workshops are structured so as to empower youth to feel legitimate in identifying forms of oppression and working to overturn them.

7.2. Becoming Citizens at their Own Pace:
From Civic Participation to Social Justice

To begin the first discussion on social change and activism, Maxime, one of the mediators, asks that the lights be turned off. The youth and mediation team are seated around five tables in a large room of the YMCA. A photograph of a woman is projected on a screen. "Does anybody know this person?" asks Maude, the other mediator. "Yes, it's Rosa Parks," answers Raffik. The young people all seem to recognize her. Apparently somewhat surprised that they know of her, Maxime asks: "Wow! That's great! Where did you hear about Rosa Parks?"

"At school," says Raffik. "Yeah, she's the one who refused to give up her seat to a white man on the bus," another youth adds. The mediation team goes on to talk about racial segregation in the United States and how Rosa Parks' gesture triggered a 381-day bus boycott in the state of Alabama, where 75 percent of passengers were African American at the time [1955 to 1956]. The mediators also mention that this action had a considerable impact on the Civil Rights Movement, which sought to abolish racist laws in several states. Though some of the young people speak, their self-consciousness is palpable. Maxime continues with another black and white image. It shows two men operating machinery in what appears to be a cave. After a few seconds, one of the students guesses that they are miners. The mediation team then facilitates a discussion on events surrounding the Asbestos Strike and the role of activism in social struggles, like the creation of unions to improve the working conditions of labourers. Then they present a final example to the group. This time, it is a photograph of the façade of a two-storey, industrial red brick building. Spontaneously, Karim exclaims: "Yeah, that's the building right over there." Many recognize the site, but nobody is able to name it or explain why it represents an example of social change.

The above excerpt takes place during the first workshop, where the youth learned and shared their knowledge about social change and activism. The examples clearly illustrate how youth acquire a perspective on social change in the workshops that is both historical and contemporary. The mediation team deliberately selected Bâtiment 7 to provide a significant, local example of activism in their own neighbourhood. To help students see how accessible social change is and their role in it, the mediator adds the following to his definition: "Change is accessible to everyone, and it comes in all shapes and sizes, large and small." In the second workshop, the youth discover even more examples of activism during a guided tour of key sites in their neighbourhood. The tour guide highlights several examples involving grassroots action against gentrification and in favour of social housing.

After visiting Le Ber Park, which today hosts the Festi-Pointe festival organized by neighbourhood youth to mobilize the community, the 23 students present today stop a few blocks further in front of the Alexandra Hospital, where tuberculosis was once treated. There is nothing spectacular about the red brick building. With the darkness, cold and ambient noise, many of the youth, some of them with only a sweatshirt for a coat, seem to have trouble understanding the guide's explanations. The latter engages with them a lot, asking them questions and then providing explanations. The youth learn that the former hospital was converted into social housing and that Pointe-Saint-Charles is one of the neighbourhoods in Canada with the highest proportion of social housing thanks to the mobilization of residents over the decades. The guided tour ends inside Bâtiment 7, otherwise known as B7, where the group takes refuge from the cold and wind to continue the discussion. The youth are particularly surprised to learn that the group Collectif 7 à Nous was able to purchase this enormous building for only $1. They listen and ask the guide about the years of persistence and mobilization needed to accomplish this. At one point, the group passes an office with two men inside, and the guide explains: "These are the coordinators of B7, but they are not the bosses. Decisions concerning B7 are made collectively; self-management means there is no boss." After exploring several projects on site, the youth learn that real estate developers want to build hundreds of condos around Bâtiment 7, despite all these successful initiatives. The guide then leads a discussion on gentrification and invites the young people to take part in a demonstration against the construction of condos.

During both the discussions and the tour, the youth are very attentive. They ask the adults questions and demonstrate some of their knowledge about their neighbourhood, but their shyness is noticeable. Issues surrounding gentrification, self-management, and democratic decision-making seem less familiar to them. In the following excerpt, the guide reacts to one student who seems disappointed at the reasons why residents objected to the building of a baseball stadium and casino.

Ismaël, who seems annoyed, says: "You guys are such a drag... I would've liked having a stadium here." The guide responds: "You have every right to think that. We can talk about it more. You can explain your point of view if you want. It's true that a stadium sounds like fun, but the problem is that the developers wanted to build 4,000 condos around the stadium. In a neighbourhood of 15,000 people, this would have led to more gentrification and increased rents. Several residents would have had to move as a result. There also would have been a lot more tourists and so more prostitution, bars, etc. The 7 à Nous citizen committee, which created this place, prioritizes services for long-term residents, like a local hospital, a high school, neighbourhood grocery stores, and so on." A discussion ensues on the positive and negative potential impacts of development projects on the neighbourhood, with the youth, guide, and mediation team expressing multiple views.

As this example illustrates, the workshops are an education initiative in which citizenship is implicitly conveyed as combining the individual and collective analysis of power relations with the practical skills needed to transform these through democratic decision-making processes. All the historical and contemporary examples presented to the youth focus on forms of injustice or oppression and illustrate actions in favour of just social change. The mediation team and guide share perspectives that are explicitly critical of power relations and consistent with a vision of citizenship oriented towards social justice (Westheimer & Kahne, 2004). Other times, the youth are exposed to more individual and participatory concepts of citizenship, like during the vox pop activity below.

While Kirianne, Zoé, and Cilia are conducting their interview in the metal sculpture studio, another team of four students is at the Bâtiment 7 bistro. The room is packed, and there are people of different ages sitting around the 20 or so tables, even a few children. It is a very friendly and noisy atmosphere. After the project is explained to a woman and a man in their fifties, the two long-time residents agree to an interview. "What does civic engagement mean to you?" asks Amadou. Having observed in previous interviews that people do not always understand the question, he reformulates it: "What are the little things or major things you do personally to be involved in Pointe-Saint-Charles?"
"We were involved as parents at the school before," answers the woman. "Another example, is that you can get involved in Le Détour, right here," she points to the door, "so your family members can save money."

"What is Le Détour?" asks Hamid.

"Le Détour is a grocery store," she explains. "If you volunteer, your relatives become members, and they don't have to volunteer because you're the one who's going to do it." The man adds: "It's anything, it's from the moment you get involved, just like you're doing now, that's civic engagement. It can be lots of things."

During the vox pop workshop, the youth encounter definitions and examples of civic engagement that oscillate between individual, participatory, and emancipatory concepts of citizenship. The suggestion to volunteer or get involved in organizations can encourage youth to take action and participate in existing structures (Westheimer & Kahne, 2004). Youth can thus contribute to the collective life of the neighbourhood in ways that do not explicitly involve protesting social injustice.

While the youth often listen, pose questions, and discuss with the adults during different activities, they are also sometimes invited to share their own perspectives on social change. In the first workshop, for example, the students are encouraged to identify something they would like to change as part of the forum theatre exercise.

Maxime presents the exercise as a theatre of the oppressed, an activity based on imagining collective solutions to social injustices. Then he asks: "And you? What would you like to change in the neighbourhood? Or at school? Or in your life in general? What seems unjust to you?" A brainstorming session ensues. One student says that more affordable housing is needed, while another answers, "Bill 21, it's not fair that people can't wear their religious signs or dress how they want." The mediation team notes that these are good examples. Then it's Cilia's turn: "What I find problematic is at school, when different groups don't talk to each other. Often, there are the Black students on one side and the others on the other side; they don't mix. It's really too bad."

The youth show that they are very capable of identifying forms of injustice that concern them. However, over the course of the five workshops, they are still just becoming acquainted with the structural causes of oppression and social injustice. During the vox pop and group discussions, they seem reluctant to discuss these causes with each other or the adults. This is evident, for example, when it comes to exploitation of the working classes or gentrification and "renovictions."[5] Each week, the review exercises clearly show that the youth retain the theoretical ideas presented to them but do not actively formulate their own critical and structural analyses of social injustice based on what they have learned. This is consistent with the fact that youth tend to first experience citizenship through an individual and participatory lens. When asked about forms of civic engagement they have observed or participated in, most youth give examples involving aiding others or volunteer work, like helping an elderly or blind person cross the street or lending a hand in a home-work support organization. The threefold pedagogical strategy at the heart of this citizenship education initiative thus welcomes their ini-tial concepts of citizenship, connects them with neighbourhood resi-dents with varied concepts of citizenship, and guides them in their gradual exploration of more critical and emancipatory concepts of citizenship.

7.3. Empowering Youth as Equal Partners

Over the course of the workshops, the students explore concepts and local practices of engagement through group discussion, exchange with the mediation team, and meetings with neighbourhood resi-dents. The process is thus very relation-focused and consists of sup-porting and empowering youth by developing egalitarian modes of cooperation with adults. The vox pop activity illustrates these learn-ing dynamics through encounters in which adults recognize the youth as competent citizens who are essential to sustaining com-munity life. The youth prepare questions and conduct interviews with people randomly selected in a given place. They ask questions, make sound recordings of the exchanges, take notes and, most importantly, talk to people they would probably never have met otherwise.

> During an interview conducted at Le Détour grocery store, the adult interviewed appeals to the critical autonomy he believes they have. When Hind asks him, "What should youth do; how should they get involved to help the community?", the man responds: "I find it hard to tell youth what to do [...] I feel like it's up to them to decide [...] Youth need to involve themselves in things that interest them [...] Now that I think of it, I have trouble with the idea of youth as a category [...] It's so diverse, I don't feel like there's the same interest across the board." Hind and the two others working with him welcome this invitation to critically reflect on the category

of "youth." The three reporters for a day nod their heads while seeming to consider the implication that young people have both the freedom and ability to choose. The man then adds: "I think it's good to latch onto existing structures and transform them, to develop a curiosity for existing institutions and structures or make them into something totally different." This presents the students with a broad range of possibilities for civic involvement. Youth are considered here to be competent and capable of contributing to existing structures and reshaping them.

This exchange is representative of many other conversations in which adults do not hesitate to champion young people's ability to get involved and work with them to transform organizations and institutions.

Meanwhile, a francophone woman in her sixties is being interviewed by anglophone students. She answers them in English, in a passionate outburst that seems to surprise them. When Jackson asks her, "In your opinion, what is the place of youth in the future of the neighbourhood?," she responds: "Young people have a very important place because a lot of people my age can't be involved anymore or they die. Youth are essential to maintaining the spirit of the community. You are the ones building the future. I don't see enough young people your age. I think it's important to pass this spirit on to more youth. It has to be preserved. You should meet Natasha from the Société historique."

This woman's testimony places less emphasis on autonomy than on the transmission needed for youth to continue the activist tradition, without imposing orders on how this should be done. Like many others, this dialogue implicitly values young people as equal individuals on par with adults. The students hear adults expressing their hopes for the next generation and receive several invitations to get involved in the local activist tradition.

In parallel to the connections they are gradually establishing with adults in their neighbourhood, the youth are also developing relationships with Exeko's mediation team. Using words, gestures, and attitudes that foster equality and cooperation, the mediators are able to build relationships with youth that realign hierarchical dynamics based on age, authority, and level of expertise. We see this during the forum theatre exercise in the first workshop, in which the students identify an unjust situation and improvise a skit about it with the adults.

Maxime presents the activity's structure: "The first step is to choose an issue, then we create a sketch based on it, then we act out the sketch. Some will be the actors and others will be spectators who can intervene in the situation. The idea is to begin with a problematic issue and aim for a more favourable outcome, going from negative to positive. The spectators have to propose changes to the actors to help them reach a positive outcome." After deliberating, the students choose the situation mentioned above: students of different ethnic backgrounds not talking to each other in the school cafeteria. The two facilitators from Pathways to Education *and the other mediator, Maude, play the roles of students. Three students and Maxime play the spectators. Zoé shouts: "Action!" The improvised scene begins then, at one point, Amadou yells "Cut!" and whispers an instruction in Hamid's ear. Zoé restarts the scene and Hamid timidly walks over to the other table to show something to Maude, who is playing the role of a student who hesitates to pay attention to him. The scene begins again and is interrupted and modified like this several times.*

Throughout the exercise, youth and adults are in a position of reciprocity; they must improvise and modify the unjust situation through the collaborative work of play. The adults are subject to the same constraint as the students: overcoming the discomfort that arises from the vulnerability in which the improvisation plunges them. By adopting this role, the mediators show that they are also in a position of learning with the students. The mediation team thus emphasizes reciprocity in learner attitudes and two-way transmission of knowledge between adults and students, highlighting the limits of the adults' knowledge.

The intentional and consistent validation of the students' words and knowledge plays a central role in fostering cooperation between the youth and the mediation team. Throughout the activities, the mediators encourage the youth to express their ideas and opinions, ask questions, and initiate discussion. For example, during the tour of Bâtiment 7, one young woman says that "a beer brewed only by women is sexist." The mediator, Maude, listens attentively to the student's explanation and shows respect for her point of view. She then takes the opportunity to discuss the sexism experienced by women in jobs traditionally reserved for men. In addition to welcoming and mobilizing different perspectives, the mediators also often remind the students that participation in the activities is voluntary, and that they are free to simply observe or stay on the sidelines. This is one of the many pedagogical strategies employed by the team to recognize the youth's autonomy and decision-making power. Overall, the students' response creates a dynamic of reciprocal learning and reflection (Zeldin et al., 2014, p. 338). However, while they make many of the decisions involved in the activities, the youth never attempt to change the structure or nature of the activities themselves, even though the mediators give them several opportunities to do so.

7.4. "#Pointe-Saint-Charles, c'est chez nous!" Students' Views on the Activist Tradition

From one workshop to the next, the students discover their neighbourhood's many stories of solidarity and struggle. They acquire this knowledge in a relational and experiential way by meeting people in places marked by a still-thriving activist tradition. Not only are these encounters empowering and fun but they also provide access to real situations where a critical concept of citizenship is being enacted. The students discover where they stand while gradually exploring this concept.

In silence, the 13 students present today at the YMCA scribble in their notebooks while listening to the audio clips from the previous week's recordings. Both excited and embarrassed to hear their own voices, they are brainstorming ideas for messages or soundbites to print on shirts the following week. Maude writes the following questions on the board: "What message do you want to send? What are your dreams for the neighbourhood? What ideas learned here could add to your message?" Posters and books that she has laid out on a table are another possible source of inspiration. For around 20 minutes, the students work in teams creating their message while the mediators walk around and participate in their discussions. The implicit goal is to help them reach a position by making their personal views political. When the teams all seem satisfied, they present their ideas to the larger group for feedback. Aïsha explains her team's message: "Our slogan is: #Pointe-Saint-Charles, c'est chez nous (#Pointe-Sainte-Charles is our home). The hashtag is really connected to our generation with social media, and it's our neighbourhood; it's our home." Mélanie shyly follows with a second slogan: "Ours is: Pour nos prochains, Sauvons notre Coin (For our neighbours, save our hood)." She explains that it's an acrostic and the letters PSC refer to Pointe-Saint-Charles. Next, Kim presents a third slogan: "Listen to the kids, we are the future." And she offers the following explanation: "We are the generation who is going to grow up and fight climate change and all that. We are the future. So we are just saying: listen to us, to the kids, 'cause we actually know a lot more than you might think, and we actually have ideas that are progressive to help the world change."

These messages reveal what the students have learned from the workshops. The first team expresses both a sense of neighbourhood belonging and pride in identity. The second team emphasizes altruism and solidarity. More militantly, the third team asserts the importance of intergenerational equity and responsibility for the future and the environment. All these messages echo the ideas covered in the workshops. The adults' remarks seem to have particularly influenced the students. The messages directly resonate with the adults' invitations to claim and forge their place in the neighbourhood as the next generation.

The following week, during the silkscreen workshop, the students bring their messages to life by printing them on shirts. The atmosphere is one of mutual support and collaboration. Several express a feeling of satisfaction and pride, as the program coordinator confirms:

> When we saw the shirts, we said: "Wow, it's our students who did this!" It was a tangible way to end the cycle of activities, and the students were very proud. Being able to discover their neighbourhood like this was extremely positive for them. They saw the importance of involvement in their neighbourhood and understood that it's within their reach. They felt more connected to the reality around them, this reality that is theirs too. One young woman said that she now felt she could have an impact, regardless of the neighbourhood she is living in in the future: "Here, it's the Pointe-Saint-Charles neighbourhood, but I could use this approach somewhere else."

These comments highlight the material and symbolic benefits of this brief citizenship education initiative. The student's comment shows that she now feels capable and legitimate in applying what she has learned far beyond the workshop context. On a symbolic level, the youth are recognized not only as capable residents but also as essential to maintaining community life. In taking a position, they identify with their neighbourhood and claim it as their own. The material benefits no doubt cement this sense of belonging. Both the students and facilitators from *Pathways* express their interest in Bâtiment 7. In the second workshop, one female student states: "I'm so happy to have discovered B7. I live two minutes from here, but I didn't know it at all." Access to this unique, self-managed, social infrastructure is a particularly positive outcome. It allows young people to take part in a vibrant activist culture that, beyond its ideas, values, and critical discourse on forms of injustice, offers a tangible and accessible space, both as a community and as an ecosystem of services.

The guided tour of the neighbourhood ends with a formal invitation from one of the mediators: "Bâtiment 7 is here for you, for the community. Feel free to come back. There are many ways to get involved in the neighbourhood." Over the course of the meetings, notably in Bâtiment 7, the youth discover opportunities that are directly related to their immediate interests, such as getting hired to help organize the Festi-Pointe festival, freely accessing recreation spaces like the Press Start arcade, volunteering at the grocery store in exchange for food discounts, learning about bike repair, cabinet-making, and much more. The brevity of the workshop series no doubt limits the students' ability to fully assimilate a social justice–oriented concept of citizenship and build relationships with adults. But by discovering Bâtiment 7 and Pointe-Saint-Charles's engaged residents, youth will be able to continue exploring their neighbourhood's activist tradition going forward.

7.5. Community-Based Citizenship Education

This citizenship education initiative is anchored in the physical, social, and political environment in which the students live their lives. In learning about the activist history of their neighbourhood during meetings with residents engaged in a variety of practices, youth are invited to participate in and discover an ecosystem where diverse concepts of citizenship coexist. They are introduced to structural analysis of social injustice by learning about labour struggles, mobilization for social housing, and self-management. The workshops respect the students' pace of assimilation while promoting a liberating and pragmatic concept of citizenship. Through the interactions between students and adults, different methods emerge, which Exeko's mediation employs to build bridges between people who would perhaps never have met. This strategy gives rise to learning based on *in situ* experimentation with citizenship. From forum theatre and guided tours to vox pop and silkscreening, the ways in which youth take positions on issues show that their learning is grounded in their physical, social, and political environment, and this has an important impact on the type of citizenship they develop. While the brevity of the workshop series can seem like a limit since youth only just began to reflect on these issues and find their voices, it could also be considered a strength given the students' ability to see themselves as empowered, legitimate, and competent residents of their neighbourhood in such a short time. This youth empowerment is a step towards creating a space in which everyone feels like a valid and capable contributor to collective reflection on social injustice—a space where everyone feels entitled to name forms of oppression and work on transforming them.

References

Beauchemin, W.-J., Blémur, D., Duguay, N., Goulet-Langlois, M., & Lorgueilleux, A. (2015, January). *La présomption de l'égalité des intelligences : des principes, une posture et la mise en pratique.* Exeko. https://omec.inrs.ca/wp-content/uploads/2020/02/Exeko_PEI-Janv2015_v3.pdf

Goulet-Langlois, M. (2017). Arts, philosophie, marginalisations sociales et émancipation : la médiation intellectuelle, une pratique frontalière des sens. In Casemajor, N., Dubé, M., Lafortune, J.-M., & Lamoureux, È. (Eds.), *Expériences critiques de la médiation culturelle* (pp. 259–285). Presses de l'Université Laval.

Office québécois de la langue française. (2020). Réno-éviction. In *Grand dictionnaire terminologique.* Vitrine linguistique. https://gdt.oqlf.gouv.qc.ca/ficheOqlf.aspx?Id_Fiche=26558204

Westheimer, J., & Kahne, J. (2004). What kind of citizen? The politics of educating for democracy. *American Educational Research Journal, 41*(2), 237–269. https://doi.org/10.3102/00028312041002237

Zeldin, S., Krauss, S. E., Collura, J., Lucchesi, M., & Sulaiman, A. H. (2014). Conceptualizing and measuring youth-adult partnership in community programs: A cross-national study. *American Journal of Community Psychology, 54*(3-4), 337–347. https://doi.org/10.1007/s10464-014-9676-9

Notes

1. Press Start is an arcade created and managed by a youth group in Bâtiment 7.

2. The demographic information provided indicates the typical composition of the group of students having participated in the five workshops. From one week to the next, the number of students varied from 5 to 23, with an average of 12 students per workshop. A core of around 10 students have participated in a least four of the five workshops.

3. All the first names used in this chapter are pseudonyms, apart from this one, referring to a co-author of the text.

4. One or two facilitators from the *Pathways* program are present at the workshops. Their presence aims to encourage the participation of students they know very well and with whom they work (e.g., for homework support) throughout the school year, and even from one year to the next. During the *idAction* workshops, they take part, like the students, as participants rather than facilitators.

5. According to the Office québécois de la langue française (2020), renovictions are a practice in which an individual or business owner of a rental unit evicts the occupants to make renovations.

C) Experiences in Citizenship Education Based on Representative Democracy and Public Action

A Democratic and Political Experience: Citizenship Education at the Commission jeunesse de Gatineau

Mariève Forest and Stéphanie Gaudet

Abstract

This chapter focuses on the Commission jeunesse de Gatineau, one of the oldest youth commissions in Quebec. This initiative recognizes the full potential of youth citizenship. It enables secondary school students to influence municipal decisions concerning youth and create projects that contribute to raising local public awareness of social issues. Youth members, who represent the majority and have exclusive voting rights, develop different working relationships with the adults. By participating on the Commission, they are transformed, take part in transforming their community, and develop their autonomy while remaining anchored in collectives. The program offers a unique form of citizenship education based on representative democracy and public action.

*I*t's close to 9:30 on a Saturday morning in the fall of 2017. Around 15 students aged 12 to 16 are quietly streaming into the room next to the city council chamber. Some are smiling enthusiastically, while others look busy, or somewhat shy. They sit down around a large oval table. One of the students is more enthusiastic than the others: She is the youth co-president. The only adult present seems relaxed, happily greeting each student as they come in. We are at the Commission jeunesse de Gatineau, one of the first municipal youth councils in Quebec.

In this chapter, we look at the Commission jeunesse de Gatineau initiative, emphasizing its educational, democratic, and political potential. We identify different features of democratic citizenship education, focusing on the particular possibilities of the municipal political context in which the Commission operates.

The first section below provides background on the Commission's principles, mandate, and functioning.

8.1. The Commission jeunesse de Gatineau

The Commission jeunesse was created in 2000 in Gatineau, inspired by the Healthy Cities and Towns network and the children's and youth municipal councils that have existed in France since the 1960s.[1] The idea for the Commission was born following a broad consultation with more than 3,000 secondary school students on quality of life in the city.

The Commission jeunesse brings together secondary school students to reflect, discuss, and decide on aspects of municipal life affecting youth. More broadly, it presents itself as a "municipal school for civic participation." It also describes itself as "a representative youth body that leverages a sense of belonging in the school and urban environments to encourage adolescent engagement" (Commission jeunesse de Gatineau, 2018). The Commission's mandate highlights four priorities: (1) positioning Gatineau teens as credible and necessary members of the next generation; (2) initiating projects; (3) galvanizing active youth participation; and (4) contributing new perspectives and making a difference by participating in municipal decisions.

The Commission jeunesse is composed of students from the 13 secondary schools situated within the municipality's territory. With two seats per school, the Commission allows for a maximum of 26 students. To ensure socio-demographic, geographic, and interest-based representation, the current members use a criteria chart to appoint new delegates. The year of our study, 23 students were members of the Commission jeunesse. The majority were female (14) and in Secondary IV (10 and 11) and V (19). We noted an over-representation of students from private schools and international education programs (11). This over-representation is consistent with broader trends, given that youth councils often reproduce a society's existing social relations, and socio-economic elites, whatever their age, are more involved in political activities than members of other social classes

(Collins et al., 2016). One member is elected youth co-president each year. This demanding role includes serving as the spokesperson, planning meeting agendas, and mobilizing other students.

The City of Gatineau appoints three city councillors to serve on the Commission, one of whom is designated the other co-president by the mayor. This member plays a more active role that includes representing the Commission at council meetings and public events. City council members do not have voting rights.

A city employee is designated officer for the Commission jeunesse, while also serving on the strategic planning team for the municipality's sports, leisure, and community development commission. Her role is central, because she facilitates the participatory governance strategy promoted by the city. She is also responsible for the quality of the youth–adult partnership.

The formal meetings of the Commission jeunesse are held one afternoon per month. The meeting agendas and minutes are posted on the city's website. During official sessions, the members welcome and listen to invited guests, and later discuss issues with them. On the days the Commission sits, the members usually also meet in the morning for working sessions. Between the monthly meetings, the students and designated officer communicate primarily through Messenger.

Before directly analyzing this experience, we will outline some theoretical points in relation to municipal youth governance bodies, examining the latter's democratic and political characteristics.

8.2. Theoretical Considerations

8.2.1. The Dynamics of Municipal Youth Governance

At least four dynamics of municipal youth governance have been identified in the literature (Augsberger et al., 2017, 2018). First, these youth councils have official relationships with and access to municipal decision-making authorities, either directly (through budgets and recommendatory powers), or indirectly (as consultative bodies). Second, these councils are informed by a positive youth-development approach (Bundick, 2011; Crocetti et al., 2014). This is based on supporting different aspects of youth development with positive initiatives rather than focusing on risk prevention. Examples include building political leadership skills and knowledge and mobilizing youth communities. Third, municipal youth councils put young people at the heart of the operations, policies, and decisions affecting them. Fourth, these councils usually provide authentic experiences: Youth initiate projects that have a real impact on their community and engage in dialogue with community and political partners who take their perspectives into consideration. We observed all these characteristics at the Commission jeunesse de Gatineau.

8.2.2. The Democratic and Political Characteristics of Municipal Youth Governance

In addition to showing how these municipal characteristics shape the Commission's work, we also want to highlight the less-studied democratic and political dynamics of these structures. As mentioned in Chapter 1, what sets democratic citizenship education apart for Westheimer and Kahne (2004) is that it incorporates a vision of social justice. Youth experimenting with democratic citizenship seek to transform their society into a more just one. This dynamic is clearly present at the Commission jeunesse, since youth are asked to identify and propose solutions to social problems that affect them.

We posit that the political and democratic dynamics of this type of governance are also revealed in moments of instability and tension. Exchanges between members of the Commission are often marked by instability due to their spontaneous nature, the delicate proposing of compromises, and the critical reflexivity that youth engage in. Following Audric Vitiello (2013, 2016), we see these unstable moments of collective, public deliberation as indicators of the Commission's democratic nature. The unstable nature of these democratic citizenship experiments can be observed in the movement and tension between opposing principles that inform youth–adult relationships: training and transformation, power and equality, and empowerment and collective engagement. This chapter will examine the Commission's democratic citizenship education experience through the lens of these three relationships and show how they foster democratic action.

8.3. Training and Transformation in Youth–Adult Relationships

At the Commission jeunesse, youth have relationships with adults that involve training and transformation. Depending on the roles of those involved, the relationships take different forms and evolve according to the context. Here, we seek to elucidate how the relationships between the adult allies[2] and the youth develop, conflict, combine, and evolve, both through training—information sharing and coordination—and transformation—advice, support, mutual listening, and recognition.

First, youth relations with the officer depend in part on training through the transmission of organization-specific and partnership-based knowledge. These knowledge-transfer activities are particularly important between the officer and the youth co-president, who is also the Commission's spokesperson. The officer is responsible for organizing meetings, acting as liaison with the municipality, developing educational material, communicating with invited guests, and so on. Her presence thus shapes the Commission's knowledge-transfer activities and dictates the efficiency of its overall operations. Working in close communication with the two co-presidents, the officer prepares the meeting agendas. While the agendas are primarily joint endeavours, the officer occasionally plays a more dominant role. Her authority is generally accepted by the members of the Commission, given her corporate memory of past decisions and actions, and familiarity with the boundaries of the municipal context in which the Commission operates. For example, during our observations, the Commission's main goals and projects were based on proposals submitted by youth during the 2015 Youth Summit two years earlier. This organizational memory, held primarily by the officer, was sometimes integrated into activities, as in the excerpt below describing new city councillors being welcomed to the Commission.

We are at an early December working session. The new city councillors are sitting on the Commission jeunesse for the first time, since the elections were held in November.[3] The youth spend over an hour presenting the Commission and the roles of each person. The 2015 Youth Summit and the one planned for 2018 are discussed. Anabelle,[4] the youth co-president, explains: "The CJ[5] created its projects, like the field action, after the Youth Summit. This year, the CJ is organizing its second field action project, which will address gender and LGBTQ2+ issues. Last year, we focused on seniors' isolation." Brigitte, the officer, adds: "The goal of the 2015 Summit was really to highlight Gatineau youth's concerns and prioritize them, rather than making a simple grocery list. The subjects covered during this event were communication, school life, public places, and the city. For example, Brigade 51 was created after this Summit. [...] The CJ doesn't want to have a Summit every year, because it would be too much." Anabelle adds: *"We achieved all the priorities identified by the students, so it will be interesting to do it again with a new action plan."*

Youth also have a more subordinate relationship to the officer when the latter is working to advance the Commission's projects between the monthly meetings. Some students noticed an asymmetry and loss of control over projects they were supposed to be in charge of, as the following excerpt illustrates:

> It's a remark I made [during a Commission jeunesse working session], that youth should be more at the centre of the projects. It runs too much on its own. I want to contribute something, but I need the opportunity to do so. They asked our opinion for the survey. They could have shown us how to create a survey. To build a project put together by youth.

This comment is a reminder that decision-making can involve youth participation at all stages, not only in the identification of projects or priorities, but also in their design (Akiva et al., 2014). However, the youth still seem able to negotiate and change things, because, after this discussion, the youth co-president and officer sought to partially correct the situation.

The working sessions, in which youth review modes of operation, establish guidelines, and take charge of projects, also tend to favour training-based relationships. The officer, youth co-president, and invited adults share all kinds of information to help students understand upcoming activities and the general context in which the Commission operates. In interviews, youth note the importance of what they have learned about meeting minutes rules, the workings of municipal commissions, and political dynamics, among other topics.

That said, adult allies often adopt positions that depart from knowledge transfer in favour of transformative relations based on advice and support. In these cases, youth have opportunities to co-create and transform rules, procedures, and other elements. This was evident when they were debating how to promote municipal election simulations in their schools. Some of the dialogues with adults reflected asymmetries, because students had to be taught about polling stations and how these would function in their schools. But the officer's remarks still emphasized youth responsibility: "This presentation aims to clarify your role. [...] It is important to understand what a polling station is. [...] You will be responsible for your own station." After this lesson, discussion turned to how students could help manage their school's polling station and promote the event. During these exchanges, the adults did not give orders. On the contrary, the students were asked to identify different options and determine the best practices based on their expertise within their school.

Overall, our observations confirmed that the adults are generally very open to youth taking part in developing or transforming activities, either through creativity, reflexivity, or dissent. The adult allies actively seek to develop reciprocal relations. Youth are continually asked to propose ideas and share their opinions. We also noted on several occasions that students could challenge the adults. The officer, however, who was seen to embody the very principles of the Commission jeunesse in her way of being, acting, and speaking, was rarely criticized.

8.4. Power and Equality in Youth–Adult Relationships

While the students usually work with adult allies in the morning sessions, they are joined by adults of different statuses and profiles during the Commission's official public sessions in the afternoon. These adults are typically members of the city council or spokespersons representing local community or public organizations in Gatineau. We observed the vigilance needed to maintain the power–equality dialectic in these youth–adult relationships. The perpetual interplay between hierarchy and equality of individuals and roles not only prevents adults from dominating, but also prevents youth from having so much control they are cut off from the halls of power.

The officer plays a central role in keeping adult allies from exercising too much influence. The Commission's three city council members are tasked with reporting what has been discussed to city council. This increases the city's recognition of the issues affecting youth and their citizenship. These adults also share their perspectives with the youth. However, even with the adults who serve an official role on the Commission, the officer ensures that youth play a lead decision-making role. This is evident in her remarks to a newly elected councillor who, participating in his first assembly, generously offered to help with a project. The officer responded by saying: "We can add you to the [Messenger] chat, no problem." She went on to explain, however, that the Commission jeunesse favours an approach that is "by and for" youth, so "the youth have to make the decisions."

Likewise, the influence of invited adult guests is mitigated by different operating rules and the high ratio of youth to adults. These adults, received by the Commission during official sessions, generally represent organizations seeking input, support, or participation. These youth–adult interactions often involve egalitarian relations marked by difference: The students present themselves and speak as municipal citizens on par with the adults, but also as citizens who have expertise in youth matters. This seems to give them more confidence, as does being members of a collective in which they constitute the majority. This reduces the sense of exclusion and incompetence that youth often experience in political contexts (Augsberger et al., 2018). The literature shows that youth develop a positive relationship with politics when they have real influence on their projects and when they make recommendations (Blondiaux, 2008). The Commission jeunesse seems to have had a real impact on the city council, municipal staff, different partners, and other youth over the course of its history.

The Commission jeunesse culture welcomes disagreement between adults and youth and recognizes the equality of all members. The dialogues that took place during the presentation of the *Défi des 30 heures de la faim* (30-hour hunger challenge) clearly illustrate that opposing views are expressed and given equal consideration. Two teachers in charge of the *Défi* presented the project to the Commission, then asked for the youth's input and invited them to collaborate on improving and disseminating it. The members responded with interest, and their curiosity proved to be an important factor. They seemed to want to be sure of the initiative's value but also understand their potential role in it. The dialogue we witnessed reflects the climate of openness, but also the students' right to oppose the views of the adults or other youth, as in the excerpt below. This example also illustrates relations between citizens who adopt an approach based on discussion (Galichet, 2002), where equality is reflected in the use of language, common pursuit of truth, self-expression, and room for dissent. It also recalls the Commission's learning-by-doing approach to democratic citizenship education through participation in public debates that have a real impact on collective life (Vitiello, 2016).

Following the presentation of the Défi des 30 heures de la faim *at the Commission jeunesse, Mathilde asks the first question: "Is your project safe? Are you sure it poses no danger?" One of the teachers mentions that one person vomited last time. However, he tries to reassure Mathilde by adding that he doesn't mind if people eat during the challenge and that only two of the 125 participants felt ill. Kassandra intervenes and says that she already participated in it but not completely. She adds that people eat a little but still experience what it's like to be hungry, having problems of concentration, for example. Mathilde remains skeptical: "I'd say that's two cases too many. Also, does it really represent the reality of people living in poverty?" The teacher is sympathetic to her concerns: "You're right, it's two people too many. Also, it's rare to not eat for 30 hours."*

As we have observed elsewhere (Gaudet et al., 2019), though adult guests sometimes adopt an adult-centric perspective and try to limit youth input, the officer and councillors work to minimize the defeatist effects typical of adult-centric initiatives. In outnumbering the adults, youth are also more inclined and able to establish egalitarian relationships with them (Augsberger et al., 2018).

8.5. Experiential Learning: Youth Empowerment in Collective Contexts

As the literature has shown, the development of independent, reflective thinking engages collective practices (Vitiello, 2016). We can better understand how youth experiment with their citizenship in democratic and municipal political contexts by examining this perpetual interplay between individual and collective will. Our study of the Commission jeunesse revealed three facets of this individual-group dynamic: addressing injustice by developing critical thinking *on* a collective, like the LGBTQ2+ community; developing shared positions *with* members of a collective, like the Commission jeunesse; and recognizing a political community that requires active *presence within* a collective, like a municipality.

Our observations were more informative in this regard than our interviews. When interviewed, youth focus more on how the Commission transformed them by improving their ability to develop and express personal perspectives: "It emboldened me to take my place, to express my opinions. I did this less before, I was shyer. After a while, I was getting positive reactions, and it gave me confidence." These remarks remind us that acting in a democratic context entails exploring one's autonomy as a person: being able think for oneself, present critical perspectives about one's surroundings, and act independently. In other words, one has to practise autonomy to become autonomous (Vitiello, 2016).

Our ethnographic observation of the Commission jeunesse allowed us to go beyond these notions to examine a movement involving both the autonomy of individuals and their grounding in collectives, like the municipality, the Commission, and the youth population in general. For Vitiello, the emancipatory potential of democratic education depends on fostering the emergence of this dialectic between a person's autonomy and ability to associate it with collective contexts.

The continual back-and-forth between individual and collective will at the Commission is expressed through identification with collectives, group deliberation and decision-making, and reflection on the political community's interests. The Commission's members develop critical and creative thinking by connecting personal opinions to collective practices, forging ties that can be critiqued, modified, or explored through dialogue.

Taking this idea further, Philippe Chanial (2016, p. 269), explains that empowerment in a democratic context requires not only recognizing "the virtues and virtualities inscribed in the former world" but also conceiving the world as external to the self, which allows us to see one or more differences between what is and what should be. We thus become aware of our cultural heritage and can partly distance ourselves from it to question its legitimacy. While Westheimer and Kahne (2004) do not explicitly evoke this type of dialectic, they distinguish democratic citizenship education by its ability to form citizens who not only identify and denounce injustice but also commit to working for social change.

8.5.1. Recognizing and Addressing Collective Injustices

At its core, the Commission jeunesse responds to a form of injustice: the limited recognition of youth contribution to municipal life and public decisions. Members are asked to recognize youth citizen experiences and include these in their socio-political efforts. For example, after the youth submitted their annual report of priorities to city council in the spring of 2017,[6] the Société de transport de l'Outaouais (STO)[7] met with the Commission that fall to present its youth services and discuss possibilities for improvement. In doing so, the STO placed importance on the voices of hundreds of youth who contributed to the Commission's work.

Other injustices frame youth engagement, if only for a time. The annual "field action" project, which aims to raise Gatineau residents' awareness of an important social issue affecting youth,[8] typically speaks to injustices that extend beyond youth experience. During our study, the project focused on issues affecting LGBTQ2+ individuals. Members of the Commission mobilized other city youth to conduct information activities about the LGBTQ2+ community. These included discussions and the production of a short video, which was then disseminated (mainly on social media) to sensitize Gatineau residents to this group's realities and lived experiences.

These activities encourage youth to go from independent thinking to a more critical collective perspective, to recognize and act on injustices that may concern them or not. However, the Commission is still relatively moderate in terms of its latitude for expressing critical positions. The adult allies, and to some extent the youth, focus on projects that are acceptable and feasible. Unlike movements based on protest or radical action, the Commission seeks to understand, recognize, and address social injustices within the municipal public space.

8.5.2. Forming Common Positions and Collective Decisions

Going from critique to action—which can be done with, on, or against others—makes the link between individuals' autonomy and heteronomy even stronger (Vitiello, 2016). This heteronomy is reflected in the fact that youth are required to co-construct the Commission's priorities and positions on social problems and how to address them. They are then asked to adopt or at least recognize these official positions when it comes time to act on them.

A quick review of the Commission's functioning reveals the collective dynamics of youth empowerment in this context. The Commission forms opinions and recommendations that it shares with its partners or city council. It sometimes decides to partner with other entities to undertake projects. The youth members thus have to agree on "the" position of the Commission: What recommendations will it make? How will these be communicated? Whom will it collaborate with and how? This necessary cohesion leads one student to compare the Commission to a political party:

> One of the co-president's roles is a united CJ. [...] Last year I was
> thinking some things I held back from sharing because I wanted
> to focus on the discussions. This year for the 30-hour hunger
> challenge, I disagreed and I said so. [...] We are like a single-party
> system. It's very similar to a political party: there is debate, but
> once we've voted, we have to come together. This allows us, and
> has allowed us, to go further.

In addition to learning how to debate, the Commission's members
thus also learn to develop common positions. Youth willingly submit
to opinions they do not share, or not entirely. While voting is often
used to establish a majority, many dialogues and debates—especially
those involving the Commission's official commitments—require
agreement among members to put forth a common position. Our
observations reveal that this consensus is sometimes more apparent
than real. According to Philippe Urfalino (2007), decisions based on
apparent consensus are not uncommon, given that collective decisions
are often made when criticism or protest is absent. An "apparent"
consensus usually reflects more or less broad support. In such cases,
some comments are always suppressed by individuals who understand the limits of the context they are working in, the general attitude toward the project in question, and the organization's desired
level of efficiency.

Several discussions surrounding the 30-hour hunger challenge,
particularly those leading to adopted recommendations, illustrate
this transition from personal critical expression to shared collective
decision-making. Initially during the presentation of the project,
youth posed numerous questions and expressed firmly held positions.
Several were hesitant to commit to the project. They criticized the
relevance of a 30-hour fast, arguing that it did not reflect the reality
of hunger in Outaouais and could affect young people's mental health.
Other members, notably those who had already participated in the
challenge, voiced their uncompromising support. After an in-camera
meeting, the youth announced a deferred vote on the subject. The
following month, during the working session, a period was reserved
to further explore the different positions and develop majority-
approved recommendations, as the excerpt below illustrates. The
members agreed on three recommendations to present at the official
meeting in the afternoon. The Commission decided to provide limited
support but did not want to be directly involved in the project.

After a half-hour exchange between youth on the Défi des 30 heures de la faim, *Brigitte tries to steer the conversation towards proposals. "We want something more concrete," she says. Her comments come as no surprise to the students, who understand what she means. Xavier suggests making posters that explain food insecurity. Anabelle, the youth co-president, says, "that's already being done." However, continued discussion reveals that not all the schools are doing this. Brigitte tries to focus the discussion again: "The school has a lot of power over how the project is run. Do you want to have participants on site during the challenge to verify dietary profiles with a nutrition expert? Or we could come up with a promo tool on food insecurity [to explain] the challenge." Amélie agrees with Brigitte: "At the start of the challenge, we could ask them a question like 'What do you think fasting will feel like?' and after, 'How was your fasting experience?'" Many express support for this proposal and want to clarify the details, as when Anabelle proposes: "Maybe a group feedback session to share some thoughts on it?" Other ideas are proposed that are somewhat unclear. When Brigitte thinks a proposal is more precise, she takes the time to reformulate it and ask the group's opinion. She considers the students' reasons for and against different ideas to judge emerging points of consensus. Finally, she says enthusiastically: "Okay! We have three solid recommendations: 1) A video to promote the project and discuss food insecurity. 2) The inclusion of experts to give talks on different issues. 3) Before-and-after questionnaires to prompt reflection on food insecurity. Who wants to present these three ideas to the CJ this afternoon?" Xavier and Marc-Antoine energetically raise their hands. Amélie does too but more discreetly. "Amélie!" proclaims the youth co-president.*

8.5.3. Having a Political Community as a Horizon

To conclude, direct analysis of the Commission's municipal dimension allows us to go beyond the first two processes linking the individual and the collective, acting *on* and *with* a collective, to recognize a political community that requires acting *in the presence of and within* a collective. This location within a political community (the municipality, in this case) sets it apart from school or community youth initiatives that are more removed from the world of politics. While schools take a certain distance from the political community (Vitiello, 2010), the Commission seeks on the contrary to immerse youth in municipal politics. The fact that it is a municipal body, and thus part of a government, allows the perspectives developed within it to make a valuable contribution to the city's political community as a whole.

This political orientation was already apparent during the discussions surrounding the 30-hour hunger challenge, which dealt with poverty in the Outaouais region, its harmful impact on residents, and possible ways to address it. However, other activities revealed that many youth were not accustomed to reflecting on the "common good" of Gatineau. Identifying municipal priorities sometimes required lengthy discussion, especially among new members who had never given much thought to the future of their city. The excerpt below is about preparations for the Youth Summit. The objective was to identify the issues and needs of Gatineau youth through direct mobilization. The Summit, more overtly than any other activity, aimed to influence the city's political agenda. It was particularly important in terms of the possibilities it created: intervening in municipal affairs, engaging adults and students in Gatineau youth issues, and shaping and legitimizing the Commission's projects and policies. The Summit also helped the Commission establish itself as the voice of Gatineau youth.

The members of the Commission jeunesse are discussing possible themes for the Youth Summit. Michaël says that physical activity is a problem in school because there are only two classes for every nine days. "In my case, they cancelled my Phys Ed classes when I came back from a long hospital stay. Could we present something to have more Phys Ed classes?" Two students begin discussing why this is not a municipal issue. Another adapts the idea by mentioning poor food selection in the cafeterias. Michaël then tries to reframe his initial idea by suggesting they address the issue of physical activity or nutrition. The officer says: "Don't censor yourselves. The strategic committee [composed of a few youth assigned to the project] will make the final choice of themes." Jacob proposes several ideas at the same time: "The problems of developed countries are stress, smoking, physical activity, diet [...]. I think one of the problems for youth is attachment to culture. Youth aren't attached to their culture, there's no cultural identity. We're not attached to Québécois culture. We don't listen to Québécois content anymore. We'd rather listen to mainstream music. So it's [more or less] cultural health that's a problem." The officer recognizes the value of this idea and suggests: "Could we say cultural identity?" Jacob agrees: "Yes. We lack cultural identification."

8.6. What Youth Gain from Their Commission Experience

Youth learn a lot from their time at the Commission jeunesse and recognize the value of the factual, practical, and social knowledge they have acquired. More importantly, youth testimonies reveal that they associate their Commission experience with a period that not only transformed them but also allowed them to explore transforming their community.

Youth recount learning the facts of municipal politics, municipal operations, and deliberative assemblies. Many were able to build on this knowledge despite having little interest in these dynamics before getting involved, as this young member explains: "Before coming to the Commission jeunesse, I had no idea what a councillor was; now I work with them every month!"

Youth also develop important practical citizenship skills in their roles as leaders, project managers, and team players: "That's what I liked about the CJ: You build a project with your peers and achieve your goal; it's not just some passing idea, it becomes a reality." They become skilled participants in democratic dialogue by leading and contributing to deliberative assemblies, formulating and expressing individual opinions, and collectively developing recommendations. As one young woman recalls, speaking requires considering the broader context: "It helped me learn to speak well, at the right time. To know how to express myself and to whom."

Finally, youth acquire equally important soft skills. They develop civic-minded attitudes that foster a sense of autonomy, responsibility, and empathy. This helps them "realize that people think very differently, and that's a good thing."

Thanks to this unique learning experience, the Commission jeunesse has influenced the life trajectories of several young people, who appear transformed: "After I arrived, it took me two months [...] it's like the flower blossomed, in the end." Experimenting with ways to transform their city seems to have made their Commission experience particularly memorable: "What I really like about the Commission jeunesse, is being able to come together with other young people and make a difference in Gatineau."

Conclusion

Several factors contributed to the success of this transformative, democratic, citizen experience. First, youth found a space in which to pursue projects that concretely benefitted their municipality. Second, they had the support of adult allies who facilitated the expression of diverse opinions, while also guiding them toward shared positions. Third, youth were recognized by municipal stakeholders who were willing to integrate their perspectives.

That said, our observations also revealed some of the limits of the Commission's transformative and democratic scope. Youth enrolled in private schools and international education programs are over-represented, potentially reducing the diversity of perspectives. While this elitist dynamic is not unique to the Commission, it remains problematic when the latter claims to speak for the "youth of Gatineau." Likewise, as a municipal body, it tends to restrict the expression of opinions that are too critical or fall outside the municipal framework. Greater consideration and priority are given to ideas that are considered more acceptable and feasible.

This initiative, which immerses youth in a democratic education experience based on representative democracy and public action, introduces them first and foremost to a concept of liberal citizenship. It is important to note, however, that the youth are exposed to several co-existing concepts of democratic citizenship education, given their involvement in deliberative, participatory, critical, and multicultural citizenship discourses, as discussed in Chapter 1. Clearly, the Commission jeunesse reveals the extent to which youth citizenship practices surpass those of many adults. It also shows the importance of developing a sense of belonging to a collective—the collective being the Ville de Gatineau, in this case—when it comes to sparking civic engagement and resolving collective problems.

References

Akiva, T., Cortina, K. S., & Smith, C. (2014). Involving youth in program decision-making: How common and what might it do for youth? *Journal of Youth and Adolescence*, 43(11), 1844–1860. https://doi.org/10.1007/s10964-014-0183-y

Augsberger, A., Collins, M. E., & Gecker, W. (2017). Best practices for youth engagement in municipal government. *National Civic Review, 106*(1), 9–16. https://doi.org/10.1002/ncr.21304

Augsberger, A., Collins, M. E., & Gecker, W. (2018). Engaging youth in municipal government: Moving toward a youth-centric practice. *Journal of Community Practice, 26*(1), 41–62. https://doi.org/10.1080/10705422.2017.1413023

Blondiaux, L. (2008). *Le nouvel esprit de la démocratie : actualité de la démocratie participative.* Seuil.

Bundick, M. J. (2011). Extracurricular activities, positive youth development, and the role of meaningfulness of engagement. *The Journal of Positive Psychology, 6*(1), 57–74. https://doi.org/10.1080/17439760.2010.536775

Chanial, P. (2016). Rendre justice à ce qui est : ou l'émancipation comme parturition. *Revue du MAUSS, 48*(2), 259–274. https://doi.org/10.3917/rdm.048.0259

Collins, M. E., Augsberger, A., & Gecker, W. (2016). Youth councils in municipal government: Examination of activities, impact and barriers. *Children and Youth Services Review, 65*, 140–147. https://doi.org/10.1016/j.childyouth.2016.04.007

Commission jeunesse de Gatineau. (2018). *La ville de Gatineau sans la commission jeunesse c'est comme un road trip sans musique. Bilan 2017.* https://publications.virtualpaper.com/ville-de-gatineau-acl/vp_bilan-2017/

Crocetti, E., Erentaitė, R., & Žukauskienė, R. (2014). Identity styles, positive youth development, and civic engagement in adolescence. *Journal of Youth and Adolescence, 43*(11), 1818–1828. https://doi.org/10.1007/s10964-014-0100-4

Galichet, F. (2002). La citoyenneté comme pédagogie : réflexions sur l'éducation à la citoyenneté. *Revue des sciences de l'éducation, 28*(1), 105–124. https://doi.org/10.7202/007151ar

Gaudet, S., Forest, M., & Caron, C. (2019). *Une expérience d'éducation à la citoyenneté : la Commission jeunesse de Gatineau* [research report]. CIRCEM. https://doi.org/10.20381/ruor-24538

Urfalino, P. (2007). La décision par consensus apparent : nature et propriétés. *Revue européenne des sciences sociales, XLV*(136), 47–70. https://doi.org/10.4000/ress.86

Vitiello, A. (2010). *Institution et liberté : l'école et la question du politique.* L'Harmattan.

Vitiello, A. (2013). L'exercice de la citoyenneté : délibération, participation et éducation démocratiques. *Participations, 5*, 201–226. https://doi.org/10.3917/parti.005.0201

Vitiello, A. (2016). L'autonomie en devenir : l'émancipation comme (trans)formation infinie. *Revue du MAUSS, 48*(2), 211–227. https://doi.org/10.3917/rdm.048.0211

Westheimer, J., & Kahne, J. (2004). What kind of citizen? The politics of educating for democracy. *American Educational Research Journal, 41*(2), 237–
269. https://doi.org/10.3102/00028312041002237

Notes

1. https://espacemuni.org/programmes/communautes-en-sante/lapproche-villes-et-villages-en-sante/

2. The main adult ally is the officer. The adult co-president and other municipal staff members responsible for helping the officer can also be considered adult allies.

3. Usually, the councillors are present from the first annual assembly in September. However, in an election year, they take up their function later, in this case, in December.

4. All the first names used here are pseudonyms.

5. The members usually refer to the Commission jeunesse as the "CJ."

6. For the past several years, the *C'est parti, je vote* project [Let's go, I'm voting] organizes school visits to raise youth awareness of municipal politics and allow for exchange with city councillors. The councillor is always accompanied by a facilitator. At the end of each session, the youth are asked to identify municipal policy priorities. Improving public transit was cited several times in the 2017 report submitted to city council.

7. Outaouais Public Transit Agency (OPTA).

8. This project stemmed from a recommendation proposed at the 2012 Youth Summit. Youth asked the Commission jeunesse to take a position on social issues potentially affecting all Gatineau citizens.

CHAPTER 9

Learning Democracy Through Adversity: The *Forum jeunesse de l'île de Montréal* and the *Prends ta place à l'école* Program

Sophie Théwissen-LeBlanc, Stéphanie Gaudet,
and Alexandre Cournoyer

Abstract

This chapter focuses on the *Forum jeunesse de l'île de Montréal* (FJÎM) and the *Prends ta place à l'école* program. This initiative offers training and support to the student councils and assemblies of two Montreal school boards. As part of the initiative, youth interact with several adults (administrators, school board members, including the chair, teaching and support staff, and FJÎM facilitators) who have varied and sometimes conflicting functions, approaches, and interests. Youth experienced tensions between their rights and desire to be heard and different administrative obstacles, but also benefitted from adult support when facing political challenges. This program offered a unique form of citizenship education based on representative democracy and public action.

When you know there are people behind you, who are there for you and encouraging you to continue, you want to continue.

James

Juliette[1] and Jeremy were there [for us]; they were part of the whole structure of the school board, but they really wanted to show us [...] the importance of getting involved and that, in the end, it's not for nothing [...] It's really going to benefit you and your society. But the problem is that their work stopped there. They couldn't come and see how our school principals were treating us. It was really like a utopian world of student engagement. At the TUCÉ [Table unifiée des conseils d'élèves], it was really that, it was the utopia of what it should be like to be engaged in a school, of how easy it should be to be heard by your principal. How your projects shouldn't kill you, and you shouldn't kill yourself for them. It was really with good intentions that they managed and led the TUCÉ; it's just that [...] they couldn't come and see with their own eyes what was really happening in our [schools].

Faïha

This chapter focuses on a youth experience with facilitators from the *Prends ta place à l'école* program offered by the *Forum jeunesse de l'île de Montréal* (FJÎM), a civil society organization that supports the political engagement of youth aged 12 to 35. These youth participated in the program as members of the student assembly, a governance body at the school-board level. The two assemblies we observed brought together 12-to-17-year-old youth from different secondary schools on the island of Montreal. Their role was to discuss issues and projects affecting students in their respective school boards and participate in monthly meetings, activities, and training offered by the FJÎM.[2]

This experience in representative democracy took place outside of school but within the broader framework of the school system. It symbolizes a third place of democratic citizenship education, because it was run by a civil society organization.[3] Participation in student assemblies allowed students to go beyond school walls and attend meetings at their school board offices, where they connected, discussed, and organized events with their peers from other schools.

Unlike the other case studies presented in this book, this one does not make use of observational ethnographic methods to examine student assemblies. It is based instead on life history interviews combined with engagement pathway calendars (see Gaudet & Drapeau, 2021). This data is complemented by document analyses and interviews with adults responsible for the supervision and functioning of the two assemblies. This methodology provides access to experience as it is both lived and recounted, i.e., to the objective unfolding of events and their subjective interpretation. The interviews were conducted one or two years after the end of the project; this practice generates more reflexive and analytical research material, since youth are able to have a more detached and critical view of their engagement experience. We decided to include this case in our book, because it sheds light on youth democratic citizenship education in the broader school system, which has rarely been documented from the students' perspective. Given the many organizations and bodies involved, we have included the table below listing the principal stakeholders and their roles.

Table 9.1. Principal Stakeholders and Roles

Abbreviation/Name	Role
AESCSDM	Montreal school board student association
AMÈS	Secondary school student activist association (created and run by youth)
Comité d'élèves	Secondary school student committee mandated by the *Education Act* (commonly called the student council)
Concertation Montréal (CMTL)	Civil society organization dedicated to political engagement in Montreal that supports the FJÎM
CRÉS	Secondary school student committee (created and run by youth)
CSDM	Commission scolaire de Montréal (Montreal school board)
CSMB	Commission scolaire Marguerite-Bourgeoys (Marguerite-Bourgeoys school board)
Forum Jeunesse de l'île de Montréal (FJÎM)	Civil society organization promoting youth engagement in Montreal
TUCÉ	Marguerite-Bourgeoys school board student association

9.1. The FJÎM and *Prends ta place à l'école*

The FJÎM was created in January 2000 as part of the 1998–2001 action plan of the Secrétariat à la jeunesse du gouvernement du Québec.[4] In 2015, after the Quebec government cut funding to the youth forums, it was integrated into the non-profit organization Concertation

Montréal (CMTL).⁵ The FJÎM has launched several projects since its creation, including the democratic participation and citizenship education project *Prends ta place*, which is aimed at Montreal youth aged 12 to 30. The school component, *Prends ta place à l'école*, offered training and support to secondary school student councils and assemblies in Montreal.

The facilitators of FJÎM were two young women in their early 20s who helped youth understand their rights, the organizations' structures, and their power in the project and the governing bodies involved in it. These two facilitators were not part of the school structure. Their approach was based on the participatory-democracy and civil society model promoted by the FJÎM.

The FJÎM works regularly with other youth organizations. For the *Prends ta place à l'école* project, this involved working with the *Commission scolaire Marguerite-Bourgeoys* (CSMB) and the *Commission scolaire de Montréal* (CSDM). These were small government school boards that supervised the management of local schools. They were run by elected members of the community. The Quebec government abolished them in 2020.

9.2. The Initiative and the Role of Youth

The FJÎM supports students in fulfilling their role by providing training on school elections, deliberative meetings, the Quebec *Education Act*, and the powers of student councils. This non-profit organization also brings together politically engaged adults and other youth who are interested in socio-political issues. The youth participating in this project are required to sit on their school's student councils. At the time of our study, the *Table unifiée des conseils d'élèves* (TUCÉ) of the CSMB united delegates from 12 secondary schools, for a maximum of 24 delegates. The *Association des élèves du secondaire de la Commission scolaire de Montréal* (AESCSDM) included the same number of delegates and constituted the first body of its kind in Quebec.

During the summer of 2016, we conducted interviews with 14 former members of student councils and school board assemblies. Among these young adults, 9 were affiliated with the CSMB and 5 with the CSDM, across 12 secondary schools. More than half of these youth could be identified as belonging to a cultural minority group, reflecting Montreal's multiethnic demographics. These youth took part in training and other activities offered by *Prends ta place à l'école* in their roles as representatives of their schools.

These youth can be considered engagement "virtuosos," and their schools seem to have been important spaces of democratic experimentation in their development. In many cases, they were elected to the student council by acclamation or co-option. In retrospect, some admit to having had limited knowledge of the goals and functioning of a student council when they joined. In interviews, they report how their involvement quickly escalated from that point on: participation in school activities, committees, protests, and so on. It was often an adult from their school who asked or encouraged them to apply for the position on their school board's student assembly. The stories we collected reveal that students' ambitions and enthusiasm tended to grow until they encountered various obstacles that we term "political challenges" (Cournoyer, 2019).[6] Their engagement pathway stories include episodes marked by adversity, such as bureaucratic interference in their projects, authoritarian or manipulative treatment from principals or school boards, and lack of interest from other students.

9.3. Socio-historical Context: The Maple Spring

The participants lived through a particular socio-historical period marked by the 2012 Maple Spring (*Printemps érable*), a student movement and strike that mobilized the entire Quebec university and CEGEP student population (Tremblay et al., 2015). Interviewees reported being inspired by the older students' solidarity. Several secondary students tried to independently mobilize their own groups at the time. Some of our study participants were key players in movements like the Association militante des élèves du secondaire (AMÉS) and the Comité représentant des élèves du secondaire (CRÉS). Pierre recounts: "Me and someone from another school who contacted me, we created an activist association separate from the AESCSDM, without adults." Simon explains that the CRÉS was also founded to be a space without adults: "I said to myself that youth should be the voice for youth and represent youth, and that adults shouldn't be making decisions for us."

These spaces created by youth for youth were short lived. The AMÉS came to end within the first year after many of the students who were deeply engaged in it completed their studies. The CRÉS was absorbed into the CSMB to become the TUCÉ. According to Luc, this transition had advantages and disadvantages: "We got a budget, we got an official administrative place in the family tree 'thing,' where the commission's decisions are made," but also "we got more bureaucracy."[7]

9.4. Relations with Adults

9.4.1. Support, Trust, and Respect in Youth–Adult Relationships

All the youth we met recognized the value of their interactions with the adults who accompanied them throughout their journey. These adults were a source of inspiration, support, and social recognition. Simon, who contributed to creating the CRÉS to build something that was truly "by and for youth," acknowledged "support from the principal and some teachers" when asked what stimulated his political participation.

The youth especially appreciated the horizontal relationships that some adults sought to create with them. Speaking of one adult from the AESCSDM who made a particular impression on him, Mikaël expressed his appreciation: "I really liked how he talked to me, because I was only 16 and he talked to me like I was his equal, and it was really interesting to be able to discuss with an adult who respects you." Faïha expressed her gratitude toward the TUCÉ, where the leaders "made us feel important [...] almost like we were adults; we had a mic; they gave us a project." These comments highlight the benefits of the youth-adult partnerships observed. The adults guided the students rather than imposing control over their deliberations, solutions, and decisions (see Zeldin et al., 2017). Based on trust, reciprocity, and power-sharing, these partnerships promote youth empowerment.

The positive influence adults had on respondents' engagement journeys stemmed from the interpersonal relations they created in their roles as facilitators. In most interviews, youth mentioned the quality of support and connection with the FJÎM facilitators, especially when conflicts arose. Pierre reported feeling pressured by the school board to take a position in a political debate: "Juliette and Vicky made me realize that just because the chair tells you to do it or proposes something, doesn't mean you have to do it [...] They really helped me relax during that very intense period." A sense of adversity sometimes stemmed from negative feelings due to conflicts.

In these cases, the FJÎM facilitators offered youth emotional support to help them maintain their commitments. Andrée said she thought her student president "did not feel like he was all alone" and that he "would have quit" if Vicky or Juliette had not been there. The respondents also appreciated the facilitators' dedication and authenticity. Pierre noted that for "Vicky, it wasn't just her job [...]; it was something she really cared about."

This emotional support was sometimes provided by another adult, like a representative from the school board partnering with the FJÎM. Emmanuel described how he reached out to one such adult after conflicts with his school principal: "I texted Mr. Lavoie. I was just like, 'Okay, I didn't come to the council meeting [...] this is why' [and he responded] 'No problem, as long as you keep up the good work you're doing'[...] I adore Mr. Lavoie."

Geneviève recounted how this same official listened to and supported her when she was "extremely upset" about the token inclusion of youth at a school board conference: "I spoke about this to Mr. Lavoie and the school board's assistant director, who strongly supports the *Table unifiée des conseils d'élèves* [...] That put my mind at ease somewhat [...] It calmed me a bit."

9.4.2. Complex Relations with the Bureaucracy: Barriers and Instrumentalization

As members of the school board student assemblies, youth interacted with adults who were not there to support them but fulfilled other functions as officials, administrators, or supervisors. These included adults who were elected to the school boards, held positions of institutional power (school principals, commission chairs), or occupied other positions of authority (teaching staff, SCGCIS animators, and parent representatives). The stories collected reveal that youth faced many political challenges involving a range of issues and factors.[8]

Students experienced more friction with adults in positions of authority at their schools and school boards than with the other adults. The most common challenges included tokenism, instrumentalization, and manipulation.[9] Tokenism has often been identified in scholarly studies as an important source of frustration that undermines youth motivation and interest in civic engagement and political participation (O'Connor, 2013; Weller, 2007). Showing openness toward youth without recognizing their agency and decision-making abilities makes them less enthusiastic about civic involvement (Boyer et Gaudet, 2021).

Interviewees vividly recalled times when they felt they were included to boost their school's or school board's image, without their voices really being heard or respected. Simon remembered a frustrating incident when he was invited to a school board conference but had no opportunity to contribute in any meaningful way: "We were invited like [...] again. I had the impression that I wasn't the only one who had the impression, that we were a bit like [..]. that we were there kind of symbolically. Just to say 'Look, we're making room for youth.'"

Luc recounted a similar situation when he was invited by one of his school's administrators to participate in a public event: "I really had the impression that the vice-principal wanted to look good by bringing a student. [...] Like saying 'Hey, check out how we include our students and give them power; look, we brought one.'"

Youth were wise to this tokenism and sensitive to their voice and presence being instrumentalized. Without specifically using this term, Faïha recalled how annoyed she was by the controlling attitude of the adults on her school board: "When it involved doing [...] things to get the school board to collaborate with us, that's when you saw it was all [...] it was just an image." Omar shared a similar remark about certain activities proposed to the student assembly by his school board: "It's like they were using students to promote their image."

Participants lived through very specific political events. During this period, debates on the role and mission of school boards were being held throughout the province. The boards were using pressure tactics to protest government proposals. Many youth were at the centre of these highly publicized political debates. In 2014, the CSDM encouraged students to participate in protest movements that took them all the way to the Quebec National Assembly (Leduc, 2014). Instead of focusing on their own projects, many student representatives were pressured into taking part in these protests against the planned reforms. Two years later, Pierre felt he was "instrumentalized" as a member of his school board's student assembly:

> It was my first meeting with the executive committee. I was
> super stressed as usual, and then she [a member of the board
> administration] came in and said to us: "Okay, they want to

merge the school boards; you're all going to be scrapped. There will be major cuts; it's going to be awful. You have to do something; I don't really know what." So, it was like, we talked about that for the whole meeting instead of talking about what we wanted. And this took up two months of our meetings.

Similarly, Andrée recounted: "That year was the dismantling of the CSDM. It went all the way to Québec City [parliament]. We were, like, really manipulated."

In the schools, part of the tension between youth and the administration was related to the very existence of the student councils, which were required under the *Education Act*. This obligated secondary schools in Quebec to ensure the creation of these bodies, referred to as student committees, and declare that "students shall determine the name, composition and operating rules and elect the members of the committee" (Québec, Ministère du Travail, de l'Emploi et de la Solidarité sociale, 2024, p. 34). Student councils were thus imposed on school administrations, which required delegation of power to students.

Many stories collected attest to the reluctance of some school administrations to accept this governing body. Emmanuel reported that his election as school president elicited resistance from the administration and some teachers, who wanted to maintain control: "The principal said to me [...] 'don't take this as a sword of Damocles, but it's just to warn you, because if this doesn't work, we'll have to reconsider the votes.'" Two other students described the strategies they adopted in response to their administration's behaviour. Nicolas recalled that "if you didn't want them to walk all over you, you had to know how to play their game." A partner of the FJÎM and *Prends ta place* project also reported seeing school administrations creating barriers to youth initiatives, and sometimes to adult allies as well. He explained that "the recommendations we submitted were rarely considered by the school administration." This was confirmed by Luc, another participant: "In a lot of student councils, not a single school administrator met with them for the whole year."

Some respondents reported that their engagement was positively or negatively affected by a change in their school's or school board's administration. This reveals the extent to which school administrators can influence the quality of the youth experience within their student councils. Several students interviewed said they had good relationships with their principals or school board representatives.

Sometimes there was tension with other school staff members, such as teachers, recreation technicians, and the SCGCIS animators who assisted the student councils. Students say these tensions stemmed from certain adults wanting to control the council's policies or minimize its resources and recognition. According to one of the FJÎM partners, this resistance was due to a misunderstanding of the council's role and functioning, the school staff's vaguely defined responsibilities toward it, and other types of pressure: "We realized there was a clash between the goals the school board gave us and the facilitator's view of things." Since the school staff "felt totally overworked," this could "demoralize the youth." Nevertheless, several interviewees described having very positive relations with school staff members (as with some administrators), sometimes even creating friendships.

9.5. What Youth Gained from the Experience

Despite the challenges, over half of the youth interviewed considered their participation on the school board assemblies and work with the FJÎM to be their most meaningful social and political engagement to date. Most of them continued to be politically involved after completing their secondary studies. The most significant aspects of this experience were the following: building positive interpersonal relationships with the adult allies (the FJÎM facilitators and adults in their schools), connecting with other youth, sharing and celebrating success stories in the student assemblies, learning and developing skills through participation in decision-making bodies, and having new opportunities to participate in the community.

9.5.1. Networking, Recognition, and Success Stories

Meetings with the TUCÉ and the AESCSM, guided by the FJÎM, were singled out as a highlight of the democratic citizenship education experience. Respondents mentioned several benefits of the assemblies. According to Geneviève, "It created a network, motivated us, and gave us ideas for how to initiate projects or which projects to pursue." James found that sharing experiences was enriching: "In many other schools, they had the same types of problems [...] This made us feel less alone." Mikaël said he was able to "build a network of contacts."

Respondents found meeting with other engaged, informed, and motivated youth to be very positive, because they often faced apathy among other schoolmates. They complained of students, including other council members, being uninformed about the role and functioning of the council. Several students recalled feeling disappointed and even frustrated by this. Luc remarked: "I don't know if this came from students not informing themselves, or if it was the school structure that kept students from knowing about it, but [...] there were some who didn't even know what my role was." Their experiences with the TUCÉ or AESCSDM were apparently more satisfying. According to Emmanuel, the students there were very motivated and driven: "It was really a student council elite at the TUCÉ."

The student assembly meetings were also a source of motivation. According to Geneviève: "Being recognized as a member of the student council at the Table unifiée was very, very rewarding for the students. I think we were praised a lot for our engagement. We were valued a lot. This really motivated me." For James: "The TUCÉ is something that gives you a major boost. It gives you a shot of energy to continue on the council."

9.5.2. Knowledge and Skills Acquired

The *Prends ta place à l'école* citizenship education experience offered by the school boards and the FJÎM combined institutional and political knowledge transmission with problem-solving experimentation. Faced with adversity, the students had to learn to negotiate, question things, choose their battles, overcome challenges, and manage their emotions. The main skills developed in this project were related to the transmission and transformation of democratic culture. Youth acquired experience in public speaking, deliberative assemblies, and collective decision-making. This experiential learning increased Mikaël's motivation:

> Being able to get involved in a cause that matters to me is really something that changed me and allowed me to get involved in many other causes and care about other things. [...] Also, it developed my democratic point of view and helped me get interested in politics, in subjects like that.

These remarks reveal a link between the perceived authenticity of participation and the democratic citizenship learning experience. This authenticity stems from learning in concrete situations, applying this learning in meaningful ways, and feeling empowered to act.[10] The students who spoke of authentic experiences took part in real collective decisions and actions in their schools. Beyond these experiential lessons, they also learned how representative bodies function. They acquired knowledge about assembly rules and procedures, school and school board administration, project development, and teamwork.

Many students found the courses offered by the FJÎM to be very useful, both in form and content. Luc recalled the following: "There were several training sessions [...] So I knew a little more about what I was getting myself into, and this was precious knowledge." What he learned "is still part of [him] today". Emmanuel said he developed his capacity to "speak in public, how to present a project and have it accepted." The courses taught Mikaël about his rights and responsibilities, and about his council's and assembly's rules and operations. He also learned about leadership, democracy, the Morin Code,[11] "how to make a point, present a document, present himself, stand out, and discuss."

For others, the training sessions covered things they already knew. James found the training too theoretical: "They taught us how to argue, how to organize your argument when there was a problem." Maria felt the courses did not affect her much. Others, such as Simon, recognized their pertinence but would have preferred more action: "I didn't feel like wasting my time with this stuff about procedures. [...] Beyond my pride, I'm still aware of the importance it can have, [the fact] of being structured and [...] I think it was very beneficial overall". Omar thought the courses had interesting content, but that "there was nothing very productive [...] I wouldn't say it was a waste of time [...], but it's time that [could have been spent on other things]." According to Nicolas, the training did not prepare students for the complexity of the challenges they were going to face: "The big problem with these training sessions is that they're very well-meaning. You know, 'get involved, it's going to be amazing and everything.' [...] In the end they're very good for consensual projects [...] They're not made for being subversive."

5.3. Impact on Students' Engagement Pathways

Some students spoke of people associated with the FJÎM and the *Prends ta place* project having an impact on their social and political engagement beyond their secondary studies. For Geneviève, FJÎM's facilitators and partners helped shape her identity and degree of "awareness of different causes." Faïha recalled how a facilitator from the FJÎM encouraged her to join the Forum jeunesse: "She approached everyone on [the school board] and really reached out to me personally and encouraged me to apply." Likewise, Nicolas recounted: "It was Vicky who asked us, 'Hey, does this interest you?' Then I submitted my application and everything. Then I found myself at the *Congrès de la francophonie,* and it was really interesting."

9.6. The Challenges of Participatory Citizenship

The stories collected reveal that the *Prends ta place à l'école* project was grounded in a liberal and participatory concept of citizenship education (Sant, 2019).[12] It emphasized youth education and participation on representative bodies to develop students' democratic skills and knowledge (about elections, for example) and engage them in the democratic processes of their school and school board. The training sessions offered as part of the project were consistent with these goals. They covered topics like the functioning of student councils and school boards; the roles, rights, and responsibilities of elected officials; leadership, public speaking, and deliberation; assembly procedures; and so on.

After taking part in this project and benefiting from the guidance of adult allies, youth gained a better understanding of institutional operations, the role of political representation, and the skills needed to demonstrate leadership, work collectively on projects, and participate in and even preside over meetings. This took place within pre-established systems and structures, like the student councils mandated by the Quebec government, the schools and school boards, and the student assemblies.

However, in addition to acquiring these formal skills and knowledge, students also faced challenges working with adult authorities. In exploring this world of political conflicts and emotions, they discovered a less sanitized image of democracy than the one provided by the liberal citizenship education programs in their schools. The CRÉS and AMÉS were just two examples of students transcending the school system's boundaries to create movements by and for youth. This was not a new phenomenon: Quebec's secondary students have a long history of political engagement (Dupuis-Déri, 2020).

The *Prends ta place à l'école* program jointly offered by the FJÎM, CSMB, and CSDM incorporated several concepts of democratic citizenship education. Above all, it immersed students in a liberal democratic experience based on representative government. Youth also took part in participatory and deliberative democratic processes, like debating issues and developing projects. Finally, and somewhat unexpectedly, the project engaged youth in an agonistic democratic experience, which, for Ernesto Laclau and Chantal Mouffe (2001), is the very essence of democracy, since dissent is vital to democratic debate.

References

Boyer, S., & Gaudet, S. (2021). La citoyenneté démocratique des enfants à l'école primaire. *Revue des sciences de l'éducation*, 47(2), 174–196. https://doi.org/10.7202/1083983ar

Cournoyer, A. (2019). Apprendre la démocratie à l'école secondaire : trajectoire de participation sociale et politique des adolescents. [Master's thesis, University of Ottawa]. https://ruor.uottawa.ca/handle/10393/39890

Dupuis-Déri, F. (2020). Histoire des grèves d'élèves du secondaire au Québec : démocratie et conflictualité. *Revue des sciences de l'éducation*, 46(3), 67–94. https://doi.org/10.7202/1075988ar

Education Act, CQLR c I-13.3 (2024). Retrieved from https://www.legisquebec.gouv.qc.ca/en/document/cs/I-13.3

Gaudet, S., Claude, M., Cournoyer, A., Portilla, J., & Déry, J. A. (2017). Apprendre la démocratie en milieu scolaire : analyse des trajectoires de participation sociale et politique des jeunes participant à *Prends ta place à l'école*. [Final report]. CIRCEM and Forum jeunesse de l'île de Montréal. https://doi.org/10.20381/ruor-20227

Gaudet, S., & Drapeau, E. (2021). L'utilisation combinée du récit et du calendrier de vie dans un dispositif d'enquête narrative biographique. *Recherches qualitatives*, 40(2), 57–80. https://doi.org/10.7202/1084067ar

Laclau, E., & Mouffe, C. (2001). *Hegemony and socialist strategy: Towards a radical democratic politics* (2nd ed.). Verso.

Leduc, L. (2014, December 9). La CSDM invite ses élèves à manifester. *La Presse+*. https://plus.lapresse.ca/screens/864b7252-a84e-492a-90ce-0995eecc6b7bl_0.html

O'Connor, C. D. (2013). Engaging young people? The experiences, challenges, and successes of Canadian youth advisory councils. In Nenga, S. K., & Taft, J. K. (Eds.), *Youth engagement: The civic-political lives of children and youth* (pp. 73–96). Emerald Group.

Sant, E. (2019). Democratic education: A theoretical review (2006-2017). *Review of Educational Research, 89*(5), 655–696. https://doi.org/10.3102/003465431 9862493

Tremblay, P. A., Roche, M., & Tremblay, S. (Eds.). (2015). *Le printemps québécois : le mouvement étudiant de 2012*. Presses de l'Université du Québec.

Weller, S. (2007). *Teenagers' citizenship: Experiences and education*. Routledge.

Zeldin, S., Gauley, J., Krauss, S. E., Kornbluh, M., & Collura, J. (2017). Youth-adult partnership and youth civic development: Cross-national analyses for scholars and field professionals. *Youth & Society, 49*(7), 851–878. https://doi.org/10.1177/0044118X15595153

Notes

1. All the names used here are pseudonyms. Juliette and Vicky are facilitators from the Forum jeunesse de l'île de Montréal (FJÎM), and Jérémy Lavoie is a school board officer.

2. Since our study was conducted in 2016–2017, the FJÎM has continued supporting youth engagement on student councils, but the *Prends ta place* program no longer exists.

3. The notion of democratic citizenship education in third places was outlined in Chapter 1.

4. https://www.fjim.ca/.

5. https://concertationmtl.ca/.

6. "Political challenge" here refers to the adversity that student representatives often face from educational institutions and the people who represent them. It is a challenging part of the citizenship education experience, which creates a negative perception of it. For more on this subject, see Alexandre Cournoyer's master's thesis (2019), which was also based on this field site.

7. The participant is referring to the organization chart. We have kept the verbatim reference (family tree "thing") to maintain the respondent's voice.

8. Spiritual care and guidance and community involvement leader.

9. See Chapter 2, which addresses these challenges in the discussion surrounding types of youth participation.

10. See the discussion of philosopher John Dewey's ideas on education presented in Chapter 1.

11. The Morin Code is a procedural guide for deliberative assemblies.

12. The different concepts of citizenship education are discussed in Chapter 1.

Doing Democracy with Youth: Four Lessons from the Third Places of Citizenship Education in Quebec

Stéphanie Gaudet and Caroline Caron

Throughout Quebec, children, adolescents, and young adults have access to activities that encourage them to participate in their communities. With the support of programs offered by non-profit organizations, youth undertake collective projects outside of school to address different problems: environmental issues, human rights violations, social inequalities, and discrimination, among others. These organizations and the adults who run them operate primarily with government funding slated for youth programs. Youth often lead and carry out the projects themselves.

The book is the product of a large-scale research partnership and innovative methodology. It presents seven initiatives and organizations using ethnographic data collected from participant observation and interviews.[1] The case studies provide unprecedented access to the inner workings of Quebec's youth organization ecosystem. Our in-depth analysis of young people's lived experiences is informed by the theory of differentiated youth citizenship, which builds on political scientist Ruth Lister's (2007) concept of minoritized citizenship.[2] Particular attention is paid to social learning processes. As John Dewey observed ([1916] 1997), collective efforts to address problems are always opportunities to learn about, experience, and uphold democracy.

A common theme that emerged from the diverse approaches to citizenship education documented in this book is the notion of a democratic ethos (Trudel & Martineau, 2021). This is an important theoretical contribution, because it reveals the pertinence of making democracy central to citizenship education, not only as an organization and institution but also as a culture in constant evolution. As we have shown, this democratic culture embraces diverse concepts of citizenship. While some of these have already been identified in the academic literature (Sant, 2019), our observations revealed two more: eco-citizenship and care-based citizenship.

The cases presented in this book highlight the social contribution of this diversity. Each project, program, or initiative teaches youth something different based on its own theories and practices and the specific context in which it is applied. Each is unique in how it teaches youth to live, think, and act democratically and use their individual abilities to work together for social change. These initiatives actively take part in "doing democracy" with young people through different ways of living and thinking about it in their everyday lives. Overall, this research highlights the importance of recognizing the diversity of third places, which represent non-formal and informal participatory spaces of citizenship education. The results of our collaborative research in Quebec also converge with those of the PARTISPACE[3] research project in Europe (Walther et al., 2019). Together, these results confirm that there is no single (or magic!) recipe for proactively developing and supporting youth participation. If anything, they foreground how crucial the diversification of places, spaces, support, and resources is to the vitality of this democratic culture.

When public policies include youth participation, this inevitably leads to the creation of programs and positions for youth professionals (Becquet, 2021). Our multisite study helped clarify the ways in which youth develop their agency when adults relate to them as mentors, rather than as supervisors or authorities. We were able to observe the quality of these interventions. Many of the adults lacked social work training, which seemed to contribute to the success of the different projects and the quality of the youth experience within them. Our observations on youth-adult mentorship relations in democratic learning contexts are consistent with past findings in the literature on youth intervention and well-being (Brion-Meisels et al., 2023), and the different forms of youth-adult co-construction in local initiatives (Zeldin et al., 2017). This represents an important avenue for ongoing research, and Quebec offers an excellent context for it, given the current proliferation of youth social innovation projects based on the mentorship approach.

Several times over the course of our research, youth described the richness of their learning experiences and the connections they made while participating. Another recurring topic of interest was how to deal with emotions in a social engagement context. We were not able to address this theme in depth, but we think it is an avenue worth pursuing. In all our case studies, we saw youth experiencing strong emotions, both positive and negative. This theme seems very promising for future studies, as Cécile Van de Velde (2021) has suggested regarding youth anger in engagement and activist contexts.

Public Policies that Support Youth

While the current socio-political context often relies on quantitative criteria to evaluate the merits and benefits of public investment in youth initiatives, the cases presented in this book offer instead a qualitative view of young people's individual and collective contributions to democracy. As this book shows, our partner organizations are important social spaces for democratic citizenship education in third places. Though very different, their youth citizenship programs complement the democratic citizenship education provided in schools. Rooted in the activism that shaped Quebec civil society in the twentieth century, the projects and programs analyzed here employ three distinct types of citizenship education. The projects focused on participatory democracy (the Institut du Nouveau Monde and Oxfam-Québec) engage students and support their participation in several ways. The programs focused on social change (YWCA Montréal, the Centre de pédiatrie sociale de Gatineau, and Exeko) raise youth awareness of social inequalities and encourage them to express their agency. The initiatives focused on representative democracy and public action (the Commission jeunesse de Gatineau and the Forum jeunesse de l'île de Montréal) introduce youth to an authentic representative government experience by means of formal bodies created for this purpose.

In their constant quest for funding, partner organizations all too often find themselves competing. This book, however, documents and confirms their rich complementarity. The project was based on a comprehensive epistemological, theoretical, and methodological approach. Each chapter highlights the specificity of the initiative analyzed while seeking to answer the broader research questions: How do youth experience these democratic citizenship education initiatives? How do the projects educate them about democratic co-existence? What have we learned from the case studies as a whole?

Our partner organizations often mentioned the challenges of recruiting and retaining youth. We would like to conclude by highlighting four lessons from this multisite ethnography to encourage continued experimentation in youth citizenship education. These "lessons learned" include best practices and courses of action that could be useful to organizations going forward.

Lesson 1: Make Youth Feel Welcome

The partner organizations showed how important it is to make youth feel welcome, and they provided many examples of ways to accomplish this. This seemed essential to the quality of the youth's experience, especially in terms of the perceived authenticity of the project's power, influence, and impact. This welcome takes place in three types of spaces: physical, relational, and dialogical.

The third places of citizenship education require physical spaces to host and meet with youth outside the school and home. These include different venues or public gathering places that are adapted to make youth feel welcome.

This physical third place also has a relational dimension. Each organization creates a unique relational space where links are forged between youth, as well as between youth and adults. In all our cases, the quality of these connections seemed intimately tied to the organization's ability to attract and maintain the participants' interest and motivation. The democratic education experience is created through a web of encounters and interpersonal relations. These often give rise to friendships that reinforce youth's sense of belonging and support for a project or cause. The adults' role is crucial, because they are responsible for creating a welcoming physical and relational environment. The adults find concrete ways to make youth feel welcome, starting with an insistence on horizontal relationships. Overall, the activities offered are interesting and enjoyable, and the approach is inclusive and caring. Several youth participants in our study said these adults left a lasting impression on them.

The third places of citizenship education are also dialogical spaces that welcome and encourage youth input. The partner organizations were successful at respecting young people's voices and creating conditions that support their expression, especially among those who find speaking difficult. The organizations also play an important role teaching youth the soft skills needed to deal with differing views and conflicts. The third places of citizenship education give youth a listening ear, but also show them how to listen to others. On several occasions, we observed the facilitation team's ability to impart these skills in concrete discussions, debates, and decision-making situations.

In the projects analyzed, the facilitation teams help youth express themselves, manage conflicts, and cope with disappointment, disagreement, adversity, injustices, and actions that do not always yield the desired results. Youth thus learn to deal with political emotions. They are taught how to formulate an opinion when angry, pursue dialogue despite feeling unheard, and convince others who think they are mistaken. The adult facilitators also guide youth confronted with institutional or symbolic barriers that sometimes infantilize them. This emotional guidance requires a lot of tact, humanity, pedagogical skill, and experience with young people.

The adult partners in our research often defended youth and enthusiastically promoted their causes, while also providing the support needed to overcome difficulties and adversity. Several youth recounted how these adults helped them develop their knowledge and skills, boost their self-esteem, and maintain their trust in collective action. The facilitation teams were decisive in the organizations' ability to ensure that youth feel welcome.

Lesson 2: Propose Meaningful, Concrete Goals for Immediate, Authentic Action

The partner organization initiatives we observed were based on projects, activities, and events that engage young people from diverse populations in ideas and issues that interest them. Youth tend to remain committed when organizations make every effort to support them. This includes helping them set goals and see the concrete impact of time and energy devoted to a collective project. Whether in the context of a four-day event, a workshop series spread over several weeks, or a year-long project, the participatory experience is more authentic and positive when it is concrete, engaging, and immediate.

It is very important for organizations to be honest and transparent about the degree of participation and power the youth will have. As we have seen with the ladders and participation types outlined in Chapter 2, consulting youth is not the same as giving them the means and power to act for themselves. Different projects can involve different degrees of youth participation, but it is important to not disappoint them. Organizations should think about this before launching any kind of youth initiative. What exactly is the organization willing and able to offer? To whom? For what purpose? What is expected of the youth? What power will the youth actually exercise? What is the intended impact? What measures will be taken to ensure the project is relevant to youth's lived experiences? This issue is not as simple as might seem at first glance. The organization has to reflect on its governance and the kind of youth–adult relationships it is able to create. This reflection is essential, because disappointing experiences can leave a bitter taste and discourage future involvement, especially when youth feel unheard, disrespected, or tokenized.[4] The organizations are responsible for ensuring that the citizenship education experience does not end in bitterness and cynicism.

Lesson 3: Expand Youth Horizons

Since the third places of citizenship education are associated with physical and relational spaces outside the school and home, they can greatly enrich young people's social reality and expand their horizons. Youth generally meet new people, develop friendships, and encounter difference in these spaces. The initiatives help them expand their interests and knowledge, develop new skills, and discover themselves as individuals and citizens. They have opportunities to build meaningful relationships with adults who hold less authority than the adults in their families or schools. Also, the teaching and mentoring offered by several organizations introduce youth to inspiring adults they can identify with and emulate. All these encounters are opportunities for youth to discover and understand the social and political world surrounding them and envision their individual and collective futures. It is one thing to know that inequalities exist; it is another to work with other citizens to understand the causes, protest, and take action to address them. These projects and initiatives allow youth to engage in the burning issues of our time while also combatting anxiety, cynicism, and disempowerment. Inspiring hope and teaching youth the power of solidarity greatly expands their horizons as citizens in the here and now.

Lesson 4: Recognize and Support the Work of Facilitators

In the vast world of youth organizations, some have difficulty recruiting and keeping participants until the end of the project. The seven cases presented in this book seem rather exemplary in this regard and provide useful models. As noted above, this book helps us fully appreciate the facilitators' personal and professional dedication to and respect for the youth. The success of the projects is often directly proportional to the connection and enthusiasm created among participants thanks to the guidance and support of these adult allies.

We should add that these facilitation teams are sometimes too modest. In their efforts to support and empower youth, they sometimes downplay the roles they play avoiding and resolving inevitable pitfalls in order to focus on youth success. The organizations adopt a "by and for youth" philosophy that is consistent with the differentiated citizenship approach. However, this philosophy does not do justice to the educational impact and pertinence of the positive youth–adult relationships we witnessed in the seven partner organizations. Having observed some of the institutional obstacles these adults face, we feel their essential roles and abilities merit greater recognition, both within their organizations and in society at large, among funders in particular. Another aspect of this lesson is for the organizations: The success of these youth projects largely depends on the quality of the facilitation team, which requires adequate budgetary, material, and human resources.

It is important to note the precarity of this work and the limited resources of organizations offering youth citizenship education programs in Quebec's third places. Fluctuating budgets and short-lived programs condemn the organizations to piecemeal operations, each project depending on often-isolated sources of funding. We have seen how much time and energy these organizations devote to meeting criteria to qualify for one-time funding programs. Any waste of public funds is probably due to this deplorable situation.

The lesson for both the organizations and public authorities is that youth programs need access to dedicated and continuous resources. Recurring initiatives help attract and retain youth, because participants bring in other youth over time. Meanwhile, piecemeal approaches too often go hand in hand with funding programs that target specific youth groups and problems. While this funding is clearly justified, the negative effects of this fragmentation cannot be denied. Of course it is important to address gun violence, sexual and gender diversity, academic success, and young people's financial autonomy in the job market. But programs should also aim to create socially diverse spaces that bring youth together. Otherwise, some projects could end up excluding youth who do not meet the criteria set by the organization or funder.

Class, in particular, can be a factor of exclusion or self-exclusion. Organizations and funders could find ways to avoid situations where educated and privileged youth are the only participants in initiatives, or admit only "disadvantaged," "vulnerable," and "at-risk" youth. Reaching a plurality of youth and exposing them to social diversity is perhaps an even greater social and political challenge today, as pernicious forces seek to undermine the legitimacy and authority of Western democracies and their institutions.

References

Becquet, V. (2021). Introduction. In Becquet, V. (Ed.), *Des professionnels pour les jeunes* (pp. 7–26). Champ social. https://doi.org/10.3917/chaso.becqu.2021.01.0007

Brion-Meisels, G., Vasudevan, D. S., & Fei, J. T. (2023). Youth-adult partnerships that foster individual and collective wellbeing. In Lester, J. N., & O'Reilly, M. (Eds.), *The Palgrave encyclopedia of critical perspectives on mental health* (pp. 1–5). Palgrave Macmillan. https://doi.org/10.1007/978-3-030-12852-4_101-1

Dewey, J. (1997). *Democracy and education: An introduction to the philosophy of education.* The Free Press. (Original work published in 1916)

Lister, R. (2007). Why citizenship: Where, when and how children? *Theoretical Inquiries in Law, 8*(2), 693–718. https://doi.org/10.2202/1565-3404.1165

Sant, E. (2019). Democratic education: A theoretical review (2006-2017). *Review of Educational Research, 89*(5), 655–696. https://doi.org/10.3102/003465431 9862493

Trudel, S., & Martineau, S. (2021). Axel Honneth et l'éducation : entre émancipation, ethnicité démocratique et compétence civique. *Formation et profession : revue scientifique internationale en éducation, 29*(2), 1–11. https://doi.org/10.18162/fp.2021.644

Van de Velde, C. (2021). "Different struggles, the same fight"? A comparative analysis of student movements in Chile (2011), Quebec (2012), and Hong Kong (2014). In Bessant, J., Mejia Mesinas, A., & Pickard, S. (Eds.), *When students protest: Universities in the Global North* (pp. 33–50). Rowman & Littlefield.

Walther, A., Batsleer, J., Loncle, P., & Pohl, A. (Eds.). (2019). *Young people and the struggle for participation: Contested practices, power and pedagogies in public spaces* (1st ed.). Routledge. https://doi.org/10.4324/9780429432095

Zeldin, S., Gauley, J., Krauss, S. E., Kornbluh, M., & Collura, J. (2017). Youth-adult partnership and youth civic development: Cross-national analyses for scholars and field professionals. *Youth & Society, 49*(7), 851–878. https://doi.org/10.1177/0044118X15595153

Notes

1. See Chapter 1. The Methodological Appendix provides a detailed account of our qualitative approach to this collaborative research.
2. See Chapter 2.
3. https://partispace.eu/
4. See Chapter 2.

Methodological Appendix

Stéphanie Gaudet

T his collaborative project represents a way of doing sociology that combines different types of knowledge and seeks to democratize their production and use (Soulière & Fontan, 2018). It not only studies democracy but also puts it into action by examining democratic citizenship education and including the viewpoints of individuals affected by our research. Drawing on scientific, practical, and experiential knowledge, we co-constructed a research project that became a multisite ethnography involving researchers and organizations with different epistemological positions and approaches to democratic citizenship education. Our observation grids and analyses were inevitably influenced and enriched by these different viewpoints, while also maintaining a degree of objectivity (objectivation) and comparability. Our knowledge mobilization plan was developed with different uses in mind. We created several tools besides our academic publications to reach different audiences: videos, documentaries, bulletins, reports, and a website.

In giving a voice to civil society stakeholders, researchers adopt a public sociology position that highlights the sociologist's role as liaison between civil society and the state (Gaudet, 2020). By bringing attention to citizens rendered invisible by society—children, adolescents, and young adults—we also shed light on categories of the population that face epistemic injustices (Fricker, 2007). Our research goals and methods were informed by both participatory ethics and an objectivizing, engaged approach (Genard & Roca i Escoda, 2019). This project was also conceived with diversity, equity, and inclusion in mind before the policies now imposed by funders were articulated in those terms. The organizations we chose to work with support youth who are among the most vulnerable due to their identity or class. University students played a decisive role in this collaborative project. The chapters co-written with them attest to our teamwork approach and desire to include them in different stages of the research process.

The modelling of a collaborative research methodology is a lengthy process, and this project stands out for the richness of the instruments developed in advance. We co-created the project with youth participation experts from both academia and different practical sectors (primary and secondary teaching, communities, associations, and para-governmental organizations). Here we present the methodologies used at different stages of our research.

Preparatory Consulting Methods

Co-creating a research project is an ambitious undertaking, and we had no recipe or guide to help us. We built a method inspired by the public participation expertise of the Institut du Nouveau Monde (INM), which has developed interesting and useful design and consulting tools for researchers. Co-creating required uniting people who had never worked together and, in some cases, never conducted scientific research. The preparatory work was thus very important to the project's success and was an integral part of the research methodology. This included designing an iterative survey based on the Delphi method (Booto Ekionea et al., 2011) to prepare for an upcoming symposium on youth citizenship and democratic citizenship education. Using online questionnaires, we consulted participants on important citizen qualities to be developed, existing resources, and educational spaces. This method allowed us to identify points of consensus. We then explored these during the symposium and discussed disagreements not addressed during the online consultation (Gaudet et al., 2017).

This two-day symposium was held at the University of Ottawa. It brought together around 50 people and made use of different discussion formats: World Café, workshops, conferences, and an open forum. These were organized in collaboration with the INM.[1] The last activity, the open forum, grouped people according to the questions and projects they wanted to address or pursue. Six proposals emerged from this forum, and the results presented in this book stem from one of these proposals.

Developing the Collaborative Ethnographic Methodology

The ethnographic approach was considered the best method for addressing the research question co-created during the symposium: "How are youth and facilitators experimenting with different citizenship education initiatives outside the school program?" The ethnographic approach entails being immersed in a setting and doing participant observation on the practices and interactions that play out. This makes it possible to document social relationships in real situations, within the complex contexts and social dynamics that structure the interactions. It is also a data-generating method that adheres to the project's iterative grounded theory approach. The following chart represents our modelling of the collaborative research process just before entering the field:

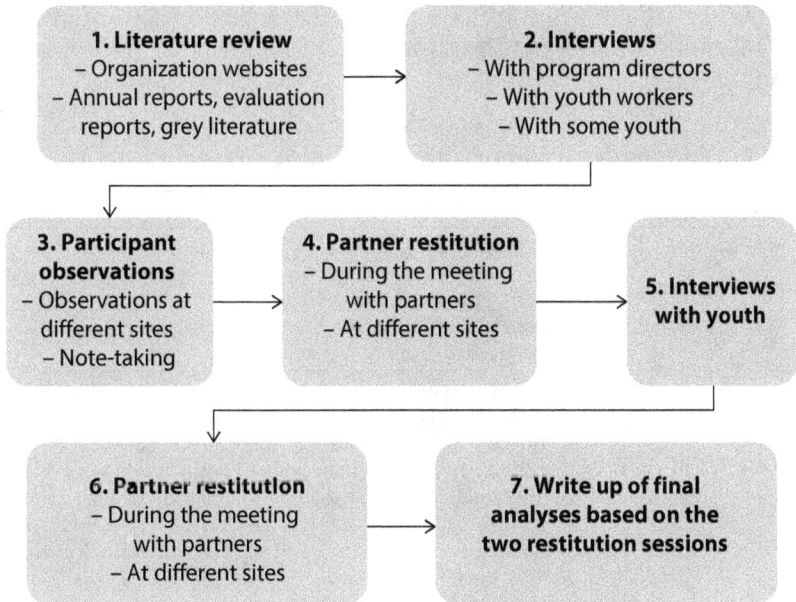

1. Literature review
– Organization websites
– Annual reports, evaluation reports, grey literature

2. Interviews
– With program directors
– With youth workers
– With some youth

3. Participant observations
– Observations at different sites
– Note-taking

4. Partner restitution
– During the meeting with partners
– At different sites

5. Interviews with youth

6. Partner restitution
– During the meeting with partners
– At different sites

7. Write up of final analyses based on the two restitution sessions

FIGURE A.1. Data-generating processes and partner relations.

The ethnographic approach is particularly useful for documenting little-studied phenomena and understanding group cultures (Cefaï, 2010; Gaudet & Robert, 2018). It is an embodied method in which the researcher's physical appearance, identity, presence in the field, and relationships with participants influence the experience. Given the very different types of initiatives and timeframes involved, research team members adapted their observations and approaches to the field site in question. The fieldworkers were mostly research assistants whose age gave them easier access to interactions. They recorded their observations in a grid based on the literature review of citizenship education practices. Their entry into the field and types of observations depended on the practices being observed. Working with engaged, dynamic students on a municipal council for a year requires different field adaptation than does working with younger or more vulnerable youth. Sometimes it is a difference in social status, rather than age, that calls for adaptation (Gaudet et al., 2020). This is why it is important to understand the effects of the actors' different social positions. As the adults, the fieldworkers have to adapt and find ways to work with youth that respect their voices and space.

Table A.1. Observation Grid and Ethnographic Conversations

Observation categories	Related questions
1.Socio-demographic information	How many people participated in the activity? Does this number change over the course of the activity? Does it seem typical? How many are women? Racialized? From immigrant backgrounds? Others? What is the approximate age of the youth participating in the activity?
2. Nature of the activity	When does the activity take place? How long does it last? How are the activities linked or connected? What happens during the activity? What do the people engaged in the activity do? What are their goals? How are speaking roles distributed? Who speaks? When? For what reasons? For how long? Who is/are the leader or leaders? What are their roles? What spaces do the activities take place in? How do people occupy these spaces (seated in circles, standing and mobile, etc.)?
3. Educational approach	Is it an activity that promotes experimentation (artistic, teamwork, brainstorming, project development)? Is it an activity that promotes discussion and debate? Is it an activity that aims to mobilize or create consensus about values (whether emancipatory or *status quo*)?

Observation categories	Related questions
4. Theories on citizenship	What information, data, notions, or concepts are mobilized during the activity? By whom? Is it information that promotes citizenship education based on civility (respect, politeness, volunteering, sharing, etc.) and adherence to rules of social harmony? Explain. Is it information that promotes engagement in social institutions—academic, administrative, political, community, etc.? Explain. Is it information that promotes questioning the established order? An emancipatory project? For example, does it question political representation or power relations based on age, sex, or ethnicity? What positions are discussed and adopted by the educators and the youth? (This element generally requires more interpretation and identification of tendencies, smaller groups defending values).
5. Know-how (or practical knowledge) about citizenship education	What do the educators ask the youth to "do"? Or: What results in terms of "activities" are expected of the youth? What actions taken during activities could be applied to future civic engagement? What skills related to management or organization are transmitted, required, or shared? What skills related to public mobilization or interaction are shared?
6. Soft skills transmitted by the activity	What qualities (critical perspective, sense of justice, obedience, openness to the other, speaking ability, attention, consensus-building, dynamics, etc.) are youth asked to adopt to successfully complete the activity? What qualities do youth exhibit during the activity? What qualities are promoted via the comments or attitudes of other youth or adults?
7. The facilitator's pedagogical approach	How is knowledge shared by the activity's leaders (personalized interventions, formal presentations)? What type of involvement (sharing an opinion, listening, creating, formulating a discourse) is expected of the youth? What type of relationship does the facilitator establish with the youth? How does this relationship change over time? What types of content are shared the most (theoretical, practical, or social?) How are youth invited to participate in the activity? How are they selected, when necessary? How is the students' success or performance evaluated? Based on what criteria?
8. Youth attitudes to the activity and teaching	How would you describe the youths' receptiveness (or non-receptiveness) to the proposed activity? What are their concerns? What stimulates them? How would you describe the youths' overall attitude to the activity (hesitant, surprised, engaged, critical, frustrated, etc.)? How does this attitude change over time? Do some individuals or small groups have particular reactions? How would you describe them?
9. The climate (or atmosphere) in which the activity takes place	How would you describe the atmosphere of the activity: cordial, serious, conflictual, friendly, engaging, relaxing, stimulating, etc.? How does this climate change over the course of the activity? Between different activities? Are there several group dynamics? What distinguishes them? Are there tensions between youth or between youth and adults? How would you describe the nature and evolution of these tensions?

The multisite ethnographic approach is quite recent. It is distinguished by the fact the field sites emerge from the objects observed rather than from the locations (Meyer et al., 2017). Our selection of field sites was based on the diversity of democratic citizenship education experiences. The observers followed the grid while adapting it to the objects of study and actors involved. For example, in the case of the Exeko project, one of the organization's facilitators acted as a research assistant and participated in an autoethnography while working with another assistant. This site was more informed by the action research tradition, and the presence of two people in the field made it possible to cross-validate observations. The specific features of the field sites are described in the table below.

Table A.2. Observations Based on Field Sites

Initiative	Duration	Data Generation
The INM Summer School	49 hours over 4 days (summer 2017)	Participant observations (welcome and networking activities, conferences, panels, debates with elected officials, dinners, get-togethers, group discussions during the courses) and interviews. Seven research assistants and two researchers worked at this field site.
Oxfam-Québec's World Walk in a secondary school	40 hours over 1½ years (2018–2019)	Participant observations (lunchtime activities, World Walk planning committees, World Walk event) and interviews. One researcher and one research assistant worked at this field site.
Commission jeunesse de Gatineau (CJG)	100 hours over 1 year (2017–2018)	Participant observations (informal meetings, CJG meetings, youth-initiated activities [video shoots, vote simulation planning, parties]) and interviews. Two researchers and one research assistant worked at this field site.
YWCA Montreal: *Strong Girls, Strong World* video project	50 hours over 7 months (2017–2018)	Participant observations (prep meetings, video shoots and editing sessions, event) and interviews. One student did her master's thesis on this field site, and her work was supervised by two researchers.
Children's Rights Committee of the Centre de pédiatrie sociale de Gatineau	25 hours over 2 years (2018–2020)	Participant observations (11 meetings and 2 marches were observed). One doctoral student assisted in this field survey, supervised by one researcher.
Exeko workshops	15 hours over 2 months (fall 2019)	Participant observations based on action research. One representative from Exeko and an assistant carried out the fieldwork.

Initiative	Duration	Data Generation
Student councils and associations supported by the FJÎM	30 hours of interviews over 1 year (2016–2017)	Interviews (with youth and facilitators), life history calendars. One researcher and four assistants worked at this field site.

The Limits of the Ethnographic Approach

The ethnographic approach focuses on *in situ* practices. It provides access to representations, interactions, practices, and experiences as they unfold or a few weeks later. This type of data contrasts with the retrospective life tories we did with youth from the Forum jeunesse de l'île de Montréal (FJÎM). Life histories encourage people to recount and situate their stories in time and develop reflexivity about their lived experiences (Gaudet & Robert, 2018). Accordingly, the data generated by the FJÎM field site is a lot more critical and reflective, because it was produced one or two years after the youth's involvement. This gives them more perspective on their experience. Life histories, however, are much less rich when it comes to describing *in situ* practices and interactions.

Analysis

Analysis is often the black box of the research process, especially in the case of ethnography. Due to the iterative aspect of qualitative research, our work is often informed by sensitizing concepts (Charmaz, 2014) like critical citizenship (Westheimer, 2015) or participatory democracy (Blondiaux, 2008). But we also discover practices and concepts that have not yet been theorized. This is called grounded theory analysis. It involves working with observation materials arising from pre-existing theories but also observations and concepts emerging from the field.

To analyze our material, we began by reading our notes to identify themes and map out cross-cutting categories. We used data analysis software (NVivo) for some field sites, but manual annotation and analytical rewriting for most (Paillé & Mucchielli, 2012). This attests to the ongoing pertinence of traditional, non-computer-assisted methods. By continually going back to the field notes and theoretical literature during the analysis, we were able to identify a diverse range of democratic citizenship discourses. However, we did not have theoretical grids to compare these. Edda Sant's article (2019) helped us develop our theories and identify new discourses around concepts like care and eco-citizenship.

Our overall research process was informed by eight important qualitative research criteria: a worthy topic, rich descriptions, analytic coherence, sincerity of the researcher, credibility of the material produced, theoretical resonance, contribution to knowledge, and ethics (Tracy, 2010). Continuous teamwork helped ensure consistent credibility in the data generated, as well as the richness and coherence of the analysis. The co-construction of the project with different stakeholders also ensured its pertinence.

Methodological Reflections

Leaving the Field

Entering the field has been amply addressed by sociologists and anthropologists. This includes taking the first steps, identifying the "gatekeepers," building trust, and developing self-reflexivity (Cefaï, 2010). In our case, this entry was quite simple, because the people we met were generally happy and grateful for our interest in their often-unacknowledged work. Little, however, has been written on leaving the field (Debonneville, 2017). In collaborative research, this is a crucial stage because it affects partner relationships. Withdrawal may be due to external phenomena like an illness, the end of a student contract, or the departure of an organization's contact person, which is quite common in the community setting. In our project, the COVID-19 pandemic affected our research process and had an important influence on our exit from some fields.

Leaving a collaborative field is a delicate matter. Partners often have many expectations of the research team and are unfamiliar with the constraints of academic research, such as the teaching load, administrative responsibilities, and the universities' neoliberal demands for efficiency and productivity. In our case, some of the exits went well and others, not so well. With some partners, either a major staff change in the organization or a research assistant completing their studies brought a natural end to the fieldwork. At other field sites, the pandemic abruptly ended the research relationship, with some students abandoning their studies. Sometimes, tensions or communication problems within the team weakened relations with the partners. In most cases, the end of the project meant the end of the ethnographic engagement, but the partner's expectations often live on. Leaving a field that includes civil society stakeholders is thus never definitive, and it is worth maintaining the relationship whenever possible.

The Limits of Collaborative Research

This project was rooted in a knowledge ecology perspective (Godrie & Dos Santos, 2017) that recognizes diverse, interrelated forms of knowledge and privileges horizontal personal relationships. Though we still defend this ideal model, it poses some problems, notably with respect to participants' sometimes very high expectations. Both civil society partners and students contributing to the project have high expectations about their participation and involvement at every stage of the research, production, analysis, and dissemination process. We tried our best to respond to these, but scientific research imperatives, theoretical and empirical rigour, and academic time constraints prevented us from applying this model perfectly. The timelines of universities and partner organizations are often difficult to synchronize.

Since research projects aim to develop scientific knowledge, they have to meet certain criteria. They must recognize existing contributions to knowledge, incorporate objectivation without claiming pure objectivity, apply a valid and transparent methodology, and open data construction and analysis to peer evaluation. As contributors to scientific knowledge, we must adhere to our discipline's social science paradigm while also engaging with and respecting other forms of knowledge.

However, the limits of this ideal knowledge ecology model soon become evident in a collaborative research project. Hierarchies persist despite efforts to reduce them, because the researchers responsible for the project must meet academic and administrative demands (institutional and funding regulations and rules). For all our best intentions and time devoted to working with our partners, we are still accountable to two knowledge paradigms, one based on science and the other on civic, practical, and experiential knowledge. Sometimes the two are in competition. Partners must defend the political interests of their organization, and it would be naïve to deny the pressure this places on scientific work. Since partnership-based research depends on collaboration, we have made some compromises, omitted some minor points, and also learned from these conciliations. The ethical and political questions raised by collaborative work were present at every stage and could be said to constitute an important characteristic of this approach.

References

Blondiaux, L. (2008). *Le nouvel esprit de la démocratie : actualité de la démocratie participative*. Seuil.

Booto Ekionea, J.-P., Bernard, P., & Plaisent, M. (2011). Consensus par la méthode Delphi sur les concepts clés des capacités organisationnelles spécifiques de la gestion des connaissances. *Recherches qualitatives, 29*(3), 168–192. https://doi.org/10.7202/1085878ar

Cefaï, D. (Ed.). (2010). *L'engagement ethnographique*. École des hautes études en sciences sociales.

Charmaz, K. (2014). *Constructing grounded theory* (2nd ed.). Sage.

Debonneville, J. (2017). La "sortie de terrain" à l'épreuve de l'ethnographie multi-site. *SociologieS*. https://doi.org/10.4000/sociologies.6432

Fricker, M. (2007). *Epistemic injustice: Power and the ethics of knowing*. Oxford University Press.

Gaudet, S. (2020). Sur le terrain de la sociologie publique : enjeux éthiques d'une recherche collaborative sur les expériences d'éducation citoyenne des jeunes. *SociologieS*. https://doi.org/10.4000/sociologies.15416

Gaudet, S., Boyer, S., & Gaudet, J. (2017). *Les qualités du citoyen démocratique* [working paper]. CIRCEM. https://doi.org/10.20381/ruor-21364

Gaudet, S., Drapeau, E., Marchand, F., & Forest, M. (2020). Repenser le rapport social d'âge sur le terrain : ethnographies de la Commission Jeunesse Gatineau et du Comité des droits de l'enfant du Centre de pédiatrie sociale de Gatineau. In Côté, I., Lavoie, K., & Trottier-Cyr, R.-P. (Eds.), *La recherche centrée sur l'enfant : défis éthiques et innovations méthodologiques* (pp. 219–246). Presses de l'Université Laval.

Gaudet, S., & Robert, D. (2018). *L'aventure de la recherche qualitative : du questionnement à la rédaction scientifique*. University of Ottawa Press.

Genard, J.-L., & Roca i Escoda, M. (2019). *Éthique de la recherche en sociologie*. De Boeck Supérieur.

Godrie, B., & Dos Santos, M. (2017). Présentation : inégalités sociales, production des savoirs et de l'ignorance. *Sociologie et sociétés, 49*(1), 7–31. https://doi.org/10.7202/1042804ar

Meyer, M., Perrot, A., & Zinn, I. (2017). Entre ambition « tout-terrain » et impossible ubiquité : les ethnographes en mouvement. *SociologieS*. https://doi.org/10.4000/sociologies.6521

Paillé, P., & Mucchielli, A. (2012). *L'analyse qualitative en sciences humaines et sociales* (3rd ed.). Armand Colin.

Sant, E. (2019). Democratic education: A theoretical review (2006–2017). *Review of Educational Research, 89*(5), 655–696. https://doi.org/10.3102/003465431 9862493

Soulière, M., & Fontan, J.-M. (2018). Les recherches conjointes : Un fait socio-anthropologique contemporain. *Recherches sociographiques, 59*(1–2), 15–24. https://doi.org/10.7202/1051423ar

Tracy, S. J. (2010). Qualitative quality: Eight "big-tent" criteria for excellent qualitative research. *Qualitative Inquiry, 16*(10), 837–851. https://doi.org/10.1177/1077800410383121

Westheimer, J. (2015). *What kind of citizen? Educating our children for the common good.* Teachers College Press.

Note

1. A synthesis of the discussions can be found here: https://educationet democratie.ca/symposium-2016/syntheses-des-discussions/.

Bibliography

Akiva, T., Cortina, K. S., & Smith, C. (2014). Involving youth in program decision-making: How common and what might it do for youth? *Journal of Youth and Adolescence, 43*(11), 1844–1860. https://doi.org/10.1007/s10964-014-0183-y

Amboulé-Abath, A., Campbell, M.-È., & Pagé, G. (2018). La pédagogie féministe : sens et mise en action pédagogique. *Recherches féministes, 31*(1), 23–43. https://doi.org/10.7202/1050652ar

Ampleman, G., Denis, L., & Desgagnés, J.-Y. (Eds.). (2012). *Théorie et pratique de conscientisation au Québec.* Presses de l'Université du Québec.

Angba, L., Tremblay-Perron, D., & Fauser, R. (2016). *Mettre en place un comité des droits des enfants dans un centre de pédiatrie sociale en communauté : démarches et conseils.* Fondation Dr Julien.

Augsberger, A., Collins, M. E., & Gecker, W. (2017). Best practices for youth engagement in municipal government. *National Civic Review, 106*(1), 9–16. https://doi.org/10.1002/ncr.21304

Augsberger, A., Collins, M. E., & Gecker, W. (2018). Engaging youth in municipal government: Moving toward a youth-centric practice. *Journal of Community Practice, 26*(1), 41–62. https://doi.org/10.1080/10705422.2017.1413023

Bachelet, M. (2022, August 3). *La crise et la fragilité de la démocratie dans le monde* [speech]. Opening workshop for the International Association of Jesuit Universities, Boston College. https://www.ohchr.org/fr/statements-and-speeches/2022/08/crisis-and-fragility-democracy-world

Bacqué, M.-H., & Biewener, C. (2015). *L'empowerment, une pratique émancipatrice ?* La Découverte.

Baillargeon, S., & Shields, A. (2019, September 28). 500 000 citoyens emboîtent le pas à Greta Thunberg. *Le Devoir.* https://www.ledevoir.com/environnement/563659/marche-historique

Beauchemin, W.-J., Blémur, D., Duguay, N., Goulet-Langlois, M., & Lorgueilleux, A. (2015, January). *La présomption de l'égalité des intelligences : principes, posture et mise en pratique.* Exeko. https://omec.inrs.ca/wp-content/uploads/2020/02/Exeko_PEI-Janv2015_v3.pdf

Beaud, S., & Weber, F. (1997). *Guide de l'enquête de terrain : produire et analyser des données ethnographiques.* La Découverte.

Becquet, V. (2018). Comprendre l'instrumentation des questions de citoyenneté dans les politiques d'éducation et de jeunesse : une typologie des dispositifs d'action publique. *Lien social et Politiques, 80,* 15–33. https://doi.org/10.7202/1044107ar

Becquet, V. (2021). Introduction. In Becquet, V. (Ed.), *Des professionnels pour les jeunes* (pp. 7– 26). Champ social. https://doi.org/10.3917/chaso.becqu.2021.01.0007

Becquet, V., & Stuppia, P. (2021). *Géopolitique de la jeunesse : engagement et (dé)mobilisations.* Le Cavalier Bleu.

Berger, M., & Charles, J. (2014). *Persona non grata.* Au seuil de la participation. *Participations, 9*(2), 5–36. https://doi.org/10.3917/parti.009.0005

Bherer, L., Dufour, P., & Montambeault, F. (2016). The participatory democracy turn: An introduction. *Journal of Civil Society, 12*(3), 225–230. https://doi.org/10.1080/17448689.2016.1216383

Bherer, L., Gauthier, M., & Simard, L. (dir.) (2017). *The professionalization of public participation.* Routledge.

Biesta, G., De Bie, M., & Wildemeersch, D. (Eds.). (2014). *Civic learning, democratic citizenship and the public sphere.* Springer.

Blanchet-Cohen, N. (2017). Apports des pédagogies autochtones à l'apprentissage de l'écocitoyenneté. In Sauvé, L., Orellana, I., Villemagne, C., & Bader, B. (Eds.), *Éducation, environnement, écocitoyenneté : repères contemporains* (pp. 67–80). Presses de l'Université du Québec.

Blanchet-Cohen, N., & Brunson, L. (2014). Creating settings for youth empowerment and leadership: An ecological perspective. *Child & Youth Services, 35*(3), 216–236. https://doi.org/10.1080/0145935X.2014.938735

Blondiaux, L. (2008). *Le nouvel esprit de la démocratie : actualité de la démocratie participative.* Seuil.

Blum-Ross, A. (2015). Filmmakers/educators/facilitators? Understanding the role of adult intermediaries in youth media production in the UK and the USA. *Journal of Children and Media, 9*(3), 308–324. https://doi.org/10.1080/17482798.2015.1058280

Booto Ekionea, J.-P., Bernard, P., & Plaisent, M. (2011). Consensus par la méthode Delphi sur les concepts clés des capacités organisationnelles spécifiques de la gestion des connaissances. *Recherches qualitatives, 29*(3), 168–192. https://doi.org/10.7202/1085878ar

Bourdieu, P. (1979). *La distinction : critique sociale du jugement.* Les Éditions de Minuit.

Bourdieu, P., & Passeron, J.-C. (1970). *La reproduction : éléments pour une théorie du système d'enseignement.* Les Éditions de Minuit.

Boyer, S., & Gaudet, S. (2021). La citoyenneté démocratique des enfants à l'école primaire. *Revue des sciences de l'éducation, 47*(2), 174–196. https://doi.org/10.7202/1083983ar

Breviglieri, M., & Gaudet, S. (2014). Présentation : les arrières-scènes participatives et le lien ordinaire au politique. *Lien social et Politiques, 71,* 3–9. https://doi.org/10.7202/1024735ar

Brion-Meisels, G., Vasudevan, D. S., & Fei, J. T. (2023). Youth-adult partnerships that foster individual and collective wellbeing. In Lester, J. N., & O'Reilly, M. (Eds.), *The Palgrave encyclopedia of critical perspectives on mental health* (pp. 1–5). Palgrave Macmillan. https://doi.org/10.1007/978-3-030-12852-4_101-1

Brodeur Gélinas, M., & Vanasse, G.-G. (2021, March 5). *Une éducation transformatrice : pour des jeunes au pouvoir citoyen émancipateur.* Le Réseau ÉdCan. https://www.edcan.ca/articles/une-education-transformatrice-pour-des-jeunes-au-pouvoir-citoyen-emancipateur/?lang=fr

Brunet, M.-H. (2017). Des histoires du passé : le féminisme dans les manuels d'histoire et d'éducation à la citoyenneté selon des élèves québécois de quatrième secondaire. *McGill Journal of Education / Revue des sciences de l'éducation de McGill, 52*(2), 409–431. https://doi.org/10.7202/1044473ar

Bundick, M. J. (2011). Extracurricular activities, positive youth development, and the role of meaningfulness of engagement. *The Journal of Positive Psychology, 6*(1), 57–74. https://doi.org/10.1080/17439760.2010.536775

Caron, C. (2011). Getting girls and teens into the vocabularies of citizenship. *Girlhood Studies, 4*(2), 70–91. https://doi.org/10.3167/ghs.2011.040206

Caron, C. (2018). La citoyennetédes adolescents du 21ᵉ siècle dans une perspective de justice sociale : pourquoi et comment ? *Lien social et Politiques, 80,* 52–68. https://doi.org/10.7202/1044109ar

Carr, P. R., & Thésée, G. (2017). Seeking democracy inside, and outside, of education: Re-conceptualizing perceptions and experiences related to democracy and education. *Democracy and Education, 25*(2), 1–12. https://democracyeducationjournal.org/home/vol25/iss2/4

Carrel, M., & Neveu, C. (Eds.). (2014). *Citoyennetés ordinaires : pour une approche renouvelée des pratiques citoyennes.* Karthala.

Cefaï, D. (Ed.). (2010). *L'engagement ethnographique.* École des hautes études en sciences sociales.

Cefaï, D., Carrel, M., Talpin, J., Eliasoph, N., & Lichterman, P. (2012). Ethnographies de la participation. *Participations, 4*(3), 7–48. https://doi.org/10.3917/parti.004.0005

Chanial, P. (2016). Rendre justice à ce qui est : ou l'émancipation comme parturition. *Revue du MAUSS, 48*(2), 259–274. https://doi.org/10.3917/rdm.048.0259

Charmaz, K. (2014). *Constructing grounded theory* (2nd ed.). Sage.

Coll, K. M. (2010). *Remaking citizenship: Latina immigrants and new American politics.* Stanford University Press.

Collins, M. E., Augsberger, A., & Gecker, W. (2016). Youth councils in municipal government: Examination of activities, impact and barriers. *Children and Youth Services Review, 65,* 140–147. https://doi.org/10.1016/j.childyouth.2016.04.007

Commission jeunesse de Gatineau. (2018). *La ville de Gatineau sans la commission jeunesse : c'est comme un road trip sans musique. Bilan 2017.* https://publications.virtualpaper.com/ville-de-gatineau-acl/vp_bilan-2017/

Corney, T., Williamson, H., Holdsworth, R., Broadbent, R., Ellis, K., Shier, H., & Cooper, T. (2020). *Approaches to youth participation in youth and community work practice: A critical dialogue.* Youth Workers Association.

Cournoyer, A. (2019). *Apprendre la démocratie à l'école secondaire : trajectoire de participation sociale et politique des adolescents* [Master's thesis, University of Ottawa]. https://ruor.uottawa.ca/handle/10393/39890

Crocetti, E., Erentaitė, R., & Žukauskienė, R. (2014). Identity styles, positive youth development, and civic engagement in adolescence. *Journal of Youth and Adolescence, 43*(11), 1818–1828. https://doi.org/10.1007/s10964-014-0100-4

Dardot, P., & Laval, C. (2010). *La nouvelle raison du monde : essai sur la société néolibérale.* La Découverte.

Debonneville, J. (2017). La "sortie de terrain" à l'épreuve de l'ethnographie multi-site. *SociologieS.* https://doi.org/10.4000/sociologies.6432

Dewey, J. (1927). *The public and its problems.* Holt Publishers.

Dewey, J. (1997). *Democracy and education: An introduction to the philosophy of education.* The Free Press. (Original work published in 1916)

Dewey, J. (2018). *Démocratie et éducation* suivi de *Expérience et éducation.* Armand Colin. (Original works published in English in 1916 and 1938)

Dewey, J. (2018). *Écrits politiques* (J.-P. Cometti & J. Zask, Trans.). Gallimard.

Dubet, F. (2002). *Le déclin de l'institution.* Seuil.

Dupuis-Déri, F. (2006). Les élections de Conseils d'élèves : méthode d'endoctrinement au libéralisme politique. *Revue des sciences de l'éducation, 32*(3), 691–709. https://doi.org/10.7202/016282ar

Dupuis-Déri, F. (2020a). Histoire des grèves d'élèves du secondaire au Québec : démocratie et conflictualité. *Revue des sciences de l'éducation, 46*(3), 67–94. https://doi.org/10.7202/1075988ar

Dupuis-Déri, F. (2020b). Mobilisations de la jeunesse pour le climat au Québec : analyse des dynamiques conflictuelles à l'école. *Sociologie et sociétés, 52*(2), 303–325. https://doi.org/10.7202/1088759ar

Durkheim, É. (1973). *Éducation et sociologie* (2nd ed. of the 1973 edition). Presses universitaires de France. (Original work published in 1922)

Education Act, CQLR c I-13.3 (2024). Retrieved from https://www.legisquebec.gouv.qc.ca/en/document/cs/I-13.3

Élections Canada. (2021). *Nouveaux électeurs – Jeunes*. Centre de ressources. https://www.elections.ca/content.aspx?section=res&dir=rec/part/yth& document=index&lang=f

Eliasoph, N. (2011). *Making volunteers: Civic life after welfare's end*. Princeton University Press.

Foucault, M. (2014). *Surveiller et punir : naissance de la prison*. Gallimard. (Original work published in 1975)

Fournel, A. (2016). Doute et autocorrection dans une communauté de recherche philosophique. *Recherches en éducation, 24*. https://doi.org/10.4000/ ree.5448

Fraser-Burgess, S. (2012). Group identity, deliberative democracy and diversity in education. *Educational Philosophy and Theory, 44*(5), 480–499. https://doi.org/10.1111/j.1469-5812.2010.00717.x

Freire, P. (1974). *Pédagogie des opprimés* suivi de *Conscientisation et révolution* (L. Lefay & M. Lefay, Trans.). François Maspero. (Original work published in Portuguese in 1970)

Fricker, M. (2007). *Epistemic injustice: Power and the ethics of knowing*. Oxford University Press.

Galichet, F. (2002). La citoyenneté comme pédagogie : réflexions sur l'éducation à la citoyenneté. *Revue des sciences de l'éducation, 28*(1), 105–124. https:// doi.org/10.7202/007151ar

Garnier, P. (2015). L'"agency" des enfants : projet scientifique et politique des "childhood studies." *Éducation et sociétés, 36*(2), 159–173. https://doi. org/10.3917/es.036.0159

Gaudet, S. (2018a). Introduction : citoyenneté des enfants et des adolescents. *Lien social et Politiques, 80*, 4–14. https://doi.org/10.7202/1044106ar

Gaudet, S. (2018b). La société d'acrobates : réflexion critique sur la responsabilité personnelle. In Marchildon, A., & Duhamel, A. (Eds.), *Quels lendemains pour la responsabilité ? Perspectives multidisciplinaires* (pp. 51–77). Nota bene.

Gaudet, S. (2020a). Sur le terrain de la sociologie publique : enjeux éthiques d'une recherche collaborative sur les expériences d'éducation citoyenne des jeunes. *SociologieS*. https://doi.org/10.4000/sociologies.15416

Gaudet, S. (2020b). La société d'acrobates : responsabilité, *care* et participation citoyenne des jeunes. *SociologieS*. https://doi.org/10.4000/sociologies.13229

Gaudet, S. (2021). Les initiatives jeunesse au Canada : des tiers-lieux de l'éducation démocratique. *Revue internationale d'éducation de Sèvres, 88*, 93–104. https://doi.org/10.4000/ries.11586

Gaudet, S., Boyer, S., & Gaudet, J. (2017). *Les qualités du citoyen démocratique* [working paper]. CIRCEM. https://doi.org/10.20381/ruor-21364

Gaudet, S., Claude, M., Cournoyer, A., Portilla, J., & Déry, J. A. (2017). *Apprendre la démocratie en milieu scolaire : analyse des trajectoires de participation sociale et politique des jeunes participant à* Prends ta place à l'école [final report]. CIRCEM and the Forum jeunesse de l'île de Montréal. https://doi.org/10.20381/ruor-20227

Gaudet, S., & Drapeau, E. (2021). L'utilisation combinée du récit et du calendrier de vie dans un dispositif d'enquête narrative biographique. *Recherches qualitatives, 40*(2), 57–80. https://doi.org/10.7202/1084067ar

Gaudet, S., Drapeau, E., Marchand, F., & Forest, M. (2020). Repenser le rapport social d'âge sur le terrain : ethnographies de la Commission Jeunesse de Gatineau et du Comité des droits de l'enfant du Centre de pédiatrie sociale de Gatineau. In Côté, I., Lavoie, K., & Trottier-Cyr, R.-P. (Eds.), *La recherche centrée sur l'enfant : défis éthiques et innovations méthodologiques* (pp. 219–246). Presses de l'Université Laval.

Gaudet, S., Forest, M., & Caron, C. (2019). *Une expérience d'éducation à la citoyenneté : la Commission jeunesse de Gatineau* [research report]. CIRCEM. https://doi.org/10.20381/ruor-24538

Gaudet, S., & Robert, D. (2018). *L'aventure de la recherche qualitative : du questionnement à la rédaction scientifique.* University of Ottawa Press.

Genard, J.-L., & Roca i Escoda, M. (2019). *Éthique de la recherche en sociologie.* De Boeck Supérieur.

Gilligan, C. (1986). *Une si grande différence* (A. Kwiatek, Trans.). Flammarion. (Original work published in English in 1982)

Godbout, J. T. (1987). *La démocratie des usagers.* Boréal.

Godrie, B., & Dos Santos, M. (2017). Présentation : inégalités sociales, production des savoirs et de l'ignorance. *Sociologie et sociétés, 49*(1), 7–31. https://doi.org/10.7202/1042804ar

Goulet-Langlois, M. (2017). Arts, philosophie, marginalisations sociales et émancipation : la médiation intellectuelle, une pratique frontalière des sens. In Casemajor, N., Dubé, M., Lafortune, J.-M., & Lamoureux, È. (Eds.), *Expériences critiques de la médiation culturelle* (pp. 259–285). Presses de l'Université Laval.

Groleau, A., & Nanhou, V. (2002) *Une analyse longitudinale des facteurs associés à la participation électorale des jeunes nés au Québec, Étude longitudinale du développement des enfants du Québec, De la naissance à l'âge adulte* (vol. 9, fascicle 4). Institut de la statistique du Québec. https://statistique.quebec.ca/fr/fichier/analyse-longitudinalefacteurs-participation-electorale-jeunes-nes-au-quebec.pdf

Habermas, J. (2013) *De l'éthique de la discussion* (M. Hunyadi, Trans.). Flammarion. (Original work published in German in 1991)

Hamrouni, N., & Maillé, C. (Eds.). (2015). *Le sujet du féminisme est-il blanc ? Femmes racisées et recherche féministe.* Éditions du remue-ménage.

Harris, A. (2003). *Future girl: Young women in the twenty-first century.* Routledge.

Hart, J. (2007). Empowerment or frustration? Participatory programming with young Palestinians. *Children, Youth and Environments, 17*(3), 1–23. https://www.jstor.org/stable/10.7721/chilyoutenvi.17.3.0001

Hart, R. A. (1992). *Children's participation: From tokenism to citizenship*. UNICEF, International Child Development Centre (ICDC). https://www.unicef-irc.org/publications/100-childrens-participation-from-tokenism-to-citizenship.html

Hart, R. A. (1997). *Children's participation: The theory and practice of involving young citizens in community development and environmental care*. Routledge. https://doi.org/10.4324/9781315070728

Hogan, C. (2002). *Understanding facilitation: Theory and principles*. Kogan Page.

Honneth, A. (2015). Education and the democratic public sphere: A neglected chapter of political philosophy (F. Koch, Trans.). In Jakobsen, J., & Lysaker, O. (Eds.), *Recognition and freedom: Axel Honneth's political thought* (pp. 17–32). Brill.

Institut du Nouveau Monde. (2017). *Guide de participation. Génération d'impact : École d'été 2017 de l'Institut du Nouveau Monde*.

Ion, J. (2012). *S'engager dans une société d'individus*. Armand Colin.

Isin, E. F. (2009). Citizenship in flux: The figure of the activist citizen. *Subjectivity, 29*(1), 367–388. https://doi.org/10.1057/sub.2009.25

Isin, E. F., & Turner, B. S. (Eds.). (2002). *Handbook of citizenship studies*. Sage.

Isin, E. F., & Turner, B. S. (2007). Investigating citizenship: An agenda for citizenship studies. *Citizenship Studies, 11*(1), 5–17. https://doi.org/10.1080/13621020601099773

Kallio, K. P., Wood, B. E., & Häkli, J. (2020). Lived citizenship: Conceptualising an emerging field. *Citizenship Studies, 24*(6), 713–729. https://doi.org/10.1080/13621025.2020.1739227

Kennelly, J. (2011). *Citizen youth: Culture, activism, and agency in a neoliberal era*. Palgrave Macmillan.

Kennelly, J., & Llewellyn, K. R. (2011). Educating for active compliance: Discursive constructions in citizenship education. *Citizenship Studies, 15*(6–7), 897–914. https://doi.org/10.1080/13621025.2011.600103

Laclau, E., & Mouffe, C. (2001). *Hegemony and socialist strategy: Towards a radical democratic politics* (2nd ed.). Verso.

Lamoureux, H., Lavoie, J., Mayer, R., & Panet-Raymond, J. (2002). *La pratique de l'action communautaire* (2nd ed., revised and expanded). Presses de l'Université du Québec.

Lansdown, G. (2001). *Promoting children's participation in democratic decision-making*. UNICEF Innocenti Research Centre.

Le Robert. (n.d.). Citoyenneté. In *Le Grand Robert de la langue française*. Retrieved Month Day, 2022, from https://grandrobert.lerobert.com/

Le Robert. (n.d.). Civisme. In *Le Grand Robert de la langue française*. Retrieved Month Day, 2022, https://grandrobert.lerobert.com/

Leduc, L. (2014, December 9). La CSDM invite ses élèves à manifester. *La Presse+*. https://plus.lapresse.ca/screens/864b7252-a84e-492a-90ce-0995eecc6b7b|_0.html

Lefrançois, D., & Éthier, M.-A. (2010). Translating the ideal of deliberative democracy into democratic education: Pure utopia? *Educational Philosophy and Theory, 42*(3), 271–292. https://doi.org/10.1111/j.1469-5812.2007.00385.x

Liebel, M. (2010). *Enfants, droits et citoyenneté : faire émerger la perspective des enfants sur leurs droits* (in collaboration with P. Robin & I. Saadi). L'Harmattan.

Lister, R. (2003). *Citizenship: Feminist perspectives* (2nd ed.). Palgrave Macmillan.

Lister, R. (2007). Why citizenship: Where, when and how children? *Theoretical Inquiries in Law, 8*(2), 693–718. https://doi.org/10.2202/1565-3404.1165

Mailhot, C., Gaudet, S., Drapeau, É., & Fuca, J. (2021). Éduquer à la citoyenneté démocratique par l'innovation sociale : l'idéal de l'entrepreneuriat social remis en question. *Canadian Journal of Nonprofit and Social Economy Research / Revue canadienne de recherche sur les OSBL et l'économie sociale, 12*(2), 58–73. https://doi.org/10.29173/cjnser.2021v12n2a381

Maillé, C. (2000). Féminisme et mouvement des femmes au Québec : un bilan complexe. *Globe, 3*(2), 87-105. https://doi.org/10.7202/1000583ar

Malboeuf-Hurtubise, C., Léger-Goodes, T., Mageau, G. A., Joussemet, M., Herba, C., Chadi, N., Lefrançois, D., Camden, C., Bussières, È.-L., Taylor, G., Éthier, M.-A., & Gagnon, M. (2021). Philosophy for children and mindfulness during COVID-19: Results from a randomized cluster trial and impact on mental health in elementary school students. *Progress in Neuro-Psychopharmacology and Biological Psychiatry, 107*(110260), 1–6. https://doi.org/10.1016/j.pnpbp.2021.110260

Manicom, A. (1992). Feminist pedagogy: Transformations, standpoints, and politics. *Canadian Journal of Education / Revue canadienne de l'éducation, 17*(3), 365–389. https://doi.org/10.2307/1495301

Marshall, T. H. (1950). *Citizenship and social class and other essays.* Cambridge University Press.

Mathieu, L. (2004). *Comment lutter ? Sociologie et mouvements sociaux.* Textuel.

Meyer, M., Perrot, A., & Zinn, I. (2017). Entre ambition « tout-terrain » et impossible ubiquité : les ethnographes en mouvement. *SociologieS.* https://doi.org/10.4000/sociologies.6521

Milner, H. (2005). Are young Canadians becoming political dropouts? A comparative perspective. *IRPP Choices, 11*(3). https://irpp.org/wpcontent/uploads/assets/vol11n03.pdf

Milner, H. (2010). *The internet generation: Engaged citizens or political dropouts.* University Press of New England.

Montambeault, F., Bherer, L., & Cloutier, G. (2021). *L'engagement pousse là où on le sème : le Carré Casgrain, de jardin ouvert à collectif citoyen.* Écosociété.

Moosa-Mitha, M. (2005). A difference-centred alternative to theorization of children's citizenship rights. *Citizenship Studies, 9*(4), 369–388. https://doi.org/10.1080/13621020500211354

Neale, B. (Ed.). (2004). *Young children's citizenship: Ideas into practice* (with the collaboration of C. Willow, R. Marchant & P. Kirby). Joseph Rowntree Foundation.

Neveu, C. (2015). Of ordinariness and citizenship processes. *Citizenship Studies, 19*(2), 141–154. https://doi.org/10.1080/13621025.2015.1005944

Neveu, C., & Vanhoenacker, M. (2017). La participation buissonnière, ou le secret dans l'ordinaire de la citoyenneté. *Participations, 19*(3), 7–22. https://doi.org/10.3917/parti.019.0007

Noddings, N. (2012). The language of care ethics. *Knowledge Quest, 40*(5), 52–56.

O'Connor, C. D. (2013). Engaging young people? The experiences, challenges, and successes of Canadian youth advisory councils. In Nenga, S. K., & Taft, J. K. (Eds.), *Youth engagement: The civic-political lives of children and youth* (pp. 73–96). Emerald Group.

Office québécois de la Langue française. (2020). Réno-éviction. In *Grand dictionnaire terminologique*. Vitrine linguistique. https://gdt.oqlf.gouv.qc.ca/ficheOqlf.aspx?Id_Fiche=26558204

Oldenburg, R., & Brissett, D. (1982). The third place. *Qualitative Sociology, 5*, 265–284. https://doi.org/10.1007/BF00986754

Pache-Hébert, C., Jutras, F., & Guay, J.-H. (2014). Le comité des élèves dans les écoles primaires et secondaires : une recension des écrits. *Canadian Journal of Education / Revue canadienne de l'éducation, 37*(4), 1–27. https://journals.sfu.ca/cje/index.php/cje-rce/article/view/1723

Paillé, P., & Mucchielli, A. (2012). *L'analyse qualitative en sciences humaines et sociales* (3rd ed.). Armand Colin.

Paperman, P., & Laugier, S. (Eds.). (2006). *Le souci des autres : éthique et politique du care*. Éditions de l'École des hautes études en sciences sociales.

Pateman, C. (1976). *Participation and democratic theory*. Cambridge University Press. (Original work published in 1970)

Pleyers, G., & Capitaine, B. (Eds.). (2016). *Mouvements sociaux : quand le sujet devient acteur*. Éditions de la Maison des sciences de l'homme. https://doi.org/10.4000/books.editionsmsh.9891

Prout, A. (2011). Taking a step away from modernity: Reconsidering the new sociology of childhood. *Global Studies of Childhood, 1*(1), 4–14. https://doi.org/10.2304/gsch.2011.1.1.4

Pulcini, E. (2013). *Care of the world: Fear, responsibility and justice in the global age* (K. Whittle, Trans.). Springer.

Putnam, R. D. (2000). *Bowling alone: The collapse and revival of American community*. Simon & Schuster.

Rancière, J. (2003). *Le maître ignorant : cinq leçons sur l'émancipation intellectuelle*. Fayard. (Original work published in 1987)

Roche, J. (1999). Children: Rights, participation and citizenship. *Childhood, 6*(4), 475–493. https://doi.org/10.1177/0907568299006004006

Rocher, F. (2015). Sur les dimensions constitutives de la citoyenneté : perspective des minorités ethnoculturelles et religieuses dans un Québec à l'identité incertaine. *Recherches sociographiques, 56*(1), 139-170. https://doi.org/10.7202/1030276ar

Rosanvallon, P. (2006). *La contre-démocratie : la politique à l'âge de la défiance.* Seuil.

Sant, E. (2019). Democratic education: A theoretical review (2006–2017). *Review of Educational Research, 89*(5), 655–696. https://doi.org/10.3102/0034654319862493

Sasseville, M. (dir.) (2009). *La pratique de la philosophie avec les enfants* (3rd ed.). Presses de l'Université Laval.

Sauvé, L. (2017). L'éducation à l'écocitoyenneté. In Barthes, A., Lange, J. M., & Tutiaux-Guillon, N. (Eds.), *Dictionnaire critique : des enjeux et concepts des "éducations à"* (pp. 56–65). L'Harmattan.

Sayad, A. (2014). *L'école et les enfants de l'immigration : essais critiques* (texts selected by B. Falaize & S. Laacher). Seuil.

Shields, A. (2019, August 28). Montréal figure dans les plans de Greta Thunberg. *Le Devoir.* https://www.ledevoir.com/environnement/561444/climat-montreal-figure-dans-les-plans-de-greta-thunberg

Shier, H. (2001). Pathways to participation: Openings, opportunities, and obligations. *Children & Society, 15*(2), 107–117. https://doi.org/10.1002/chi.617

Simard, M. (2013). *Histoire du mouvement étudiant québécois 1956-2013 : des Trois Braves aux carrés rouges.* Presses de l'Université Laval.

Sirota, R. (2005). L'enfant acteur ou sujet dans la sociologie de l'enfance : évolution des positions théoriques au travers du prisme de la socialisation. In Bergonnier-Dupuy, G. (Ed.), *L'enfant, acteur et/ou sujet au sein de la famille* (pp. 33–41). Érès. https://doi.org/10.3917/eres.bergo.2005.01.0033

Soulière, M., & Fontan, J.-M. (2018). Les recherches conjointes : un fait socio-anthropologique contemporain. *Recherches sociographiques, 59*(1–2), 15–24. https://doi.org/10.7202/1051423ar

Spencer, N., Colomer, C., Alperstein, G., Bouvier, P., Colomer, J., Duperrex, O., Gokcay, G., Julien, G., Kohler, L., Lindström, B., Macfarlane, A., Mercer, R., Panagiotopoulos, T., & Schulpen, T. (2005). Social paediatrics. *Journal of Epidemiology & Community Health, 59*(2), 106–108. https://doi.org/10.1136/jech.2003.017681

Théwissen-LeBlanc, S. (2020). L'éducation à la citoyenneté dans un programme jeunesse féministe non-mixte : le cas de *Force des filles, force du monde* [Master's thesis, University of Ottawa]. https://ruor.uottawa.ca/han-dle/10393/40724

Tracy, S. J. (2010). Qualitative quality: Eight "big-tent" criteria for excellent qualitative research. *Qualitative Inquiry, 16*(10), 837–851. https://doi.org/10.1177/1077800410383121

Tremblay, P.-A., Roche, M., & Tremblay, S. (Eds.). (2015). *Le printemps québécois : le mouvement étudiant de 2012*. Presses de l'Université du Québec.

Treseder, P. (1997). *Empowering children and young people: Promoting involvement in decision-making*. Save the Children.

Tronto, J. (2009). *Un monde vulnérable : pour une politique du care* (H. Maury, Trans.). La Découverte. (Original work published in English in 1993)

Tronto, J. C. (2013). *Caring democracy: Markets, equality, and justice*. New York University Press.

Trudel, S., & Martineau, S. (2021). Axel Honneth et l'éducation : entre émancipation, ethnicité démocratique et compétence civique. *Formation et profession : revue scientifique internationale en éducation, 29*(2), 1–11. https://doi.org/10.18162/fp.2021.644

Turner, B. S. (1997). Citizenship studies: A general theory. *Citizenship Studies, 1*(1), 5–18. https://doi.org/10.1080/13621029708420644

Urfalino, P. (2007). La décision par consensus apparent : nature et propriétés. *Revue européenne des sciences sociales, XLV*(136), 47-70. https://doi.org/10.4000/ress.86

Van de Velde, C. (2021). "Different struggles, the same fight"? A comparative analysis of student movements in Chile (2011), Quebec (2012), and Hong Kong (2014). In Bessant, J., Mejia Mesinas, A., & Pickard, S. (Eds.), *When students protest: Universities in the Global North* (pp. 33–50). Rowman & Littlefield.

Vitiello, A. (2010). *Institution et liberté : l'école et la question du politique*. L'Harmattan.

Vitiello, A. (2013). L'exercice de la citoyenneté : délibération, participation et éducation démocratiques. *Participations, 5*(1), 201–226. https://doi.org/10.3917/parti.005.0201

Vitiello, A. (2016). L'autonomie en devenir : l'émancipation comme (trans) formation infinie. *Revue du MAUSS, 48*(2), 211-227. https://doi.org/10.3917/rdm.048.0211

Walther, A., Batsleer, J., Loncle, P., & Pohl, A. (Eds.). (2019). *Young people and the struggle for participation: Contested practices, power and pedagogies in public spaces* (1st ed.). Routledge. https://doi.org/10.4324/9780429432095

Weller, S. (2007). *Teenager's citizenship: Experiences and education*. Routledge.

Westheimer, J. (2015). *What kind of citizen? Educating our children for the common good*. Teachers College Press.

Westheimer, J., & Kahne, J. (2004). What kind of citizen? The politics of educating for democracy. *American Educational Research Journal, 41*(2), 237–269. https://doi.org/10.3102/00028312041002237

YWCA Montréal (n. d. a). *Strong Girls, Strong World*. https://www.ydesfemmesmtl.org/services-jeunesse/programmes/force-des-filles-force-du-monde/

YWCA Montréal (n. d. b). *Mission, vision & values.* https://www.ydesfemmesmtl.org/en/about-us/mission-vision-values/

Young, I. M. (2002). *Inclusion and democracy.* Oxford University Press.

Yuval-Davis, N. (2011). *The politics of belonging: Intersectional contestations.* Sage.

Zeldin, S., Christens, B. D., & Powers, J. L. (2013). The psychology and practice of youth-adult partnership: Bridging generations for youth development and community change. *American Journal of Community Psychology, 51*(3–4), 385–397. https://doi.org/10.1007/s10464-012-9558-y

Zeldin, S., Gauley, J., Krauss, S. E., Kornbluh, M., & Collura, J. (2017). Youth-adult partnership and youth civic development: Cross-national analyses for scholars and field professionals. *Youth & Society, 49*(7), 851–878. https://doi.org/10.1177/0044118X15595153

Zeldin, S., Krauss, S. E., Collura, J., Lucchesi, M., & Sulaiman, A. H. (2014). Conceptualizing and measuring youth-adult partnership in community programs: A cross-national study. *American Journal of Community Psychology, 54*(3–4), 337–347. https://doi.org/10.1007/s10464-014-9676-9

Author Biographies

Co-Editors

Stéphanie Gaudet is Full Professor and Director of the Centre for Interdisciplinary Research on Citizenship and Minorities (CIRCEM) at the University of Ottawa. She studies social and political participation, notably among youth, life trajectories, and qualitative methodology. She leads a partnership research project on citizenship education experiences in community and organizational settings (educationet-democratie.ca) and a research project on youth social and political engagement pathways (both through SSHRC). In 2018, she published French (UOP) and English versions (Sage) of *A Journey Through Qualitative Research: From Design to Reporting*. Her work has also appeared in academic journals including *Lien social et Politiques, Journal of Gender Studies, SociologieS, Revue des sciences de l'éducation, Recherches qualitatives,* and *Revue canadienne de politique sociale.*

Caroline Caron is Full Professor in the Department of Social Sciences at the Université du Québec en Outaouais. She specializes in gender relations in media and communication, as well as youth media and adolescent civic engagement in the digital space. She has recently conducted pioneering studies on the civic uses of videoblogging among young YouTubers in the Canadian context. Her research often focuses on engagement practices outside adult-run institutional frameworks. In 2016, she was awarded the Canada Prize in the Humanities and Social Sciences by the Federation for the Humanities and Social Sciences for her book *Vues, mais non entendues : les adolescentes québécoises et l'hypersexualisation*. Her work has appeared in academic journals including *Journal of Youth Studies, Approches inductives, Lien social et Politiques, Communication,* and *Convergence.*

Editorial Collaboration

Sophie Théwissen-LeBlanc holds a master's degree in women's studies from the University of Ottawa. Her master's thesis focused on citizenship education for adolescent girls and young women in a Montreal-area feminist organization, the results of which were published in the journal *Recherches féministes*. She has contributed to several research projects on youth, gender, media, and citizenship as a research assistant or as a professional.

Contributors

Brieg Capitaine is Associate Professor at the University of Ottawa's School of Sociological and Anthropological Studies. He holds a PhD in sociology from the École des hautes études en sciences sociales (Paris) and is interested in the civil sphere and social movements. With Geoffrey Pleyers, he co-edited the book *Mouvements sociaux. Quand le sujet devient acteur* (Éditions de la MSH, 2016) and the special issue "Jeunes alteractivistes : d'autres manières de faire de la politique ?" in the journal *Agora Débats/Jeunesses*.

Hérold Constant holds a master's degree in sociology from the University of Ottawa. His thesis focuses on the relationship immigrants of Haitian origin have with work. He collaborated in the research partnership as a research assistant.

Alexandre Cournoyer holds a master's degree in sociology from the University of Ottawa. His thesis focuses on the social and political participation of young adults. He collaborated in the research partnership as a research assistant.

Emilie Drapeau is a PhD student at the University of Ottawa's School of Sociological and Anthropological Studies. Her research focuses on conjugal commitment, which she situates at the crossroads of the sociologies of the family, the couple, youth, life trajectories, and religion. She collaborated in the research partnership as a research assistant and coordinator.

Mariève Forest is a visiting professor at the University of Ottawa's School of Sociological and Anthropological Studies and a researcher affiliated with the Centre for Interdisciplinary Research on Citizenship and Minorities (CIRCEM). She is also President and Senior Researcher at Sociopol, a company specializing in applied social research, consulting, and coaching for collectives. As a researcher, she specializes in public decision-making, social policies related to official languages, social change, and citizenship education.

Maxime Goulet-Langlois is a researcher-practitioner with a passion for philosophical practices and popular education. He is currently completing a PhD in the Department of Integrated Studies in Education at McGill University. His research interests concern the professional development infrastructures used by third-sector practitioners to design their analyses of social problems. He is also a lecturer at HEC Montréal, where he teaches program evaluation.

François Marchand has been a social worker since 2007 (when he graduated from the Université du Québec en Outaouais), focusing on community action and organization. He became interested in public participation in Quebec's health and social care institutions as part of his master's degree in political science at the University of Ottawa (2015). He is currently pursuing a PhD in sociology on children's social participation (University of Ottawa).

Index

www.ingramcontent.com/pod-product-compliance
Lightning Source LLC
Chambersburg PA
CBHW050640280326
41932CB00015B/2727